Travels With Max

In Search of Steinbeck's America Fifty Years Later

By
Gregory Zeigler

6/11

Happy Travels!

Blaine Creek Press
Salt Lake City, Utah

www.travelswsteinbeck.com

Requests for permission to make copies of any part
of the book should be mailed to:

Blaine Creek Press
P.O. Box 521388
Salt Lake City, UT 84152-1388

For additional copies, go to www.blainecreek.com/books

To contact the author: gzeigler@wyom.net
To visit the author's blog:
www.travelswithsteinbeck.wordpress.com

Printed in the United States of America
Book design and map illustration by Jim Hayes,
Cenozoic Design, Salt Lake City, Utah

ISBN number: 978-0-615-37803-9

*Dedicated to independent schoolman
and Jackson Hole luminary Jack Huyler.
Jack understands the power of stories to teach,
and advocates treating the earth gently,
"'cause we're all just passin' thru."* *

*And to my children,
Jamie, Alex and Wil and grandson, Theo.*

From the poem "Just Passin' Thru" by Howard Ballew, put to music by Jack Huyler.

CONTENTS

Author's note: In order to tell a better story, I have at rare times taken liberties with the time/space continuum but all events and people are actual. Some names have been changed; most have not.

Prologue

I held a well-traveled copy of *Travels with Charley* in one hand and half a sloppy chicken salad sandwich in the other. It was February 1, 2007. I was sitting in the Salt Lake City Airport rereading the opening pages of the Steinbeck classic when it struck me that the fiftieth anniversary of Charley's trip around America was three years away. My heart raced. I was gripped with the desire to light out, retrace John Steinbeck's journey and "rediscover this monster land."

Steinbeck distilled his travels and resulting memoir down to one simple question, "What are Americans like today?" With this as my guide, I wondered how much America had changed since Steinbeck and his standard poodle, Charley, circumnavigated the United States in 1960. I wasn't so interested in how *things* had changed: computers, cell phones and the ubiquitous purveyors of designer coffee, but how Americans had changed. That was the fundamental question I intended to answer. What are Americans like *today*? Simple, right? All I needed was a way to camp, some maps and supplies, and a good dog.

Steinbeck, a major American writer and winner of the Nobel Prize for Literature, was a passionate observer who lived and loved large. The love he felt for country was often manifested in harsh criticism such as in his last book, *America and Americans*. A humanist, environmentalist and pacifist, Steinbeck imbued his work with a concern for issues that would, in subsequent years, explode upon the American consciousness. America was the author's muse, and in the late 1950s he hatched a plan to combine his love of travel with his need to reconnect with his countrymen.

To the vagabond in spirit, like Steinbeck, slow travel is an end in itself. All that matters really is what lies beyond the next hill, and the next, and hitting a large body of water, such as an ocean, is a minor inconvenience, easily corrected with a ninety-degree turn left or right. I share Steinbeck's love for slow travel. For a time, I worked near the headquarters of Grand Teton National Park, and, contrary to the typical local disdain for the big buses that paused briefly on "stop and snap" tours, I relished the purr and thrum of those huge diesel hearts. Something stirred in my belly and I wanted to climb aboard.

My favorite childhood memories are of crisscrossing this country while snuggled among my three siblings in the back of a family station wagon pulling a camper. As a young adult, in the 1970s, I drove back and forth across the states several times. Until that moment in Salt Lake City, only my nostalgia for the trips of my youth and peripatetic nature pushed me but never quite enough to get me going again; somehow family and work always intervened. But that day, in the airport, I'd hit upon a damned good excuse to travel the country once again. I knew I *would* go.

There were several elements, aside from the anniversary, which made this pilgrimage timely. During the Nixon/Kennedy race in 1960, the nation wondered if a Roman Catholic of Irish descent could be elected president. The country struggled with a similar question during the presidential race of 2008. In a post-Katrina and early-Obama era, I wanted to see how the nation was reacting to the Obama administration and then conclude my journey in New Orleans, where Steinbeck observed black children being publicly scorned by white adults for integrating schools. Barack Obama certainly could not have been elected president in 1960, but Steinbeck witnessed events that indicated nascent change.

The economic meltdown of the fall of 2008 suggested revisiting the life of the author of the depression-era classic *The Grapes of Wrath*. As the economy slumped into recession, our leaders struggled to prevent it from spiraling into a second Great Depression. Many jobs were lost, mine among them. Unemployment hit a twenty-five year high. The magnitude of the economic calamity was the major issue facing the American people in 2009. During my travels, I explored the painful realities of the economic downturn. In a time of crisis, one can discover who Americans really are.

Part One of this book describes my preparations. Part Two depicts my journey along the Steinbeck route. Part Three describes my return home. After much reflection, I chose September 7, 2009, as the day to leave our place in Jackson Hole, Wyoming, and head for Sag Harbor, Long Island—Steinbeck's point of origin for his trip. That was an exciting day. There are two moments that I find to be as exhilarating as any in the human repertoire of experience: the first expansive minutes of a journey and the heady feeling of completing the first few pages of a writing project.

As Steinbeck wrote in *Travels with Charley*:

> *Once a journey is designed, equipped, and put in process; a new factor enters and takes over. A trip, a safari, an exploration is an entity different from all other journeys. It has personality, temperament, individuality, uniqueness. A journey is a person in itself; no two are alike. And all plans, safeguards, policing, and coercion are fruitless. We find after years of struggle that we do not take a trip; a trip takes us. Only when this is recognized can the blown-in-the-glass bum relax and go along with it.*

In September of 2009, after two years of planning, *this* bum relaxed and let the trip take him.

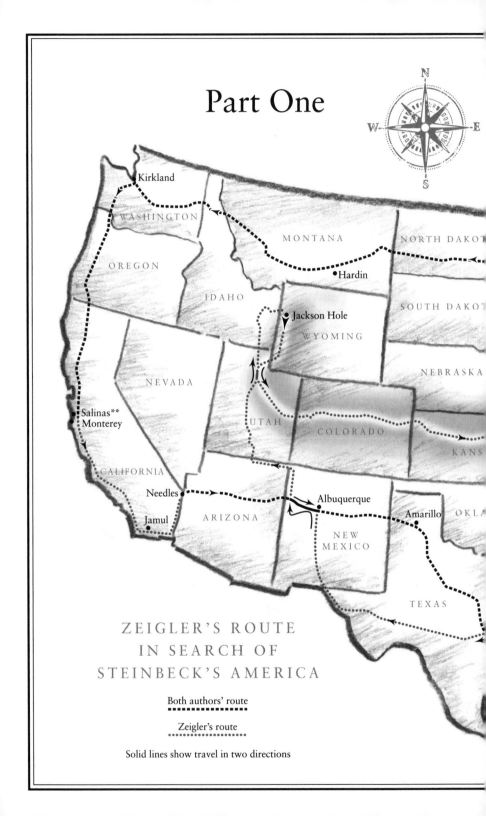

Part One

ZEIGLER'S ROUTE
IN SEARCH OF
STEINBECK'S AMERICA

Both authors' route
••••••••••••••

Zeigler's route
••••••••••••••••••••

Solid lines show travel in two directions

Preparation for
the Long Journey

*Sag Harbor was
Steinbeck's point of departure

**Salinas is Steinbeck's
birthplace and resting place

Chapter One
Leaving Tracks

In sixty years, I've left a lot of tracks.
John Steinbeck, 1962

Follow in John Steinbeck's tracks—stand where he stood, imagine what he saw, and try to determine "what Americans are like today." That was my goal. It was never my intention to diminish in any way or even imitate what Steinbeck accomplished with his trip. I don't presume to set myself beside him as a writer or pretend to offer a critical analysis of his writing. Mine was a pilgrimage fueled by admiration, firm but not fanatical. My plan was to follow Steinbeck's roadmap and, if fortunate, to offer a fresh perspective on America. Henry Miller wrote, "One's destination is never a place but rather a new way of looking at things."

During the early planning, I wrestled with questions of authenticity. Should I purchase the same brand of truck, camp in the same manner, even adopt a standard poodle like Charley? I concluded that I had to make decisions with the sort of "clear, concise, and reasonable" forethought that Steinbeck used in his trip preparations (see *Travels with Charley*).

I'm no mechanic, so I needed a familiar and reliable vehicle. I decided to camp in a safe and comfortable manner and to take a canine companion that I knew and loved. These decisions also saved money, in short supply for just about everybody in 2009. My Toyota 4Runner was my vehicle, our Airstream trailer my camper, and Nellie, sturdy grand-dog—a mutt of great heart, my intended canine companion. Nellie was ten, as was Charley. She was a chow/Lab cross and had the stubbornness and power of the chow but the tenderness and tolerance of the Lab. Our dog, Max, the tiny white Maltese, did not seem suitable. Although old dogs rule, and in the dog world ten is the new five, nine weeks on the road would surely be too hard on Max, who was fourteen and partially deaf.

Nellie's owner of record, my daughter, Jamie, lives with her husband, Paul, in a shoebox apartment in Manhattan; therefore, Nellie resides in Salt Lake City with my former wife, Merry. Ten days before my departure, my ex-wife sent an email accusing me

My trusted guide to Steinbeck's route, a 1959 Rand McNally.

of a transgression I had committed with a dog some thirty-five years ago and telling me unequivocally that Nellie was not going on the trip. I commiserated with my friend, Tommy, and he suggested a dognapping could add to the drama of this saga. Instead, I went to my wife, Dimmie, and asked for permission to take Max. Why not Max in the first place? As I said, I had chalked it up to age and infirmity. That, at least, was my excuse. The change in circumstances forced me to look deeper and examine my small-dog bias.

In addition to not being a large or even medium-sized dog, Max has some, uh, issues, which I will delve into in greater depth later. But first let me be more honest about *my* issues. I'm a big dog person, always have been. When I gave Max to Dimmie, in an attempt to replace (always a mistake) a favorite small dog of hers, I had Bandon, a robust, intelligent and, well, large Australian shepherd. It was a perfect arrangement—his and her dogs. But we lost Bandon to a bizarre illness at the age of eleven, at which point, weighing in at seven pounds and closely resembling a white dust mop, Max became top dog.

Frankly, "top dog" has always been Max's aspiration. He eschews any suggestion that he's a lap dog. He warmly greets any human being, but I have also seen him throw himself into the jaws of pit bulls—and I'm not lying. Just prior to my trip around America, Max was in San Francisco with us visit-

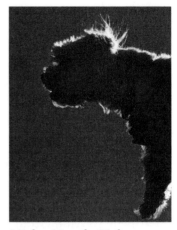

Mighty Max the Maltese.

ing our son, Wil. Max and I were sitting outside our hotel in Wil's rather seedy Tenderloin district while every manner of human being walked, staggered or wheeled by (that is, those who were not prone on the sidewalk). Max didn't remark on any of them. But when a German shepherd had the nerve to stroll down the other side of the busy avenue, Max went nuts. I have to admit the San Francisco trip caused me to look at Max from a different perspective. For all intents and purposes, he had to live in the car in San Francisco and he never had an accident (see *that* issue addressed below). Each time we put him down on the pavement, he was off down the street like a sailor on shore leave, sniffing everything in range. I remember thinking Max seemed rejuvenated; perhaps all he needed was an adventure.

Now to the big issue: Max is no longer willing to go through all those antics that dogs are trained to go through—lacking the right words—to go out. He just goes, anywhere he pleases, except in his kennel. Needless to say, this has caused some stress around our house. We are pretty fastidious people. The vet examined Max and assured us there was nothing wrong physically, that this new development was behavioral, perhaps related to senility. I say "new development," but, truth be told, Max has been so hit and miss—well, mostly hit, as in hit the floor and Oriental rugs—over the years that he might just be getting the olfactory signal that the house is a perfectly acceptable place to fire away. We certainly were not going to swat him or try to house break him all over again at the age of fourteen. Now Dimmie is one of the most loving and tolerant people I know, but even she, in moments of extreme frustration, has uttered the "eu" word—choose one: (a) euphoria (b) eulogize (c) euthanize (d) euphemism.

I'm a big believer in the power of women. By virtue of the fact that women give life, in my view, they pretty much have the right to take it away. Within reason, that is. But ambivalent as my relationship has always been with Max, I couldn't conceive of his checking out (or being checked out) anytime soon. Although for much of his life I had mostly tolerated and ignored Max, I had too many memories of our boys, Alex and Wil, holding him and playing with him. I suddenly realized that this adventure might not only revive Max, it could be a reprieve. To quote, Rowlf, the Muppet, Max might gain "a new *leash* on life." I decided Max and I were going to spend nine weeks together on the road.

So when my friend, Tommy, was told Nellie-napping was out of the question and that I was taking Max on my trip, he said, "Pretty cool, after a rich long life, to cap it off with a trip around America."

"Are you talking about Max or me?" I asked.

"Both of you," he said.

Max had nine teeth removed just before we departed. The vet reassured us, saying, "Max doesn't really need to hunt and kill his food." No kidding. At first the little guy was a bit under the weather, and chewing was really not an option. But his antibiotics and daily meds seemed to revive him rapidly, and within a matter of days on the road he was his "old" self. One morning early in the trip, while disguising his baby aspirin in some string cheese, slicing open a smelly capsule for his fish oil, and crushing his glucosamine onto his food, it occurred to me I was pretty much taking the same meds—plus my blood pressure pills.

Apart from the dog, another important decision I made was that I, like Steinbeck, had to do this alone. Dimmie is a supportive and dear friend—my traveling companion in life. There is nothing I like better than the two of us heading off on an adventure, pulling our little Airstream. But Dimmie works full-time, and nine weeks away from home was out of the question. So for the purpose of practicality and reasons of authenticity, Dimmie visited us en route three times—in Georgia, Chicago and California, just as often as Elaine Steinbeck visited John—in Chicago, California and Texas. Elizabeth Berg made a strong case for the unique experience intrinsic to solo travel in her article titled, "Amalfi Coast" in *National Geographic Traveler* (Vol. 27, No. 3). "When you travel with someone, there is a natural inclination to view things from a shared perspective that in some respects insulates you from the experience at hand or even dilutes it. Traveling solo not only gave me a clearer vision of a community and its people but of myself. And that, to borrow somewhat from Robert Frost, made all the difference." I guess you could say I was seeking that different experience.

As the trip approached, I began to organize and file my abundant notes from the previous two years of research. Many were loose, and others were tucked in various notebooks, legal pads and journals. I found some in unusual places, such as the console of my car, but none were as creatively archived as the ones Steinbeck discovered after his trip, rubber-banded to a bottle of ketchup. One day, while sorting, I stumbled upon a list I had scribbled in 1998. I was fifty-two at the time. A notation with the list indicated I had created it after reading an article about "life lists" in *Outside Magazine.* I hadn't looked at it again until that day.

The life list was not directly related to my Steinbeck odyssey, so after a quick review and a bit of nostalgia, I was setting it aside when something held me. I looked more closely. I counted four health and physical fitness goals and four that related to family. There were three goals involving volunteerism and two each for writing and intellectual self-improvement. All well and good, but this really grabbed me—eight out of twenty-five entries involved travel. One of those was "to drive and camp across America again."

Around the time I created the list, I had recently been named president of Rabun Gap-Nacoochee School in Georgia, a very well-endowed school with great potential, a plum of a job, yet none of the items on my life list related even remotely to my career as a school head. In searching for Steinbeck's tracks, I found muddy footprints of my own. Now that I am unemployed, or retired, not sure which, I should be able to complete the list, right? All I need is time.

I recently discovered that, at sixty-two, I qualified for the Golden Age Pass—free entrance to all national parks and monuments. I purchased my pass at the gate to Grand Teton National Park. It cost $10. I had scored a great deal, yet I drove away with a deep sense of unease. For the first time in my life I possess a document that expires, not in twelve months, which is typical, not even in ten years. It expires, well, when I do. All I need is time.

John Steinbeck died in December of 1968. He was sixty-six years old.

On my life list in 1998, I set a rather ambitious goal to read all the classics of American literature. Instead, I've focused almost exclusively on the life and work of one man. Besides his patent humanity and personal struggles, it is Steinbeck's love of story that most captures me. When Samuel Hamilton in *East of Eden* says,

"I eat stories like grapes," I believe Steinbeck is talking about himself. I was fascinated to learn that he bought the story of a man being rescued from starvation by the intimate gift of a woman's breast milk from a hobo who said it had happened to him. The author paid two dollars for this powerfully human and controversial conclusion to *The Grapes of Wrath,* one of the great American classics. Steinbeck's publisher tried to get him to alter it. He refused. This provocative scene became one excuse for many attempts to ban the book, but stands in today's editions.

I have never collected objects of any sort. I don't have a postcard, stamp or baseball card collection. Except for mental snapshots, I take few photographs. The only thing I collect is stories. Everybody's got one and, for the most part, people are eager to share. Often in my career, I went to fund-raising parties prepared to meet a lot of people and work the room, but I just couldn't do it. I'd fall into a story. I'd become completely engrossed in the tale old Mrs. Taylor was telling and want to spend the rest of the evening talking with her. Before I knew it, the party was over. I'd leave knowing one or two people very well but missing briefer contacts with many others. I learned during my research that John Steinbeck was very much the same way: if he was conversing with people, or just simply observing them, they had his full attention. And Steinbeck focused on people because they were interesting, not because of whatever advantage he might gain by knowing them.

Stories captivate me. One Memorial Day weekend, I was talking with a seventy-three-year-old father and his middle-aged son who had ridden their Harleys from Jackson, Mississippi, to Jackson, Wyoming. The dad put it well; he said, "Half the fun of these trips is the folks you meet and their stories." Stories constitute the fabric that binds us as people. They carry messages straight to the core of our being and speak about essential matters.

To paraphrase author Barry Lopez on the art of storytelling, sometimes people need a story more than they need food. Or as Lee says in *East of Eden*, explaining what makes stories resonate with people, "...a great and lasting story is about everyone."

As a writer, Steinbeck was brilliant at capturing and creating character-driven stories. At times, as Jackson Benson points out in *John Steinbeck, Writer: A Biography*, Steinbeck was criticized for not connecting the scenes as artfully as the traditional novel form requires. I would add, however, no one could question his brilliance at crafting the nuances of dialect and character, especially of Americans. Think of Lenny in *Of Mice and Men* and Casy in *The Grapes of Wrath*. One of the most rewarding elements of my trip was gathering the stories of typical Americans, especially "the man in the field," which is how Steinbeck described the sort of person he wanted to meet on his travels. I found Americans on my trip to be eager to share their stories, and I gobbled them up.

John Steinbeck was a complex and paradoxical man. He had a child-like enthusiasm and curiosity for detail. He was a scientist and a naturalist but also mystical and sentimental. He was often paranoid, depressed and lonely, especially as his fame grew. Steinbeck was passionate about America and, at the same time, harshly critical of it. He enjoyed great success and elaborate travel, but simplicity and privacy were what he truly sought. He was modest, shy, thin-skinned, idealistic and outraged by injustice. Steinbeck summarized his philosophy regarding the oppressed in a letter to an Ohio University graduate student, Merle Danford, in 1938, "I don't like people to be hurt or hungry or unnecessarily sad." Steinbeck enjoyed an intimate relationship with nature. Jay Parini in the introduction to the 1997 Penguin edition of *Travels with Charley* writes, "As Steinbeck moved slowly toward California, he grew steadily more disenchanted with everything except the natural world."

The author married three times and, according to his biographers, battled bitterly with his second wife, Gwyn, resulting in his turbulent relationship with their sons, Thom and John. He won the Nobel Prize for Literature in 1962, and yet he suffered vicious criticism throughout his career that insisted he had produced nothing of equivalent merit to *The Grapes of Wrath*, published in 1939. As heart disease began to take its toll near the end of Steinbeck's life and friends suggested he slow down and do less, he chose instead to drive, mostly solo, eleven thousand miles around the United States. He justified his decision in a letter written during his trip to his wife, Elaine, on October 10, 1960, from Mauston, Wisconsin, "I'm still a man, damn it. This may seem silly but to me it isn't."

As for me, I got to know Steinbeck well and had one hell of an adventure following his tracks around the country. To date, I haven't come close to reading all the classics of American literature, but I did get to recreate one of the classic American odysseys. I offer here a modern perspective on that journey, and on this great country.

Chapter Two
Where Am I?

Place where folks live is them folks.
The Grapes of Wrath

John Steinbeck had a life-long interest in *who* Americans were in relation to *where* they were. Steinbeck believed place equaled character. In his fiction, he often depicted the dysfunction that resulted from rootlessness. In his non-fiction, he railed against the impact of the mobile home on American culture.

So if place equals character, who and where am I? Except for some extended travel in Europe and Mexico, Steinbeck lived "permanently" in only two states, California and New York. I was raised in Pennsylvania and have lived in nine other states.

We bought our place in Wyoming in 1986 when I was the director of the Teton Science School based in Grand Teton National Park, but we only lived in it for one year before shoving off for jobs in several other states. In 2005, we moved back to Wyoming "permanently," but after working for both a hot air balloon company and the post office in Moose, Wyoming, for $15 an hour, I needed to seek more lucrative and fulfilling work—hard to find in Jackson Hole. So I commuted to Vancouver, Washington, for two years as an interim head of a progressive elementary school. My family remained in Jackson. I retired (again) from headmastering in June of 2008 and returned to Jackson, determined to make it "permanent." This time I even landed a suitable part-time job writing and editing for an educational website (although my job did not survive the "fall" of 2008). But that winter, an intriguing offer that would have required another move tested my resolve. Although the job was attractive, I fought and won an exhausting wrestling match with ambition. After much thought and discussion, I said no to the offer and yes to permanency in our home in Jackson Hole, Wyoming. And that at the age of sixty-two. Why is that so hard?

Being a baby-boomer growing up in a post-war time of plenty, I moved, not so much from necessity for work, but using work as an excuse. Once, after deciding as a young teacher to pull up stakes again, I took out a map of New England and drew a circle around towns with independent schools and a square around nearby ski resorts. I was a fanatic hiker, backpacker and skier and never wanted to drive more than a few hours to the nearest mountains. For a time, I was even a wilderness and mountaineering instructor. Mountains and wild places have had a special pull in my life and, although I've moved a lot, I've always lived near mountains. Another western author to whom place was very important was Wallace Stegner. Stegner moved a lot during his life. He wrote that he was always "going away east and coming home west." I realized in my early thirties that I was always traveling to the West for adventure and returning home to the East. I was determined to correct that. I moved to Salt Lake City in 1976 and have felt the West was my home since.

Put another way, I feel like I have been running from the necktie all my adult life. I was raised on a boys' boarding school campus where ties were required for most of the day. In Wyoming when I first arrived, I was informed that wearing a tie to a party guaranteed it would be cut off with scissors. During my early tenure at the Teton Science School, I was scheduled to meet the governor with my professor friend, Flo Krall, a Wyoming native. I showed up wearing a tie and Flo chided me for falling back on my upbringing. Sure enough, the governor was bare-necked when we met. Historically, a "necktie party" is a very different concept in Wyoming, reserved for cattle rustlers and horse thieves, and that suits me just fine, as long as I'm never the guest of honor.

But certain ties are hard to break. My longest tenure away from my new home, the West, was in the South. Although we kept our home in Jackson and always felt a tug to return, we lived for eight years in the Smokey Mountains on the bucolic campus of Rabun Gap-Nacoochee School. Following that, we lived for one year nearby on the bend of a rushing stream in southwestern North Carolina. Perhaps the length of our stay in the South was influenced by the fact that so many southerners are tied to place and oriented to family. For example, during my headship at the school, I participated in an educational leadership program just across the Chattooga River at Clemson University, in the South Carolina foothills of the Appalachian Mountains.

One day at lunch, I was seated across from another school principal. To make conversation, I asked him where he'd like to live in retirement.

"Oh, I'm sure I'll stay right here in Clemson. Maybe become a Walmart greeter or something," he said. "I grew up here and attended high school and college right here. Most of my family's here. I can't imagine living anywhere else." He paused, chewed and continued wistfully, "Had a brother moved to Athens, though. Don't know what got into him."

Athens is Athens, Georgia, less than fifty miles away from Clemson, *but* different state, university and football team.

That vignette reminds me of a story Utah author Terry Tempest Williams told me about Wallace Stegner. Although Stegner grew up without roots or a hometown, he always thought of Salt Lake City, where he attended high school and college, as home (even late in life when he was living in California and Vermont). Terry was assigned to drop Stegner off at the airport after a speaking engagement in Salt Lake City. Williams uttered the standard, courteous, "Wallace, thank you for coming."

"Thank you, Terry, for staying," Stegner replied.

I've finally found a place where I think I can stay. After so much wandering, my home in Wyoming is the place that defines me. Our lot beneath the cliffs of East Gros Ventre Butte, four miles north of Jackson, has a stunning view of Sleeping In-

Sleeping Indian Mountain—a part of our place.

dian Mountain, which resembles an American Indian in full headdress lying peacefully on his back. Jackson was the first place Dimmie and I moved to as a married couple. It is where our first son, Alex, was born. We struggled to hang onto our home in Wyoming while living and working in four other states, always yearning and planning to return.

Dimmie and I agree that if a wild wind blew up and blasted our house off our butte, we would settle down in the rubble and continue to stare at "our" mountain, and watch for bison, wolves, elk, swans and cranes on the twenty-five thousand acre National Elk Refuge below. I would still enjoy the sagebrush that stand taller than my head and smell like minty green tea after a rain. House or no, I would still love the quiet, the cliffs, the brilliant sunrises that light up our lot like a stage set. My job may be anywhere and I've lived in many houses, but my *home* is in Wyoming.

Don't get me wrong; living in paradise can be hell. It's damn difficult to raise children in a resort (think *party*) atmosphere. Stuff is expensive if you can find it. Real estate is outrageous if you can buy it. It's tough to make a living even if you land a job. At six thousand feet it's impossible to grow produce. It's hard to see the beauty in ten inches of wet snow in May. But this place is in my bone marrow. I know we will never give it up. I hope someday—after the age of eighty-five—surrounded by my wife, children and grandchildren, to lie down parallel to the Sleeping Indian in this place, draw my last breath and, after one hell of a wake, provide much-needed nutrients to the sagebrush.

Steinbeck's strong belief in the power of place aside, he felt ambivalent about his roots in Salinas, California. An outsider as a youth, he never felt at home there as an adult. The region and its denizens fed his fiction, but that caused resentment from those who didn't appreciate how he depicted them and from others who questioned his left-leaning politics. In addition to other affronts, local bookstores declined to carry his earlier books, and a book club, of which his mother was a member, refused to read him, saying the club only considered "decent" books.

After several failed attempts to live in central California as an adult, Steinbeck ended up fleeing, living in New York City and summering in Sag Harbor on Long Island—staying close to the sea, which he dearly loved, but far away from where he grew up. On his trip around America he stopped to visit family and, as he wrote in *Travels with Charley,* "I arrived in Monterey and the fight began." After nightly arguments over politics with his conservative sisters, and almost getting in a fight at Johnny Garcia's bar, his old watering hole, Steinbeck concluded, "Tom Wolfe was right. You can't go home again because home has ceased to exist except in the mothballs of memory. My departure was flight."

In a letter sent prior to his journey around America to Elizabeth Otis, his friend and agent, Steinbeck wrote, "I want the thing in context against its own background—one place in relation to another." He called his trip "Operation Windmills," in answer to the skepticism of so many of his friends, and chose a 1960 GMC truck he named Rocinante after Don Quixote's horse. I discovered something while reading *Don Quixote* that Steinbeck did not mention in *Travels with Charley.* Rocinante, the name of Don

Quixote's bony old nag used in tilting at windmills, defending damsels—whether they needed defending or not—and righting other perceived wrongs, means "formerly an ordinary horse." That has such delightful universal applicability. For example, I suppose I could say I was formerly an ordinary golfer, now I'm just a bad golfer.

Steinbeck's home was a Wolverine Camper that rode in the bed of the pickup. I was surprised to learn from Thomas Steinbeck that his father had never camped prior to his journey. When I asked Thomas how that was possible, he said, "Dad grew up working on a ranch in Salinas; he figured he could do anything." As I followed Steinbeck's truck tracks, I lived in my sixteen-foot Bambi, the smallest trailer made by the venerable Airstream company.

As a fellow nomad, I'm interested in the beginnings of modern American mobility. The car trailer business, begun in the 1920s, prospered during the Great Depression. According to *Airstream: The History of the Land Yacht*, Wally Byam, the father of the modern travel trailer, "…saw early on that the legions of wheat harvesters, cotton pickers, journeymen mechanics, and factory workers migrating from job to job like the Joad family of John Steinbeck's *The Grapes of Wrath*, were seeking a simpler low cost alternative to the skyrocketing rents of the city."

Early on, Byam recognized that disenfranchised folks were not his only market, for over the years he positioned his rolling silver bullets as the very highly sought-after and pricey "land yachts" of the industry. I bought mine secondhand in 2006 with money inherited from my mother, Winifred, who loved to camp. I named it for her. I like to think it takes a self-assured man to travel around the country in a Bambi named Winnie.

Airstream has never produced many Bambis. They are so compact that only one person at a time can work inside. But the

Bambi has all I need to live comfortably on the road. The starboard exterior door opens onto the cozy dining nook on the right, providing seating for four. To the left is the bathroom. Straight ahead is an efficient galley, including stove, fridge and sink, and to the rear, past a closet, the "master bedroom." Every detail is carefully designed, every surface rounded to

The Bambi eating/writing space. Max awaits the muse.

avoid painful collisions. At 6' 2", I'm grateful there is ample headroom throughout. Winnie is well insulated, quiet, and tracks beautifully on the road. My favorite features are the gleaming look of the interior and exterior aluminum skin and the tinted wrap around windows both fore and aft. The trailer is a little mobile space that is easy to clean and organize. Just as many folks in 1960 asked Steinbeck about the then-unique Wolverine slide-in camper that rode in the bed of Rocinante, Winnie was a great conversation starter because Bambis are rare.

Steinbeck admitted in Part One of *Travels with Charley* that he was guilty of a little artifice for the purpose of starting conversations. He carried several rifles, a shotgun and a fishing pole, "for it is my experience that if a man is going hunting or fishing his purpose is understood and even applauded. Actually, my hunting days are over." He went on to write, "This stage setting turned out to be unnecessary."

I gave some thought to trying to create the appearance of having a purpose. I was never much of a hunter and don't own a gun, and I hadn't fished in years. I decided that a mountain bike on the top of my car would identify me as a purposeful person who was seeking manly outdoor adventure. Of course, hunting and fishing were what this journey was about, metaphorically speaking. Steinbeck, and I, tracked American characters in their habitats and tried to catch and consume their stories. My mountain bike was the last possession to get packed when the time came to gad about the country. Although it didn't turn out to be much of a conversation starter, I found the bike to be about as useful as any conveyance when tilting at windmills.

Sometime just before the trip, as I contemplated leaving my home for several months, it struck me that a journey is only a journey when one has a desirable place to come home to. Absent that, travel is not joyous exploration; it is aimless roaming.

All decisions had been made, all preparations finalized. It was time to leave our place in Wyoming, temporarily, and travel out in search of America.

Chapter Three
To the Grocery Store and Beyond

The moment or hour of leave-taking is one of the pleasantest times in human experience, for it has in it a warm sadness without loss. It would be good to live in a perpetual state of leave-taking, never to go nor to stay, but to remain suspended in that golden emotion of love and longing; to be missed without being gone; to be loved without satiety.

The Log from the Sea of Cortez

September, 2009

My Toyota 4Runner was pulled up to the basement door under our deck. Sun warmed me as I packed the car. Far below the house, the Elk Refuge grasses, dried to a fall umber and fringed with morning sunlight, set off the beauty of the evergreens on the distant Sleeping Indian Mountain. The splendor of the day made the prospect of leaving home for two months heartbreaking and thrilling at the same time.

Max and I say farewell to our place in Wyoming.

Packing is my forte, so I asked Dimmie to be in charge of the cooler and leave the car to me. (I later discovered a tragic oversight: she inadvertently left out the jar of homemade lemoncello given to me for the road by my friend, Dick.) Winnie was in Salt Lake City for repairs and a pre-trip check-up and I had a speaking engagement there, so my first planned stop was five hours driving time to the south. Soon the Toyota was jammed with gear for the whole journey, much of which would eventually be stored in the Bambi, and I was forced to strap a plastic food tub on the roof rack next to my mountain bike and Thule storage box.

Since Max was thrust into this undertaking sort of last minute, I didn't share the whole scope of the trip with him. I told him we were going to the grocery store...and beyond. He was assigned "shotgun" for the first leg. Dimmie took a photograph, which later became the banner of the Travels with Steinbeck blog, of me holding Max in front of the packed car. We had a warm, brief goodbye. Knowing we would be together one week hence in Georgia, and planned to see our son, Alex, there for the first time in eight months, made the departure easier. Max and I headed south through the town of Jackson on U.S. 89.

I had not driven fifteen miles before the screeching of the wind in the straps holding down the food box proved intolerable. I pulled over in front of a market in Hoback Junction. It turned out that I was already in need of a bathroom anyway, the beginning of a daily struggle that I later labeled the "Battle of the Bladder." Let me just mention what I learned repeatedly and often painfully during fifteen thousand miles of driving: it is wise for a man my age to tow his own bathroom. I emptied the food in the plastic tub into nooks and crannies in the back of the car, placed the tub on the only available space, Max's seat, and plopped him on his blanket *in* the tub. He sniffed around a bit, looked up at me as if to say, "This is different, but hell, I've seen it all in my fourteen years," and did what he does best, curled up and went to sleep. I was already beginning to see the advantages of traveling with a small dog.

It was Labor Day and the normally little-used back roads to Salt Lake were jammed with all manner of vehicles pulling flatbed trailers loaded with mud-spattered ATVs—grasping summer's last. After a few hours, I drifted through the meadows north of Randolph, a town of roughly five hundred in northeastern Utah, where, according to Wikipedia, 95 percent of all votes went to George W. Bush in 2004. Randolph sits in the heart of a high, flat country dotted with tawny, round hay bales and ringed with mountains—you're as likely to see a bald eagle near Randolph as a person. Giant, insect-like, metal irrigation monsters on rubber wheels sat ready to toss water the way a cowboy throws around money on a Saturday night. The most majestic building in town, constructed of pink bricks in an unusual design with elaborate sandstone block quoins and displaying a prominent tower, was the Mormon church.

Max in the box—the benefits of a small dog.

When I was living in Utah in 1982, a buddy from Salt Lake and I biked from Ogden to Randolph and got permission from the owners of an oiled log cabin to camp in their front yard. The yard was decorated with a large, metal cowboy and his horse. The following day I completed my first one-hundred-mile bicycle ride. As I drove through on the Steinbeck journey, I noticed the cabin was still there, as was the cowboy, freshly painted black. Not much changes in Randolph.

I spent the night in Salt Lake City at my sister Jeanne's house. Max had his first walk since his dental surgery—once around a tree-lined block. He did well, even managing to jump over the occasional curb. A large, gray woman sitting on a stool weeding the garden in front of her house said, "Hello there. Cute dog."

It was a cool, breezy evening punctuated by rustling leaves. Jeanne had arranged a visit with her friends, Penny and Rick, an industrious young couple with an angelic five-week-old daughter who was African-American. Penny and Rick had desperately wanted a baby, got one, and were thrilled—race was not a factor. These folks had gone through a five-year ordeal trying to locate a child. Prior to getting Caroline, Rick said he refused to get excited this time until he was holding the baby. I asked Rick if he was sleeping through the night.

"No, I just stay up all night staring at Caroline while she sleeps," he said.

I suppose some would say adopting a child of a different race bears additional responsibility. I would argue that blended families and mixed races are the future, and the ultimate end to racial tension. Racism is spawned by ignorance. Proximity eradicates ignorance.

Caroline's adoption almost certainly would not have happened fifty years ago in Utah at the time Steinbeck was traveling around America. Race was one of Steinbeck's interests. In New Orleans for *Travels with Charley,* he witnessed adult white females, referred to as "cheerleaders" in the national media, heckling small black children as they tried to fulfill the federal school-integration mandate. A crowd of local citizens cheered on the cheerleaders. Steinbeck had no tolerance for the powerful preying on the weak. He wrote that this display of virulent racism made him physically ill.

America has come a long way in fifty years...but President Obama spoke to America's school children in September 2009, and many American families, especially in Utah and Texas, wanted their kids to remain at home. Let's set politics aside for a second. Just let me ask, what about this man would make you think you couldn't trust him with your children for a weekend, let alone have him speak to them electronically? Unless, of course, this is all about race.

Later in Sag Harbor, at a dinner party, I made this same statement. One of the guests, a middle-aged white man who appeared to be well educated and urbane, said, "Maybe the kids were being programmed to react and applaud in certain places—you never know."

As if that were possible with a single classroom, let alone with millions of students.

Steinbeck did not cross the center of the country on his trip, so it would be several days of travel before I intersected with the last leg of his loop in Georgia, but later that night at my sister's house in Salt Lake, I read portions of both *The Log from the Sea of Cortez* and *The Pearl* and learned a great deal about

The second graders ride along.

John Steinbeck's writing process—an actual experience (the marine expedition with Ed Ricketts) fed his non-fiction *(Cortez)*, and that work of non-fiction shaped his fiction *(Pearl)*. I marveled at Steinbeck's timeless control of the language and beautiful imagery in either genre.

The next morning, Max and I, accompanied by my Sponge Bob Square Pants pillow, addressed all the second graders at Rowland Hall, Jeanne's school. Max was an instant hit, as was Sponge Bob. When Jeanne asked the students what sort of instrument I might need to navigate around the country (answer, GPS), Sam blurted, "A banjo?"

I thanked Sam for that wonderful suggestion and said perhaps I would take up the banjo after I mastered the Native American flute I carry in my trailer. I promised the kids that Max would send a postcard from every state we visited, and each card would have a red rubberstamp that read "Hello From Max" with a small paw print. The task of finding postcards in every state proved more difficult than one might imagine. Jeanne later reported to me that, about halfway through my travels, one of her little guys commented that it was nice getting cards and envelopes from

Max, but it would be great to occasionally hear how Bob was doing. Sponge Bob sent an update immediately thereafter.

Getting wonky in Winnie with Buddy Bob.

After a rousing sendoff from the second graders, I picked up the Airstream Bambi at a dealership south of Salt Lake and, now with much more room in the car and Max in the back, we made our way down the Beehive State on U.S. 6 to I-70 near Green River, Utah. Central Utah on U.S. 6 was predictably sunny and dry. It is the aridity that guarantees crystal-clear views. The dry climate also means less groundcover, resulting in exposed rock in vivid colors. The town of Green River ends (or begins, depending on direction) a one-hundred-and-fifteen-mile stretch of I-70 across beautiful high-desert desolation with no services. Soon after we joined the interstate, a sign cautioned, "Watch for Eagles on the Highway."

Max and I arrived at our goal for the day, Ami's Acres, a narrow, terraced RV park above I-70 and the Colorado River in Glenwood Springs, Colorado. Our campsite was perched high on the hill, in view of all, and required extreme trailer-backing skill. It had been a long day. Truthfully, I'm not good at backing up my Airstream after a short day; my only consolation is the knowledge that smaller one-axle trailers are the hardest to back up. After I made repeated failed attempts blundering backward in my rig, and came close to rolling it down a steep embankment, a concerned fellow camper came to my rescue and guided me back.

That evening, as the sun dropped behind the ridges, I sat in my camp chair and toasted a successful second day with a single shot of Jameson's Irish whiskey and a microbrew beer. Later I climbed up a steep walk, in the dark, to the bathhouse. A lean, muscled young man stood in the dim light at the sink shav-

The rig comes together in Salt Lake City.

ing...his head. His tanned shoulders were adorned with interesting tattoos—dragons, I think. We got to chatting and I realized, while he showed me around the bathhouse, that, although I had recently gotten my first, and last tattoo (a fir sprig—upper right deltoid), I had no idea what the protocol was surrounding body art. Should I say, "Nice tats, want to see mine?" while trying not to seem *too* interested.

I opted for safer subjects such as why Tim was living at the RV Park (affordable) and his two-hour round-trip commute to his house-painting job in Vail. He told me we were camped right across from the site of the July 1994 Storm King Fire, which killed fourteen firefighters. I did a little online research later and got to a website called "Inferno." I learned that Tim was not exaggerating. The conflagration was visible from I-70. A routine fifty-acre fire started by a lightning strike was being fought to prevent it from moving to the interstate when the wind changed direction and increased to gusts of close to fifty miles per hour. Suddenly, two thousand acres were ablaze and a wall of flame rushed toward the firefighters at thirty feet per second. Ten men and four women were overtaken and burned to death, many of them young people, all of them, in my view, heroic.

The next morning, I sat outside in the sun at the campground's only "hotspot." I was trying to send my first blog post from the road, and the connection was agonizingly slow. Below me, three ravens played on air currents above the interstate and river. I learned from an email that, with a little luck, I might land an interview with John Steinbeck's son, Thomas, when I was in southern California. Another message indicated Oregon Public Broadcasting was interested in being the presenting station for a documentary about my journey. Day three, and I was already on a roll!

I-70 from Glenwood Springs to Denver proved to be a most scenic stretch of superhighway. In steep-walled canyons, above the swiftly moving Colorado River, it was as if the future, a cascade of concrete ramps, met the wilderness. A sign just before Georgetown, Colorado, on a particularly steep declivity declared, "Truckers! Lost Brakes! Stay on I-70. Do Not Exit Into Town!" It occurred to me that caution could have been phrased so much more politely with a sign reading something like, "Truckers: In the event that you have lost your brakes, it would be deeply appreciated if, rather than in the heart of our city, you could crash somewhere else."

Denver was, well, a mess, but I got through it with relative ease, and eastern Colorado delivered what I had expected from Nebraska, which I erroneously thought lay straight ahead—a flat and treeless plain. I called my friend, Clint, and mentioned Nebraska; he informed me that it was Kansas I was heading toward. We passed Bovina, Colorado—no services in Bovina, only cows. My goal for the day proved unreachable (and for that matter, in the wrong state) so I rented a room at a Comfort Inn in Burlington, Colorado.

It rained gently during the night. The next morning, after breakfast, I went out to check on the Bambi. The sky was still overcast and the air had a fresh, moist, early-morning smell. Beside the parking lot, I spoke with two oilmen. One asked about the trailer. He commented that he had never seen such a small Airstream.

He said, "Me and my buddies travel constantly for work—

New York last week, Colorado this week. We're from Oklahoma, but motels are our friends. Iowa next week."

"Good money?" I asked.

"Not any more. Not in this economy." My talker—his buddy had taken a call on his cell—was huge, at least a yard wide in his coveralls, and he sported a scraggly, caramel-colored goatee.

"Why's that?"

He made a downward gesture with his right hand. "Soon as our new president came in, my work dropped straight off," he said, as he glanced at an attractive African-American woman sitting close by at a smoker's bench.

I pushed him and asked if his troubles hadn't really started during the last administration. "Nope, it was the month he took office." (He made the hand gesture again.) "I sit at home for months at a time without work and then have to travel much farther when I do have it—gotta go where the work is, but I only have a girlfriend, so it's not too bad."

"She doesn't mind?" I asked.

"As long as a man is bringing home money, we don't mind," the woman interjected with a smile.

We all laughed. "Even if he's gone for a month?" I asked.

"Yep! If that's what it takes," she said.

I tracked down that interesting woman and we conferred in the lobby. Her name was Marquitta and she was forty-two years old. Marquitta was from Aurora, a suburb of Denver. She was traveling with her parents to her aunt's funeral in Austin, Texas, and their car had broken down—twice. They were waiting for it to be fixed—again. Marquitta was serene, articulate and comfortable in her skin. She was family-oriented. She had a husband and three daughters and talked to her mother every day on the phone. But all that had come at a price. Thirteen years prior, she had been an addict distributing a controlled substance and got caught. As one who had straightened out her life and counseled at-risk folks professionally, she felt that, because of the stigma, it was just too hard for people to turn their lives around. Housing and credit were the two big problems for a person with a criminal record.

From left, Max, Otha, James and Marquitta.

"People don't even want someone who has had a misdemeanor. Plus, programs are not gender specific and most are geared toward men. Thus, the revolving door of women going in and out of prison," she said.

When I brought up politics, Marquitta said she felt the country needed to give Obama a chance. "We are such a microwave society. We want everything right away."

"Do you experience much racism?" I asked.

"Of course I run into it…" she narrowed her large eyes and leaned in, "…but I ain't got time for that bullshit. I've gone through so much. *I've* gotten out of my way, now I can't let petty people get in my way. I just look like—this is *your* problem—and walk away."

Later Marquitta, her father, James, a ramrod-straight, handsome man who was once a civil rights investigator and pastor but quit the ministry when he lost his sight to glaucoma in 2002, and her lovely mother, Otha Lee, posed outside for a picture with Max (thrown in for scale).

I went back in the Comfort Inn to check out. I noticed the woman behind the counter was studying a large pathology text. I spoke with her. Her name was Tonya. She was thirty-six, pretty in a plain sort of way, but with one eye a bit askew behind her glasses. The big book was part of a plan to earn a nursing degree so she could return home to live near her recently widowed mother in Oklahoma. Tonya was working on legal custody of her three kids, even though their father had moved out of state before resolving custody issues. She wanted things in order. Her two-year, prenursing degree had taken over three

Tonya, an average American?

years, so far, because she was a single mom and worked two jobs. She had no health insurance. Everything costs more in such a remote location. The economy had been especially tough on her, but she didn't tie her economic struggles directly to the current administration as the oilman had.

Struggling with the economic downturn, three kids, two jobs and nursing school—think this woman is a multi-tasker? And we call folks like Tonya *average* Americans.

Rolling east again on I-70, I reflected back on Burlington. John Steinbeck had great admiration for hard-working, blue-collar Americans. I wondered how he would have reacted to Tonya, Marquitta and my oilman. I think Steinbeck would have been impressed with their resilience, civility and utter lack of bitterness during difficult times. Most of all, I think he would have admired their optimism and resourcefulness. I felt good about the good people I'd met and the stories I'd captured.

One thing I learned on my trip around this country: the less attractive the terrain, the more outlandish the attractions used to convince travelers to get off the road briefly and leave some cash. I first discovered this while crossing barren eastern Colorado and encountering a pitch for a rather unusual cow. I contemplated stopping for the heavily advertised "cow with five legs," but I didn't get to see that peculiar animal because I was already feeling rushed.

Steinbeck wrote in *Travels with Charley* that, when it came time, he did not want to leave home. That's understandable, given his diagnosed health problems and the many people who discouraged him from taking the trip. But he was powerfully motivated by a desire to escape the "sweet trap...of semi-invalidism," and to avoid trading "quality for quantity" in his life. Steinbeck was often depressed and homesick on his journey. After Abingdon, Virginia, he wrote, "The way was a gray, timeless, eventless tunnel, but the end of it was the one shining reality—my own wife, my own house in my own street, my own bed."

Although five years older than John Steinbeck at the start of my trip, I was enjoying the fortune of good health. I felt nothing but exhilaration and anticipation, and, although my schedule was a little too tight, the constant demands of driving, camping, regular blogging and speaking engagements kept me too busy to get homesick. But in fairness to John, he was in his tenth week on the road when he captured his feelings in Abingdon. I was only four days out as I approached Kansas.

The flat farmland east of Burlington, Colorado, spawned a thought: sometimes you're in Kansas before you leave Colorado.

When I finally entered Kansas, I remembered a story my brother, David, told me. Years ago, he was driving one of the flat-to-the-horizon two-lanes across Kansas, through wheat and cow country, when a stock truck passed in the opposite direction. Apparently, a cow had her butt right up against the slats of the truck and a yellow stream was ejected horizontally within twenty feet of my brother's little car. He drove directly into the spray, which blocked his vision and caused him to turn on his wipers. His thought as he pulled over to the shoulder: thank God, I'm not in a convertible.

Truth be told, Kansas was beautiful and a pleasure to cross on I-70. The terrain got rolling and pretty around Manhattan (the Little Apple). And a four-lane highway cuts way down on bovine rain. That evening, in eastern Kansas, at the end of a fifty-mile stretch of interstate without a gas station, I coasted into Mill Creek RV Park with my gas gauge reading below empty. While Judy, the owner, sold me five gallons of gas from a can, Betty, her mom, came out of the office carrying Maizie the Maltese to meet Maxie the Maltese. You would think the opportunity for at least a little Mal-teasing and flouncing would have been perfect; Maizie and Max just yapped at each other.

The attractive grounds of the Mill Creek RV Park included the Paxico, Kansas, train station, picturesque but out of service. Still, just over a fence, the tracks were active and freight trains rushed by so close you could almost spit in the boxcars. The men's room came equipped with a church pew and was situated right beside the clearly marked storm shelter.

Parked by a lake in the Midwest on private property, Steinbeck was accosted by a young man whose job it was to throw him off for trespassing. After the author artfully defused the situation, the man not only allowed Steinbeck to camp in Rocinante near the lake, he came back the next morning to fish with him.

I thought of that scene from *Travels with Charley* as I went down to Mill Creek behind the campground with three young men, a boy and a dog in search of catfish, and in so doing caught my big story for the day.

Josh's six-year-old son, Isaac, stubbed a finger on a pass thrown by his dad and wailed briefly, but was soon placated with a trip to nearby Mill Creek. The stream was running high. Mark, an electrician's apprentice, waded in and right up the middle of the rushing stream, followed by his dog. He wore his lineman's harness, with his hound dog, named Hound Dog, attached to it by a nylon rope so the dog couldn't float away. Adam, also an apprentice, scrambled, with Josh and Isaac, down to a sand bar in a bend of the creek. Isaac squatted and tossed pebbles into the current. I stood on a bank above the water and

"We're still in Kansas, Max."

watched the men cast. A bet of thirty bucks was riding on the first fish caught. Dusk came on with a riot of night sounds, as freight trains hammered by. In the haze, the moon looked like a slice of lemon.

Josh, his wife, April, Isaac and their baby girl, Ruthie, were living at the RV park while remodeling their house in Paxico. Adam, Mark and Hound Dog shared a separate trailer. Josh had never lived more than fifty miles from that spot. He liked it that way; small towns suited. Earlier, over dinner together at a picnic table, Josh had said eight of his crew of eighteen at Capital Electric, where he was a foreman, had been laid off, and several had been demoted. Work was slow. But, I thought, life goes on; houses are remodeled, catfish are caught (on a good night that is; they all got skunked that night) and boys learn to catch a spiral pass. Later, as I reflected on that richly textured evening, I was most impressed with the fact that, as a complete stranger bearing strange foods such as hummus and hardtack, which Josh had never heard of but was willing to try, I was welcomed for an evening into the world of these young Kansans.

Morning dawned, dripping with fog. I walked Max along the tracks and photographed trains barreling out of the mist. As a child in rural western Pennsylvania, I learned the thrill of stand-

Pieces of the past in Paxico, Kansas.

ing close to tracks, feeling the impact of air and sound as trains approached, and hearing the metallic cadence as they passed and departed. The thrill was not gone.

Later I drove through yellow cornrows as tall as the car and visited the Beecher Bible and Rifle Church, founded in 1857 in Wabaunsee, and the rather tacky Oz Museum in Wamego, founded the previous summer for all I knew. There was no one around at the church. Although it was pleasant enough looking, I wondered if it was a place where one checked one's rifle at the door before going inside to pound bibles. I learned later I was wrong.

The museum did provide a handy way to get my Kansas postcard for the second graders back in Salt Lake. I purchased one with Dorothy and Toto and the quote, "Toto, I've a feeling we're not in Kansas any more." I knew the kids would love it.

I climbed back in the car and quipped, "I've a feeling we're still in Kansas, Max." He extended his tongue and panted asthmatically. I took that for a wry chuckle. Wamego is in Pottawatomie County just north of the Kansas River. I read a copy of the *Wamego Times* over breakfast at a café I had learned about from a goateed fellow filling his pickup at The Pump gas station. He recommended the Friendly Cooker on Main after determining that I was an "egg and meat kinda guy" like him. On the front page of the *Times* was a picture of the cheering crowd during the Wamego Raiders' "opening kickoff" at the "home opener." On page eight there was an article about a locals' fishing trip to Green River Lake in Wyoming, about two hours from Jackson Hole.

I spent the rest of the day on the final leg of Kansas, bypassing Topeka and Kansas City, and crossing Missouri on I-70. I stopped for the night at a Comfort Inn in Warrenton, just west of St. Louis. I parked the Bambi in the motel parking lot without unhooking her from the car—a choice I often made when my stay was going to be brief. That simplified arriving and departing, but meant I had no car to drive around town.

The Hideout, offering "Beer, Food, Fun," was right up the street from the motel. The bar's dark interior was welcome after a long day in the sun on the road. The draft beer was cold. Several men dressed in black leather vests adorned with patches, and matching flame-streaked ball caps, trooped in. The men, ranging in age from thirties to sixties, were orderly but clearly had a strong sense of camaraderie; women accompanied several. I asked the young, bottle-blonde, tattooed waitress if she knew anything about the group. She said they were a motorcycle gang. That didn't seem right, even after I'd had a beer. I saw a guy wearing a blue T-shirt that read, "Cubs Baseball, An Alternative to Winning Since 1908," speaking with one of the newcomers. I intercepted the Cubs fan on his way to the restroom and inquired about the "gang." He appeared to have beaten me to the bar by several hours and slurred his reply, "BMWs, I mean POWs."

Finally, I caught one of the gray-haired members of the group and inquired again. He informed me with a smile that they were not a motorcycle gang and not POWs either. They were all veterans of Vietnam and Iraq, members of the local VFW. Earlier that afternoon, they had read the names of fourteen-hundred Missouri war dead at a replica Vietnam Memorial, and then dropped into the Hideout for a couple of beers and dinner.

I thought a lot about the men in that bar—unusual for me—but on that night I *was* thinking about the men. Even those who were a little tipsy were not in the least bit threatening. But then perhaps that impression was distorted by the fact that I was exceeding my usual two-beer

The Beecher Bible and Rifle Church.

limit. After two beers and dinner, I requested the bill from my waitress, and I was pretty certain she had heard me. She came back a few minutes later without the check, smiled, and shouting over the music and chatter, asked if I wanted another beer. That is a remarkable marketing technique, I thought, and went for it. That gave me more time to observe the men in the room and to appreciate the talents of "Bob, the One Man Band," who had just started his first set. I realized every man I had approached on the trip thus far had been warm and helpful. I found that reassuring. My bill, when I finally received it, for fish, chips, slaw and three beers? Twelve dollars—and thirty cents.

The next morning, in the motel breakfast room, I met two folks from—where else—eastern Kansas. Sometimes you're still in Kansas even after you've crossed to the other side of Missouri. Jane and Carroll were heading home to their farm in Green, Kansas. They were returning from Pittsburgh and a conference on Welsh heritage, a particular interest of Jane's. We sat at a round table and sipped coffee. I asked about the farm. Carroll said they raised grain after many years of rearing hogs. He was tan, sturdy, stocky, and seventy-one years old. When he lifted his cup there was a barely perceptible shake. Jane was buxom and bright-eyed, in her mid-sixties, with shiny white hair. They both had thick hands that looked powerful enough to crack walnuts. Jane said they had slept half the nights on their two-week trip in their Pontiac Vibe. I told Carroll sleeping in his car in his seventies made him my role model.

Jane said, "Well, the seats recline partway, plus we don't sleep well. Might as well not sleep well in the car at a campground as in a motel."

I mentioned visiting the Beecher Bible and Rifle Church. Jane said she had an interest in the history of the Underground Railroad in eastern Kansas. She explained that the church was established by folks who drove their wagons from Connecticut to Kansas with their bibles visible on top of their wagons and their rifles hidden underneath—determined to fight for their belief that Kansas should remain free of slavery. She said the church is still functioning after one hundred and fifty-three years. It dawned on me that I was talking to a Kansas farm wife who sounded like a liberal.

When asked, Jane said with a fist pump, "Absolutely, I'm a child of the sixties."

Carroll said he was the more pragmatic one and that he had only recently joined Jane as a Democrat. Jane beamed at the wisdom in her husband's recent conversion. I could only imagine how long this forceful "child of the sixties" had been working on him. Carroll told me with pride how many four-year college degrees there were in their two families. He said one of their two sons (now both college educated) had considered dropping out of college at one point, "but he was afraid of what would happen when he told his mother."

I inquired about the economy.

"Grain has collapsed, but not necessarily because of the

economy," Carroll said.

Then Jane proceeded to give me a lecture in buying futures that she said are controlled by hedge funds, during which I smiled, nodded and remained clueless. I did learn one thing; grain sales have little to do with actual supply and demand. I asked how many other Democrats there were in Green.

"Uh, one other family," Jane said. "And oh, my sister-in-law, Helen, too."

Forty percent of the Democrats from Green, Kansas.

I had just enjoyed coffee with forty percent of the Democrats from Green, Kansas. I asked what the Obama chatter was like out there. Jane said people are tolerant and giving in general, but the talk was getting nasty.

"Too much radio," Jane said.

"Too much Rush," said Carroll.

I asked Carroll and Jane to meet me outside before they left. I photographed them in front of their Vibe and said goodbye. On the road, I smiled, remembering that Carroll had called their car his "Obama machine" because he bought it using the government "Cash for Clunkers" program.

In a suburb of St. Louis, close to the Illinois line, I realized I hadn't found a Missouri postcard. My rig, including car, is over thirty-five feet long and, remember, I don't back up well, so I enter every gas station and parking lot anxiously, planning my escape. I considered several places with no luck; some were too small and crowded to chance getting stuck, and others I stopped at had no postcards. Desperate, I finally grabbed some materials on an Arby's counter, free for the taking, a Rams pro football schedule, which I discovered later had a Bud Light ad on the back, and an announcement for a local tent revival, a "Power Weekend" with the Winds of Pentecost Church, conducted by an evangelist who had reportedly died and been revived thirty minutes later by God. (When the envelope arrived, my sister called and said she got a chuckle out of my choice of Missouri materials, but still she tacked them up on the map for the kids with the other postcards and notes.)

I got lost trying to find my way back to the interstate and stopped at a gas station. A helpful man consulted with a friend in a separate car and got me back on track immediately. An unoccupied recent-model pickup truck at that same gas station had a bumper sticker carrying a picture of Obama with one word below it: "Joke."

At long last I was forced to leave I-70 in St. Louis, Missouri. From there I followed I-64 and I-57, past the town of Zeigler (no relation) in southern Illinois, a town with a strange and violent coal mining history from its founding in 1914 to the early 1950s, and took I-24 across western Kentucky to Nashville, Tennessee. Then it was I-40 to Clyde, North Carolina, and finally, smaller roads to Rabun Gap in north Georgia. That leg of the trip took over two days. All together, during my first week on the road, I drove twenty-three-hundred miles.

I got a call from my son, Alex, while crossing Kentucky. We chatted a bit about travel and he told me I was becoming a "rubber tramp." He said he had read somewhere that a "foot tramp" is a vagabond on foot and a "rubber tramp" is a vagabond in a vehicle. I told him I liked that description.

In order to tell you the *rest* of this story, I need to provide a little background. Prior to moving to Georgia, Alex had made several failed attempts to "launch." He dropped out of college and came home, got a job and soon lost it, and because he was unable to live by our simple family rules, ended up living in his car in a parking lot. All this, as you might imagine, was breaking our hearts. We felt helpless. One day after "friends" stole the wheel off his car claiming he owed them money, Alex came to us, hood up, head down and asked to come home. We agreed—if he was willing to live by our rules. We offered him our basement couch. For six months, just prior to his twenty-first birthday, Alex sat in our basement and watched daytime TV. Looking back, I think he was pondering if there was any way at all he could avoid growing up. We, of course, kept urging him to come up with a plan. One day late in the fall of 2008, he did. He said he wanted to move back to the South. Alex left for Georgia in late January of 2009.

Several months prior to our arrival in Georgia, Alex had found a job, adopted a dog, met a girlfriend and moved into a house. And he had a new plan, which was to study to become an emergency medical technician. (In the words of some of my more religious southern friends—*thank you, Jesus.*)

Now you know the story. This is the rest of our cell phone conversation as I drove across Kentucky.

"You know, Dad, it was that trip across America that caused me to grow up. When I ran out of money in Texas (we knew he was leaving without enough money to make it to Georgia) and you guys didn't bail me out and I had to get that construction job to eat and put gas in my tank, something changed."

"I know," I said. "That guy who hired you sure was the right person at the right time in your life."

"Yeah, great guy. I have great stories from my trip. My buddies are always asking me about my trip."

"It was an adventure, buddy, and all your idea. And look where you are now."

"I feel pretty good about it all. You know, Dad, I loved your stories growing up and some of my teachers' stories in school, but it was on that drive across the country that I realized it was time for me to start writing my own stories."

After Alex said goodbye, I discovered that, although not recommended, it is possible to drive while wiping at one's eyes.

I ran into the only grumpy person I encountered on the entire nine-week trip at the welcome center for North Carolina on I-40. I was on the desperate, daily, state-by-state search for postcards. I had learned by now that while some visitors' centers have 'em, most don't. This one did not. The woman behind the counter kept directing me to a truck stop that was beyond where I planned to leave the interstate and head south to Georgia. Finally I said, no doubt a little snappishly, "I've been driving for seven straight days. Don't you have anything with North Carolina on it?" She whipped a North Carolina map across the counter at me, like she was dealing a card, and flashed an automatic, pre-programmed, welcome-center smile.

Circling back to when I left Kansas: for the first time on the trip, I had experienced a little fatigue similar to the feeling Steinbeck describes often in *Travels with Charley*. In Paxico, I had been up late blogging and hadn't slept well near the train tracks, and, as a result, Missouri was a bit of a blur. However, the further east I got, forests increased in number and size, and the terrain became more varied and hilly. Reaching our major rivers, such as the Missouri and the Mississippi in St. Louis, was an important milestone. Each crossing represented significant progress and served as a harbinger of topographic changes ahead.

While driving the mountainous twists and turns of I-40 through eastern Tennessee and western North Carolina, I realized I had started this first leg of my journey in the mountains of Wyoming and over two-thousand miles later I was ending it in the Great Smoky region, a different kind of beauty, but beautiful mountains all the same. And yes, they looked smoky from the humidity, as green overlapping ridges climbed up to precipitous, blue-gray summits. Other signs of the South included: barbeque, sweet tea, obese children, boiled peanuts, many more churches, the ubiquitous exotic strangler-plant called kudzu and southern-sounding names such as Opryland, Percy Priest Dam, Caney Fork River and the Nolichucky River. While driving this remarkable country with Georgia as my goal, I recalled that when I was moving from Utah to live in the South for the first time, a friend who had traveled extensively throughout the region for work offered words of wisdom. Jim said, "Remember these three things about the South: the best ribs are at the worst-looking places; you can get away with saying the nastiest things behind a man's back as long as you follow with 'bless his heart'; and you should never eat boiled peanuts." All proved true.

I arrived at my first multi-day layover—Rabun Gap-Na-coochee School in north Georgia, an independent school for three hundred students in grades six through twelve. Not only had I served as head of school at RGNS, but our son, Wil, attended there in middle school, and Alex was a graduate of the high school. (Dimmie was deeply involved with an artist's residency program nearby called The Hambidge Center. She first served on the board and later became the director.) I was scheduled to address the school community and teach several classes over two days. Every student had purchased, and presumably read, a Steinbeck work prior to my arrival.

And I was thrilled to finally be on the Steinbeck route. Close study of my 1959 *Rand McNally Road Atlas*, cross-indexed with *Travels with Charley*, indicated that Steinbeck came through north Georgia, which he didn't mention, on his way from Montgomery, Alabama, to Abingdon, Virginia, both of which he did mention.

As Steinbeck often did when he visited with immediate family during his great trip, I prefer to "draw a veil" over my time in

Georgia with my wife and my son, Alex. Suffice it to say, I felt richly rewarded for my first seven days on the road. My dream to drive and camp across the U.S. was becoming a reality and I had met some fascinating Americans. Now I had two days and three nights with my wife and son in a place that had become, over our nine years there, very important to us as a family. I will mention one detail: Dimmie, in her endless resourcefulness, managed to smuggle on the plane several small bottles of the forgotten lemoncello and deliver them to me unharmed.

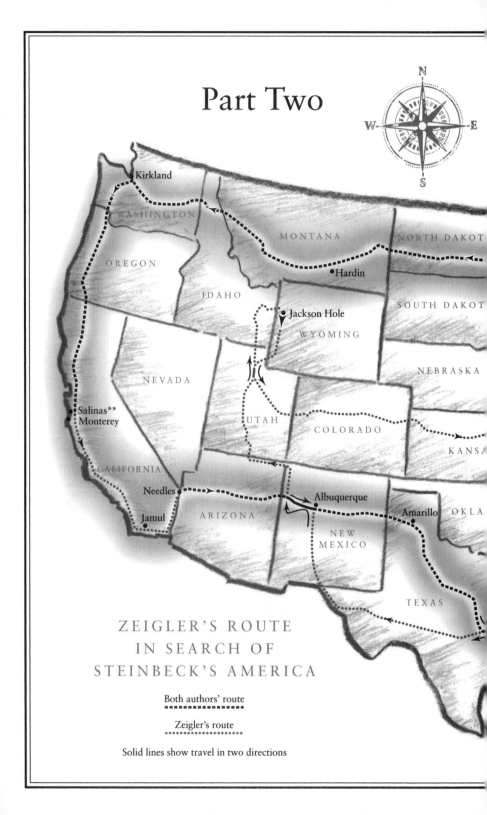

Part Two

Kirkland

WASHINGTON

OREGON

MONTANA

NORTH DAKOT

IDAHO

•Hardin

SOUTH DAKOT

Jackson Hole

WYOMING

NEVADA

Salinas**
Monterey

UTAH

COLORADO

NEBRASKA

KANSA

CALIFORNIA

Needles

ARIZONA

Albuquerque

Amarillo OKLA

Jamul

NEW
MEXICO

TEXAS

ZEIGLER'S ROUTE
IN SEARCH OF
STEINBECK'S AMERICA

Both authors' route

Zeigler's route

Solid lines show travel in two directions

The Tracks
of the Master

Fort Kent

MAINE

VT
NH

Deer
Isle

Niagara
Falls

NEW
YORK

MA

MINNESOTA

WISCONSIN

MI

MICHIGAN

RI

Sag
Harbor*

PENNSYLVANIA

NEW
JERSEY

IOWA

Chicago

ILLINOIS   INDIANA

OHIO

DELAWARE

MISSOURI

WEST
VA.

VIRGINIA

MARYLAND

KENTUCKY

NORTH
CAROLINA

TENNESSEE

ARKANSAS

SOUTH
CAROLINA

MISSIS-   ALABAMA   GEORGIA
SIPPI

New Orleans

FLORIDA

LOUISIANA

*Sag Harbor was
Steinbeck's point of departure

**Salinas is Steinbeck's
birthplace and resting place

Chapter Four
Last Things First

My long journey started long before I left and was over before I returned. I know exactly where and when it was over. Near Abingdon in the dogleg of Virginia...

Travels with Charley

Rabun Gap is a high Appalachian mountain valley ringed by forested peaks and rocky "balds." On the morning I was scheduled to speak, it was pouring rain in Rabun County—after King in Washington, Rabun is the nation's second wettest county. Heavy clouds perched on the surrounding mountains and mist floated above the lush valley floor below the school. I walked through the rain, across a circular drive and garden kindly dedicated by the school board to me and the four other educators in my immediate family, to the brick and glass Arts and Technology building. It is always a pleasure to visit the A&T. It is a beautiful new building, one of several built or remodeled during my tenure. I'm proud of it and all we accomplished. I mustered with some of the faculty in a side room off the lobby, and we all marched to music behind students carrying flags representing their states and countries onto the stage of the Rearden Theater. Dimmie, holding Max in her lap, sat with Alex in the crowd.

My address to the Rabun Gap School at the annual convocation, or academic kickoff, was titled, "The Secret to Life Is in Your Mind and in Your Art." I talked about my Steinbeck project and how it had energized me. I was one of the founders of this event and yet I felt a new freedom in my vagabondage, manifested by throwing Nerf footballs into the audience. After all, it was a "kickoff" event, right?

I taught eight classes about Steinbeck in two days and was particularly delighted with my visit to the middle school, nestled in two older houses perched on a tree-covered hill. The students had all read *The Pearl*. The kids ranged in age from sixth to eighth grade and were quite sophisticated in their assessment of the book's themes and lessons. During our discussion, a white student sat on a couch with his arm around his black buddy. I commented, referring to gender not race, "I have to say, I'm impressed with you two guys at your ability to publicly show your affection for each other."

The white boy smiled and said, "We're brothers."

That lead to a discussion of how boys and girls have different ways of communicating. Race was not mentioned. I realized I had witnessed in these two boys something that Steinbeck could not have seen fifty years ago in the South. Being a sucker for kids, I agreed to send a postcard from Max, from every state we visited, to these irresistible middle schoolers, just as we were doing for the second graders in Salt Lake City. The wonderful and unique quality about RGNS is that a large endowment, thanks to generous heirs to the Coca-Cola fortune and other donors, has made it possible to provide financial aid to the majority of the students. The result is a diverse student body who, for the most part, feel grateful rather than entitled. Rabun Gap School has many strengths, but the quality of the kids has always been chief among them.

I said goodbye to Dimmie and Alex and prepared to hit the road. Getting off the campus with the Bambi was tricky, however, because a long line of traffic, the longest I had ever seen in remote north Georgia, had formed on the county road that cuts through the school property. The cars were backed up for a mile from the parking lot of a Presbyterian church, blocking my departure. I asked a woman arriving for work on the campus what was going on. She said it was the line for a food bank set up at the church once a week. A snapshot of the times we are living in, I thought, as I left by a different exit to U.S. 441 North.

Within a few minutes of getting back on the road, I was re-minded how a memory, especially an exceedingly sad memory, can be visceral, seated somewhere in the region of the stomach and bowels. I was driving in North Carolina, a few miles from the school, when I suddenly became aware of a faint nausea. Be-fore my mind could recall what my belly knew, I rounded a bend and drove past the spot where Julia, riding her bicycle on a school-sponsored trip, had been struck and killed by a young motorist. As I mentioned, Rabun Gap is a small school with many warm and wonderful students. As head of school I got close to many—Julia among them. She was an impressive and charismatic young woman: a scholar, an athlete, an artist and a leader.

The whole tragic experience came rushing back; the wail that rose out of the throat of a freshman boy when I made the an-nouncement to the student body assembled in the school chapel; and after I excused the children to the nearby courtyard, the con-fusion and pain on the faces of faculty members, many now weep-ing. I remembered my appeal to those teachers, that although devastated ourselves, we had to be the adults who helped our stu-dents begin to process their loss. Several weeks of services and me-morials followed, and following those, in a private moment with my wife on our back deck, I began my own grieving. Julia's boyfriend, Brian, attended the school also. He chose to deal with his grief by taking a year off before college and walking the entire length of the Appalachian Trail from Maine to Georgia. Brian teaches at the school now, as does his wife. They had a baby girl recently and named her Julia.

Eventually I wrote about Julia, and my words still accom-pany the student award that is given annually in her name. "Julia was buried in her formal school dress in our cemetery on the wooded hill. It is also the resting place of the school's founder,

Andrew Richie. Julia's headstone depicts her running in her track uniform. I've been asked what was lost and what was gained in Julia's untimely death. Lost was the embodiment of serenity, grace, power and intellect far greater than most people achieve in a full life. Small consolation is what we gained, the precious reminder that any one of us, or even more tragically, any one of our children, can be stopped dead—in a heartbeat—and frozen, as Julia is depicted on her gravestone, in mid-stride for eternity." There is nothing as gut wrenching as seeing a child in pain, nothing as tragic as a child lost.

The torrential downpour continued as Max and I followed U.S. 441 and U.S. 74 through Cherokee country to reconnect with I-40 to Asheville. I'll mention one other memory from Rabun Gap before I leave the school behind and move on once again. In my second year as head of school I visited the chief of the Cherokee Nation on the North Carolina reservation tucked up in the bosom of Great Smoky Mountain National Park. My mission was to recruit more Cherokee students for our school. I asked the chief, a woman (when I later reported this to my mother she said, "The chief is a woman, well, hallelujah!"), if the school mascot, the "Indians," would affect our relationship with her community. She said it was denigrating but wouldn't stop her from sending qualified students. I returned to the school determined to be a better neighbor and, a howl of protest from alumni notwithstanding, after due process and with the help of several savvy administrators, changed the mascot to the "Eagles."

Before North Carolina had zipped by again, I remembered to get off I-26, just north of Asheville, to search for postcards. I found a Hallmark store in a small mall. I also hit an Arby's for lunch because Max had become a big fan of Arby's roast beef. Soon we were in Tennessee. Sometime during that morning, I turned on Betty, my GPS, for the first time on the trip. It was the start of an intimate two-month relationship that was at times blissful, at others frustrating, and fraught with disappointment and confusion. But, as is often the case in the blush of a new relationship, when I first met Betty, I was smitten.

On a dry run the previous spring, towing Bambi from Jackson to Phoenix (including a stretch of I-40), I wasn't looking for love, but in Surprise, Arizona, I fell hard for the kind of woman who has always intrigued me: smart, confident, a good communicator. I'm referring to Betty, of course. I'd purchased her just before the drive south but was reluctant to get involved. Prior to arriving in the Phoenix area I'd relied solely on my maps. U.S. 93 branched south from I-40 east of Kingman, past Cattle Chute Pass Road, and eventually entered the intimidating heart of Phoenix through Surprise and Sun City. I had no clue how to find Glendale, let alone my RV Park there. I turned on Betty—I had named her Betty after my excellent former assistant whose name conjured authority for me—for the first time, and she wowed me. Every turn Betty suggested caused my instincts to scream, "This doesn't *feel* right!" Still, I trusted and followed. It wasn't like I had a better idea.

And soon we arrived at the address of the Covered Wagon RV Park in Glendale. Here's the hitch about the Covered Wagon: I couldn't see it. I drove around the block three times; each time Betty reiterated, "Recalculating..." and brought me back to the same spot, reassuring me, without a hint of rancor, that we had arrived at our destination. Finally, I had to believe the park was actually there, and indeed it was, tree-covered and relatively tranquil given its urban location, but hidden behind an apartment building and sporting no apparent signage at the entrance. How much better, I wondered, as I pulled Winnie into the Covered Wagon, would we all get along with our spouses and partners if, when they ignored our instructions and kept driving in the wrong direction, we calmly said, "Recalculating…"?

Betty has been with me ever since, but our relationship has "matured," you might say. For the most part she's been a valued companion and at times nothing short of a miracle-worker. But there've been other times (no offense intended to the real Betty) I've come close to chucking her, battery charger and all, out the window.

So Max and I, now accompanied by Betty, made our way north, through the South. Tennessee was Appalachian lovely. I-26 pitched up and down steep passes bordered by high, rugged peaks. I saw signs for Rocky Fork and Rock Creek Recreation Area near Erwin, which boasts a stream-fed lake surrounded by oaks, maples, hemlocks and pines. The hills actually had rocky tops, as in the song "Rocky Top," and the folded, marbled rock looked older than that of my western Rockies. I guess that's because it is, by several hundred million years. I-26 intersected with I-81 past Johnson City, Tennessee. The weather cleared. Virginia lay ahead.

As soon as I crossed the line, I stopped at the Virginia welcome center on I-81 (Steinbeck would have been on U.S.11, which to this day parallels I-81) and asked for postcards.

"Nope," the welcoming southern gal of some years behind the counter said. "We sure don't have any postcards, darlin'. Postcards are really becomin' a thing of the past, aren't they?" Not what I needed to hear.

I settled for two "Virginia is for Lovers" bumper stickers and, after walking Max, slid back in the car. I got off onto U.S. 11 in Abingdon, happy in the absolute certainty I was on Steinbeck's actual route, even if it was the place where, as I have mentioned, he finally hit his saturation point. As he wrote in *Travels with Charley:*

The road became an endless stone ribbon, the hills ob-
structions, the trees green blurs, the people simply mov-
ing figures with heads but no faces. All the food along
the way tasted like soup, even the soup.

Although it was hot and muggy, it was great to be in Abingdon. Tucked in the heart of Appalachian mountain country in the southwestern toe of Virginia, and founded in 1778, Abingdon is a small city rich in history, with an agricultural feel and a dedica-

Abingdon, Virginia, Visitors' Center.

tion to the arts. It was the site of a significant Revolutionary War event, serving as muster ground for part of the militia that later defeated British Major Patrick Ferguson's troops at the Battle of Kings Mountain in South Carolina, a battle that Theodore Roosevelt wrote was "the turning point of the American Revolution."

I entered the Abingdon Visitors' Center, housed in a remodeled, white Victorian with large, covered porches, and chatted with frizzy, pretty Nicole. She wasn't aware Abingdon held the honor of being the last town mentioned on Steinbeck's journey. She didn't realize the fiftieth anniversary of his trip was coming up in the fall of 2010. I taught Nicole a few facts about Steinbeck and she taught me something equally as interesting. Abingdon, with a population of 7,938 and located in Washington County, may have the only theater in America where tickets can be had in exchange for food.

Barter Theater was established in 1933 when Robert Porterfield brought twenty-two fellow actors to his hometown and proposed bartering foodstuffs in exchange for theater tickets. He often paid playwrights in food as well. "Ham for Hamlet" it was called. George Bernard Shaw, a vegetarian, was paid in spinach. It is still occasionally possible to exchange food for tickets. Steinbeck did not mention Barter Theater in *Travels with Charley*, but given its provenance, I have to believe he was aware of it. Barter Theater offered *Of Mice and Men* as part of its 2009 season.

I pushed on several hours north of Abingdon because I needed to be in Harrisburg, Pennsylvania, by noon the next day for a school visit. I passed the exit for Hungry Mother State Park near Marion, Virginia. According to the park's website, local legend has it that a long-ago mother and her small child escaped from raiding American Indians and wandered in the wilderness, near present-day Marion, surviving on berries. Eventually, the mother collapsed, but her child continued downstream, finally reaching help. The exhausted child could utter only two words, while pointing upstream, "Hungry mother." Molly Marley was found dead. Today, the stream is known as Hungry Mother Creek.

I went as far as I could on that steaming day and finally quit in Harrisonburg, Virginia. I snuck Max into my motel room for a few hours because it was so bloody hot in the car. I knew when I let him out of his kennel that I was pushing my luck. Still, I gave him a hug and a little talking to. I said that I was making him a star on our blog, but even rock stars can't pee with impunity on motel room rugs. I think he heard me because he slunk into the bathroom and went on the tile floor. I banished him back to the Toyota.

I-81 crosses a very narrow strip of West Virginia and an even narrower slice of Maryland. At the West Virginia welcome center, I procured several postcards intended to attract people to "come home" and resettle in West "By-God" Virginia, but I don't remember even seeing a place to stop in Maryland (although I suppose there must have been one around Hagerstown). It turned out to be the only one, among the thirty-five individual states my tires touched, in which I got nothin'. Fortunately, my older brother, Jake, a retired teacher, lives in Delaware, close to Maryland, and he

Max with Toni Berger and CHS kids.

loves kids, so he sent Maryland postcards to the two schools from his yellow Labrador retriever, Nilla. Still on I-81, I crossed the Mason-Dixon line into Pennsylvania. In the same vicinity, Steinbeck wrote:

> *The miles rolled under me unacknowledged. I know it was cold but I didn't feel it; I know the countryside must have been beautiful but I didn't see it. I bulldozed blindly through West Virginia, plunged into Pennsylvania and grooved Rocinante to the great wide turnpike. There was no night, no day, no distance.*

After a short stay at Harrisburg Academy, which included my speaking to an Advanced Placement English class, the Steinbeck route took me back to my roots. I hadn't visited Carlisle—at the intersection of I-81 and the Pennsylvania Turnpike, where my father grew up and attended college—in over twenty years. I backtracked from Harrisburg to Carlisle and spent the night at my cousin Patsy's house. The next day I was honored to speak at Carlisle High School, my father's alma mater, to hundreds of students, in five separate groups, over four hours. I also spoke to several ninth-grade Honors English classes at Cumberland Valley High School.

I enjoyed two satisfying days with my "farm family" in Middlesex, near Carlisle, even though my close association with these good folks was mostly in childhood. My father, Jacob Zeigler, was a teacher at Kiski School, a boarding school for boys near Pittsburgh, and my brothers, Jake and David, and sister, Jeanne, and I grew up on the school campus. Dad liked to visit the farm often and ex-

My father's childhood home.

pose us to the wonders of true rural living. I remember my Uncle Paul bucking his open jeep, with several excited kids hanging on to the seats, up the steep power-line breaks in the dense forest on the slopes of the mountains near the farm. I can still hear my uncles' laughter and taunts echoing from the dairy barn at 5:00 a.m. and smell fresh eggs frying in the kitchen downstairs. Often when I entered the barn during milking, my Uncle Mike would arch a stream of milk at me straight from the cow's udder. If it hit me, he'd laugh uproariously and shout, "That'll frost yer punkins." (Translation: That will make you mad.) I loved it.

On this long-overdue visit, I stayed in my Uncle Sam's place (now Patsy's), close to the farmhouse in which my father was born. Patsy cooked for me and did my laundry. I was booked at the schools, entertained and shepherded around by my cousin Steve's fiancée, Toni Berger. Steve changed the oil in my car. The warmth and hospitality were almost overwhelming. In a humble attempt to show my gratitude, I took the whole crew out to dinner. There is something very special about being around relatives. It may be the common ruddiness to the cheeks, color to the hair and lilt of the tongue. There is a comfort—no doubt atavistic—a fullness in the heart that says, "I'm safe here, I belong here, these are my people."

I left with a photo of my father and his six brothers, and my grandmother, Rachel, her feet lifted off the ground by two of my uncles playfully grasping her arms. More importantly, I left with a renewed sense of my roots, if a bit sad that not a single one of my relatives is a farmer. But that, in its own right, is a unique American story. My father grew up with eleven siblings—six boys and five girls. He was the only one to attend high school and college. His brother, Sam, had Patsy, Shirley (living in San Diego), and Steve. Steve's house is next to Patsy's, on land once part of the original family farm, which is now mostly subdivided and leased. My Uncle Sam, a very smart and gentle, but physically powerful farmer, never attended high school; his son, Steve, my cousin, although desperately wishing to attend college, felt obligated, as the only son, to remain on the farm and help his dad. He later left farming and became a mechanic and then a job-site safety inspector. Steve's four children from a previous marriage include a veterinarian, a doctor, an HR specialist, and a carpenter. Three out of four of Steve's children have college degrees—two have advanced degrees. None is farming for a living.

It was time to push on to Connecticut. Back on I-81, we left Carlisle and traversed sunny and sylvan northeastern Pennsylvania. My plan was to vary from Steinbeck's route slightly, circling around to Middlebury, Connecticut, to avoid New York City traffic. Steinbeck's experience was enough to warn me off driving through or even near the city. On his last leg to Manhattan, he was prevented from going through the Holland Tunnel because of Rocinante's butane tank, had to take the Hoboken Ferry during rush hour, entered a one-way street the wrong way and then got lost in his own city—and that was forty-nine years ago. Campers with bottled gas are still prohibited from using the Holland Tunnel. Although I wasn't planning to cross over to Manhattan, getting around the city to Long Island, even as far south as Elizabeth, New Jersey, was not something I relished. My plan was to head to Connecticut and take the ferry to Long Island.

It was a beautiful, clear day in eastern Pennsylvania and the humidity of the South was behind us. Again at Harrisburg, I saw stone-arch bridges across the mighty Susquehanna River on its way to the head of the Chesapeake Bay. The river flowed around several verdant islands. Later, on I-81, I entered cathedrals of towering rock faces on sheer mountainsides. One such face, unfortunately, had the American flag painted on it. Trees lined the highway and mountain passes. Near Wilkes-Barre, I bumped into the Susquehanna again, after I crossed I-80 and Nescopeck Mountain. I was finally far enough north to perceive the promise of fall color in the trees.

I left I-81 in Scranton, and after a short jog on I-380, followed I-84 across the state boundary waters of the Delaware River at Port Jervis, New York, and on to Middlebury, Connecticut (southwest of Waterbury). My plan was to leave the Airstream in Middlebury at the home of the parents of a friend, and after spending the night, drive to New London, Connecticut, take the ferry across to Long Island and motor around to Water Mill, New York, which is close to Sag Harbor. I had a comfortable night in a beautiful home just outside of Middlebury. My room overlooked a moonlit lawn leading down a hill to a field, trees and a lake. But I could barely sleep for excitement as I anticipated standing in Steinbeck's shadow under the oaks at his beloved seaside cottage, and roaming his Sag Harbor streets.

Chapter Five
Sag Harbor: At the Beginning at Last

Holiday (magazine) asked White to drive coast to coast, as he had done in 1922, and write some pieces about America. He accepted but got only as far as Galeton, Pennsylvania. The assignment was passed on to John Steinbeck, who made the trip and wrote Travels with Charley.

Letters of E.B. White, collected and edited by Dorothy Lobrano Guth

Big, burly *Mary Ellen* bumped the dock. Car engines fired to life as the ferry's massive hull doors clanged open. I drove into the sunlight and onto Long Island at Orient Point. In this unpretentious seaside

New London, Connecticut, from the deck of the Mary Ellen.

village it immediately struck me that while crossing the country from Wyoming, through the South and even including eastern Pennsylvania, then New York and Connecticut, I may have—by blind, dumb luck, I assure you—chosen one of the most scenic routes across America. I had driven close to thirty-five hundred miles and crossed fifteen states and had not encountered a single unsightly industrialized area. Certainly there had been miles and miles of malls and sprawl around the cities, but rural vistas and mountainous terrain had predominated. I had already seen a beautiful part of America, yet of all the places I had visited, the one I guessed had changed the least since the 1960s was eastern Long Island.

Just outside Orient Point, I stopped at a public parking area adjacent to a white expanse of beach. It was Sunday, and a winsome, raven-haired woman stood in the gentle riffles in her bare feet, wearing a pleated blue skirt and white oxford cloth shirt—fishing. She allowed me to photograph her against the backdrop of the cerulean sound, saying with a warm smile, "I just wish I had a big fish for the photo."

Sunday on the Sound.

The terrain of Long Island was low and rolling, the antithesis of the rugged and rocky coastline of the Northwest where I had spent the majority of my recent beach time. I didn't notice any fast food restaurants or big-box stores. Eastern Long Island does, of course, have its share of Hampton "McMansions" hidden behind huge hedges and the roads were congested with weekend traffic, but the area had retained a rural, agricultural, seafaring feel and was dotted with family businesses, vineyards, produce stands and corn mazes.

Then, Betty and I had our first serious disagreement. After I passed Greenport, she kept trying to convince me to return there to take the Shelter Island Ferry. How does she even know about ferries? I wondered. I had chosen to drive around the "open crab claw" tip of Long Island surrounding Great Peconic Bay to the town of Water Mill. I was just obstinate enough to wonder how far we would travel before she gave it a rest and adjusted. She was just obstinate enough to refuse to drop it and adjust. After about thirty minutes, I tired of being told to turn around at every intersection and turned her off. I rounded the hinge of the claw and was heading east when I passed a white plaster duck, at least ten feet high, the purpose for which, apart from kitsch, escaped me. Just outside of Water Mill, I pulled into a short, isolated driveway shielded from the road by trees and onto Rogers' Farm, where I had been invited to stay with friends of a friend.

On a short drive later that afternoon to an expansive ocean beach, I discovered that Water Mill, and all surrounding towns, are picturesque, adorned with shingles, shakes and steeples—more New England than New England. I picked up a local paper with the girls' soccer team, the Whalers, featured on the front page. I couldn't wait for the next day and the chance to see Steinbeck's cottage in Sag Harbor:

> *Under the big oaks at my place at Sag Harbor sat Roci-*
> *nante, handsome and self-contained, and neighbors*
> *came to visit, some neighbors we didn't even know we*
> *had.*

I stood under those oaks at Number 2 Bluff Point Lane and imagined Rocinante packed and ready to depart on September 23, 1960. Steinbeck's cottage, a gray and white, one-story, wood structure surrounded by low hedges, was simple, secluded, and difficult to find, but lacking any kind of fence or security. His writing cabin, Joyous Garde, named for Sir Lancelot's castle, stands guard at the end of the shaded point overlooking the bay. It was fashioned after Mark Twain's writing cabin. Joyous Garde is six-sided, with windows in all directions, and intentionally built too small for a bed so it could never be considered a guesthouse. It resembles a lighthouse. Scratched in cement in the back yard, by the small pool John built for Elaine, are these words, "Layde, I take record to God. In thee I find my earthly joy."

Reference librarian Suzie Smyth at the Sag Harbor Library was very helpful. In fact, I learned on my trip that libraries are some of the warmest and most welcoming places in this country. It's gratifying to walk into a public establishment as a stranger and feel eagerly received, knowing there is no expectation of re-muneration. Suzie said her uncle had been a friend of Steinbeck's. She let me view the library's only copy of the DVD titled *Joyous*

Garde: Steinbeck in Sag Harbor, produced by Tom Browngardt. In it, long-time resident Nada Barry, whose deceased husband, Bob, was one of Steinbeck's cronies, said, "We protected John. If people asked where he lived, no one

Steinbeck's "place" at Sag Harbor.

told." Nada also mentioned baking Steinbeck a birthday cake.

Steinbeck's biographer, Jackson Benson, mentioned in an interview on the DVD, "John Steinbeck brought western consciousness about the land to the east. He recognized that the relationship of man to the land was spiritual." Various Sag Harbor residents interviewed for *Joyous Garde* reported that Steinbeck was a shy and quiet man, but a man who

Joyous Garde, Steinbeck's writing cabin.

reached out to people he liked. He was described as very funny and a good listener. He loved the Sag Harbor whaling museum and the history of whaling. It was said that Steinbeck loved to fish but often didn't bait the hook and refused to keep a fish when caught. In Sag Harbor, the DVD's narrative was particularly poignant:

> *The story goes on and nothing finishes—the story goes on and leaves the writer behind, for no story is ever done.*

Suzie brought me every biography about Steinbeck in the library's

collection. I glanced briefly at the exposé written by the author's younger
son, John Steinbeck IV, called *The
Other Side of Eden,* and while thinking that famous people have not truly
"arrived" until they have had a "tell-
all" written about them, set it aside
unopened. I photographed the library's bust of Steinbeck.

In my conversations with locals,
there were stories of Steinbeck and
his coterie of male friends hanging

*Steinbeck commemorated in
the Sag Harbor Library.*

out in an upstairs bar in the local marina discussing politics. Some
"fishing" trips involved boating to Connecticut and heavy booz-
ing. I was told a local woman was once overheard saying she expected pearls to come out of Steinbeck's mouth, but if he had been
drinking it was more like profanity.

Although I missed speaking with vacationing Nada Barry,
current owner of a gift store on Main Street called The Wharf
Shop, I was fortunate to meet Gwen, her charming and comely
forty-something daughter. We spoke about how the town had
changed and how Steinbeck might react to those changes. Gwen
said she remembered as a child hearing rumors of heavy drinking
and domestic turmoil in the Steinbeck family, but all were vague
and had faded with time. I mentioned the irony inherent in a
hand-written sign in a nearby storefront window offering a two
thousand dollar reward for the return of a standard poodle, given
that Charley was the same breed.

Gwen said, "Yes, that has caused quite a stir. All of us have
our kids out looking for that dog."

Across Main from The Wharf Shop is Marty's Barber Shop.
Marty Trunzo is a local celebrity. His unpretentious setup behind

the classic barber pole created quite a contrast to the nearby Harbor Salon, which promised "organically focused beauty." Trunzo was short and stout, had a white mustache and peered through thick glasses. He

New York's most experienced barber.

was wearing a blue smock over a red-striped polo shirt. While he trimmed my hair in his long, narrow, photo-lined establishment, we spoke of many things—from Southern cooking (which he is for) to celibacy for priests (which he is against). As soon as Marty determined I was a vagabond writer, he told me over the buzz of the clippers what the greatest book ever written was.

"*Divine Comedy,*" he said.

"*Divine Comedy* by Dante?"

"By Dante. And that goddamn Shakespeare copied off of him and put it into plays."

"You think he ripped him off, huh?"

"Well sure, sure."

"Shakespeare ripped off Dante?"

"Yeah, yeah."

"So I'll bet you've cut..."

"Well, since 1930. I'm ninety-one years old," Marty interjected.

"...easily over ten thousand haircuts."

"Oh, easily."

"Wow. And let's see, your sign in the front window says, 'Sorry, I can't handle kids, no fancy cuts, no shaves'."

"Yeah, I wanna work relaxed," Marty said. "I love what I'm doing, ya know."

"Well, you wouldn't still be doin' it if you didn't."

"There is a word that is mispronounced, misspelled and misused."

"Retire?"

"No, amateur. Few pronounce the word right. It's not amateur, it's amatora," Marty said.

"Amatora?"

"You love what you're doing."

"Oh that's good! I didn't know that."

Max in the stocks. Busted in Sag Harbor for littering.

"You love your work. Michelangelo was a teenager when he made David, and he loved his work."

Marty said he occasionally cut Steinbeck's hair. He remembered greeting Steinbeck on the street and often getting a grunt in response. Marty pointed to a picture on his wall of a gentleman standing beside Teddy Kennedy, "You need to talk to Johnny Ward. Steinbeck referred to him as 'the mayor of the village' in one of his books." I paid Marty and posed for a photo with him out front, under the striped pole.

From a bayside picnic table, behind the stocks for the public humiliation of transgressors of another era, I got John Ward on my cell and he agreed to talk about Steinbeck. I asked how he knew the author. He said he had been a drinking and fishing buddy of Steinbeck's. Bob Barry, Nada's husband, had introduced them.

I asked Ward about reports that Steinbeck was a shy man who often grunted at people in response to being greeted. He said Steinbeck was abrupt with people at times because he simply wanted to be left alone. "He didn't want to be recognized or fussed over. He didn't like celebrity. He wanted to be one of the guys," Ward said. "We had a lot of fun and good times. Steinbeck

loved to fish and drink with his buddies. He was a good friend and he
was definitely not shy."

Johnny Ward said much had
changed in Sag Harbor over the past
ten years and Steinbeck wouldn't like
it. That's ironic, I said, because Steinbeck felt that way about Monterey in
the sixties.

Schiavoni's Market.

According to Ward, Steinbeck had a small circle of friends
that he thoroughly enjoyed, but he didn't mix much beyond that
group. Several of the gang worked on the annual Whaling Festival, for which Steinbeck served as honorary chairman. Ward said,
"Steinbeck's motto regarding the festival was 'the bigger the snafu
the better. We can make a big mistake bigger next year.'"

I learned from John Ward that Steinbeck was attracted to
Sag Harbor because it reminded him of Salinas and Monterey
where he grew up. He also liked the fact that it was blue collar, off
the beaten path and close to his Upper East Side Manhattan apartment. Steinbeck bought his cottage in 1955. According to Ward,
Steinbeck had two favorite bars, the Black Buoy, and across the
street, the Sand Bar. "'If you missed the Black Buoy, you hit the
Sand Bar' was the expression in Steinbeck's time," Ward said.
Both bars are gone, having fallen prey to gentrification.

I thanked John Ward for his time and, on my way back up
Main Street from the waterfront, dropped by Schiavoni's Market,
founded in 1941 and said to have been the inspiration for the grocery store that figures so prominently in Steinbeck's last novel,
The Winter of Our Discontent. Steinbeck wrote, "Again shelves
to the ceiling, filled neatly with gleaming canned and glassed food,
a library for the stomach." Schiavoni's, too, had changed with the
times; it now looked very upscale.

I hurried to the Sag Harbor Library to collect my thoughts, review my notes and post a blog. I was flushed with the feeling of having truly connected with Steinbeck's Sag Harbor, especially after standing so close to him in his backyard. The hours flew by. I stopped briefly to let Max out of the car and glanced at the time. It was 1:30. I realized I had missed a lunch appointment with a prominent local matron, Charlotte Smith, whom I had met the day before. The irony was that Charlotte was very forgetful. Just after meeting me, she had asked her daughter how she would know I was the right man when I came to her house for lunch. When I realized my mistake, I immediately called Charlotte and apologized. I joked about my being the forgetful one. She was very gracious and extended an invitation to come by later that day, at 3:30.

Charlotte's house in Bridgehampton is a one-story, mustard-brown clapboard, with a high peak in the center. It sits behind a semi-circular driveway and is the only house on the block without hedges. I was shown into the living room by an African-American woman, Charlotte's live-in helper, walked past a baby grand piano, and sat facing Charlotte in her winged armchair, with its back to the fireplace. The room was furnished with Victorian sofas and chairs and trimmed with luxurious wood. Family photos and books cluttered the shelves and surfaces. Charlotte, red-haired and regal in her early nineties, was dressed in a brown cardigan sweater over a blue shirt and brown corduroy pants.

Speaking of a time when eastern Long Island was one of the largest producers of potatoes in America and of her first husband, a farmer, Charlotte said, "Hildreth and I enjoyed many trips that combined music and potato farming, before he passed away."

In the thirties, Charlotte studied music at New York University. After she married Hildreth, they lived on his family farm, where she taught piano and organ lessons and hosted music performances for the local community. She was also the organist at the Bridgehampton Presbyterian Church for many years, playing for a dollar a week. Robert Fordham, one of Charlotte's ancestors, immigrated to Long Island in 1640. He was the second Presbyterian pastor in Southampton.

Charlotte's daughter, Susan, was kind enough to share two personal books with me. One, titled *Reflections,* was a history and biography Charlotte had compiled for her family, and the second was a copy of a handwritten log by Charlotte's great-grandfather, Henry Augustus Fordham, who went to sea in 1850, on the whaling ship *Ontario,* at the age of fourteen. He continued on the ship for four years until the commander, Captain Brown, was killed by the tail of a whale. I know—that's a whale of a tale with a very familiar ring, but Charlotte swears it's true.

I was struck with the candor of this quote from Charlotte's *Reflections:*

> *In thinking through my reflections, several facts become apparent. The first is that each of the generations I know or knew about had problems. They were emotional, mental or financial but there is a continuing thread of faith of the forefathers that seems to have supported each one. I am proud of each and every one of you.*

Charlotte's grandfather, Henry H. Post, was a gambler, land speculator, lumberman and offshore whaler. Charlotte said the cry of "Whale Off!" brought townsmen running to the beach, stripping off wallets, rings and watches. The men would jump into whaling boats and row out to the whale with the harpooner poised in the bow.

I found many fascinating entries in the handwritten log. Here is one example.

April 23rd, 1850

*Man overboard, heavily clothed, almost drowned—
going under. Rescued. Deeply chilled. We rubbed him
with brandy and gave him some to drink.*

Many daily entries captured the tedium at sea by simply recording the weather and wind conditions and then signing off with something such as, "Nothing remarkable taken place today, so ends these 24 hours." But on the same day the man went overboard, it was written that a second man was injured when the main topsail yard broke. That must have been an exciting day at sea!

Charlotte mentioned that she loved to play piano and organ duets with her daughter, Ann Morgan.

"At the church?" I asked.

"No, right here in my living room," she said, gesturing over my shoulder.

"In your…" I said, and turned to see for the first time, although I had walked right past it, a large organ with full pipes projecting into the open loft space above the main floor.

I asked her to play for me. She demurred, but only briefly, and called for her organ shoes.

"Can't play the organ in sneakers," she said. I was treated to a private recital.

Over a very late lunch, Charlotte told me that her second husband, Dinwiddie, had been the choir director at her church. One day, after she had been widowed, he cornered her on the steps to the choir loft and declared his love for her. I asked if there had been any sign of his affection prior to that day.

"No, we just made beautiful music together," she said.

Susan remembered it differently; she said that "Din," as he was called, was an independently wealthy man, but also an alco-

holic, and that his attentions to Charlotte were both intense and prema-
ture, proffered while Hildreth was
ailing but still very much alive. That
caused some tension in the family,
Susan said.

Late that afternoon, back on the
farm, Max did indeed seem to have
a new "leash" on life. He was perky
and adventuresome. I took him on a
hike that required us to walk by the
outbuildings of Rogers' Farm. He

*Charlotte playing the organ
in her living room.*

chased Millie, the guinea fowl, until Millie bustled off, pitching a
hissy fit. Later, we spotted a white flag of a tail in the tall cornrows. Locked on the scent of the deer, Max tried to leap off the
two-track we were following and run into the field.

That evening I met, for the first time, a second cousin of mine
who lives in Southampton. Rob and I went out to dinner in Sag
Harbor. Rob, a lanky blonde with an athletic carriage, did the important work of assessing environmental impacts in eastern Long
Island. His profession had taken him onto the property and into
the homes of some of the very rich and famous, such as Calvin
Klein, who seek the proper permits to build or remodel on eastern Long Island. Over dinner, my cousin explained that the region
had been hit hard by the recession with sales off and real estate
down. Of course, he said, that is relative in the Hamptons. He
also told me of a daily protest at a local convenience store where
Mexican migrant workers were being taunted by flag-carrying citizens.

After dinner we went over to a nearby table and I was introduced to Steven Gaines, author of *Philistines at the Hedgerow:
Passion and Property in the Hamptons*. Gaines, a short, attrac-

tive, middle-aged man with an enviable full head of salt-and-pepper hair, is assumed to be the authority on all things Hampton and all persons Hampton—painter Jackson Pollock, for example. Gaines wrote this in his book about real estate magnate Allan Schneider, "It was Schneider's hallmark that he was friendly not only with the wealthy Summer Colony but with the hoi polloi, the farmers and tradesmen who were the 'real people' of the town." Gaines goes on to depict a night that Schneider was drinking heavily and while eating dinner had to have a chunk of steak removed by the Heimlich maneuver. The incident had a startling aftermath, "For a moment there wasn't a sound in the room. Then Allan pitched over to the side and hit the floor with such a thud, the walls shook." Gaines also wrote a controversial biography of Calvin Klein titled *Obsession*, in which, according to an interview with Gaines conducted by A.D. Amorosi and printed in the *Philadelphia City Paper* of August 13–20, 1998, many people felt Gaines "outed" Klein. Gaines told me that after so many years of such intense study of the Hampton community and its characters, he found the idea of getting out and following Steinbeck's route around the country intriguing.

Rob and I posed for a photo together outside the restaurant, and I bid my cousin goodbye. After one more night in Water Mill and a second in Middlebury, Connecticut, I planned to drive to Deerfield, Massachusetts, Steinbeck's first stop.

Steinbeck took three ferries from Sag Harbor on the day he left Long Island in 1960. He took the Shelter Island Ferry, then a second ferry to Greenport, and a third from Orient Point, New York, to New London, Connecticut. On September 23, forty-nine years to the day from Steinbeck's departure, I did the same.

The winding, tree-lined roads to the docks were clearly marked, and I felt a powerful sense of being right in Steinbeck's tracks. I drove on the first two short-hop ferries as if both were waiting for me. The gates swung closed behind my car. The water was flat and gray, reflecting an overcast sky. Both ferries pulled away from shingle and shake cottages lining the shore. The cross-sound ferry, called the *Susan Anne*, was the only one of the three that allowed time for getting out of the car and engaging in conversation. Steinbeck interviewed a navy man during his crossing. He spoke of war, the military and "atomic" submarines in that section of *Travels with Charley.*

> *"And now submarines are armed with mass murder,*
> *our silly, only way of deterring mass murder."*

I didn't notice anyone in uniform, but sitting on one of the open-air benches on the top deck, I saw a man wearing a shirt with the New York (City) Fire Department logo on it. I spoke with him. His name was Frank; he was a marine chemist and college professor, and a volunteer fireman on Long Island. Frank was fit and handsome—showing a bit of gray in his sandy hair—and medium in stature. He said he was wearing the shirt out of respect for his New York City comrades. He spoke of September 11, 2001, as a day he "would forever remember." Every fireman within one hundred miles was called to duty. Frank shared his memories of that time, including the remarkable ways in which nearby communities mustered firefighters and supplies to be shipped into Manhattan. He spoke emotionally about the loss of the captain of his ladder company—just one of many deaths in the region. "One line-of-duty death service is both impressive and traumatic. Nearly three hundred and fifty is...is...overwhelming," he said, shaking his head.

We sat in silence for a moment and studied the ferry's wake. A gull shrieked above us.

I asked Frank about the economy and status of local fisheries. He said the fisheries were "a mixed bag." Fluke and striped bass numbers were on the rise; however, cod stocks remained depressed. He said lobsters were nearly gone from local waters, and while there was much finger pointing, data suggests rising water temperature as the culprit. Frank echoed what my cousin, Rob, had said about the local economy. Home prices were depressed; unemployment, though a little less than the national average, had created serious problems for many families.

"One upside: enrollment at state universities is at an all-time high as students look for a more cost-effective education, while riding out the time of no jobs. I guess they see it as a way to prepare for better times ahead," Frank explained.

"When do you think that might be, Frank?" I asked.

"Like most Americans, we all hope that the next few years will be a significant improvement."

In Middletown, Connecticut, I stopped for lunch at a bar and then went into a LensCrafters looking for dark glasses. I spoke with a man behind the counter about my American adventure. He told me I really should Google his ancestor, Joshua Tefft, the last man to be drawn and quartered on American soil. I walked out, shaking my head and thinking about people and *their* stories. Stories had already become a significant part of my experience. By the way, check out Joshua Tefft. He *was* the last man drawn and quartered on American soil and, incredible as it may seem, there is ample reason to believe he was innocent of the charge of treason for which he was convicted and executed.

Winnie was waiting in Middlebury, Connecticut, on the lakeside farm of the Christels, parents of my friend, Tammy, from Jackson. Now-fallow fields, delineated by perfect, gray, stone walls, surround their spacious, brown-shingled home. My hostess, Thyrza Christel, a striking woman in her high seventies, is a member of the Whittemore family. The Whittemores made a fortune in malleable iron (iron that could hold a shape and was essential to transportation and many other fields) in the late nineteenth and early twentieth centuries. Two generations of affluent Whittemores quietly transformed central Connecticut with philanthropic projects, including parks, schools and libraries. John Howard Whittemore, who died in 1910, and his son, Harris, who passed away seventeen years later, also collected art, especially the French Impressionists. In time, the Whittemore Collection grew to over one thousand pieces. Thyrza is Harris Whittemore's granddaughter. She is a gracious, humble and private person—a living example of the Whittemore legacy.

Tammy had arrived for a visit with her parents, and the two of us enjoyed a beer on the covered porch overlooking sunny fields rounding down to the shore of the lake. Several family members who live nearby joined us for a drink and dinner. The talk was of Obama and Steinbeck. Thyrza's husband, Chris Christel, an eighty-four-year-old retired businessman and a frugal Yankee, was the sort of analytical fellow who wanted to see how much one knew before he fully engaged. He posed questions such as, "How many book sales would it take to make a bestseller in 1962?" (*Travels with Charley* was published in 1962.) I must have passed the test because, at breakfast, just before I departed, Chris confessed that he always felt Steinbeck, and especially *The Grapes of Wrath,* which he had read in school, had shaped his left-leaning inclinations. Chris, Thyrza and Tammy walked me to my rig. As I eased down their long driveway, I saw the Christels waving in my mirrors. I headed through the town of Middlebury to I-84. What better time, I thought, as I merged onto the freeway, than late September to follow John Steinbeck through all of magnificent New England?

Chapter Six
New England to Niagara

*I had promised my youngest son to say good-bye in passing.
His school is at Deerfield, Massachusetts, but I got there too late
to arouse him, so I drove up the mountain and found a dairy, bought
some milk, and asked permission to camp under an apple tree.
The dairy man had a PhD in mathematics, and he must have
had some training in philosophy. He liked what he was doing
and he didn't want to be somewhere else—one of the very few
contented people I met in my whole journey.*

Travels with Charley

I left Middlebury, Connecticut, on a stunning clear morning. Winnie tracked in my rearview mirror; it felt good to have my rig whole again. We followed I-84 to Hartford and there picked up I-91 to Deerfield, Massachusetts. Just before leaving Connecticut, I realized, once again, I had no postcards. I stopped at the only place I could find, a Conoco/Dunkin' Donuts combination, and bought the only items available with the name of the state on them—highway maps. I know, lame. What is a second grader in Utah going to do with a highway map of Connecticut? I was desperate.

While drivin' and drinkin' my Dunkin' Donuts coffee out of a paper cup (I had accidentally left my travel mug in the car, which was parked about a block away from the coffee shop to avoid any threat of backing up), I remembered that Steinbeck wrote on this leg of his journey, "American cities are like badger holes, ringed with trash—all of them—surrounded by piles of wrecked and rusting automobiles, and almost smothered by rubbish." He condemned packaging and the fact that we throw away more than we use and asserted that in Europe all of these discarded items would be utilized somehow, "In this, if in no other way, we can see the wild and reckless exuberance of our production, and waste seems to be the index." I didn't notice that much trash around cities. Perhaps we have become better at recycling and reusing, or simply hiding our trash from view. Perhaps we have stopped noticing. Either way, Steinbeck was way ahead of his time on the status of waste, which, visible or not, is dire in this country today. I

The road to Eaglebrook.

finished my coffee and, in reckless exuberance, tossed the paper coffee cup out the window. (You do know I'm kidding, right?)

The Eaglebrook School lies beyond a one-lane stone bridge on the side of a forested mountain in Deerfield, Massachusetts. Steinbeck wrote:

> *I prefer to draw a curtain over my visit to Eaglebrook School. It can be imagined what effect Rocinante had on two hundred teen-age prisoners of education just settling down to serve their winter sentence.*

On the day of my visit, the trees were in full-on fall-flash. I had a brief talk with a young teacher doing a freshwater experiment with four students on the shore of the school's centrally located lake. He said that, while Eaglebrook folks appreciated the mention by Steinbeck in *Travels with Charley,* they didn't much like the reference to boarding students as "prisoners." I followed the teacher's directions up an oak-shaded sidewalk to the administration building and met Andy Chase, the affable head of school. Andy told me that the dairyman Steinbeck referenced was apparently so contented at the farm up the road that he only just recently moved away. Although Andy couldn't join us, I had lunch at his table in the dining room with several students and his secret weapon, his wife, Rachel Blain, who teaches at the school. Dur-

ing the meal, Rachel good-na-
turedly tossed academic questions
at the young men (grades six
through nine) who circled our
table. I was reminded of my
boarding school upbringing and
my father's uncanny sense for the
teachable moment.

Outdoor science at the Eaglebrook School.

Eaglebrook is an extraordinary school, extremely well en-
dowed, in a stunning mountain setting, with the unique claim of
having three generations of schoolmen at the helm. Andy Chase
sits at the desk that belonged to his father, Stuart, before him, and
his grandfather, Thurston, before that. Johnny Steinbeck was remembered as a troubled young man. His relationship with his father was generally rocky. How sad. As a father myself, I'm
haunted by one line from *Charley*. About leaving the "prisoners"
behind at the school to continue his journey, Steinbeck wrote,
"My own son will probably never forgive me."

I left the school and pulled back onto I-91 headed for St.
Johnsbury, Vermont, which I guessed was Steinbeck's second stop.
Although not mentioned in *Charley*, it is listed as the mailing ad-
dress of a letter to Elaine, posted on the second day of his trip,
September 24, 1960:

Dear Bogworthy:

*I didn't get you written last night as I thought I might.
There was the yearly Pow-Wow when the new boys are
taken into the two tribes. It was a beautiful-big bonfire,
and Thurston Chase in a war bonnet looks exactly like
Thurston Chase in a war bonnet, glasses and all and
speaking Longfellow Indian. I swear it. He wrote it
himself in Hiawatha hexameters, and it was as sub-*

limely dreadful as anything I ever heard.

Prior to reaching Maine, where he is very specific, Steinbeck is vague about his whereabouts in New England. And he made a curious, and at first confusing, writer's choice. Relaying impressions about Vermont and its foliage in the time continuum of the trip, fall of 1960, he digressed into a discussion of Joseph Addison ("He plays the instru-

Andy Chase on the campus of the Eaglebrook School.

ment of language as Casals plays a cello.") and dropped in the date, Sunday, January 29, 1961, thus jumping forward in time to, I'm guessing, the day he was *writing* about crossing Vermont in September of 1960.

My attention to that curious detail was brief, however, for I was astonished by the physical description that followed, which (forgive me) could have been written about me: "I am very wide of shoulder and, in the condition I now find myself in, narrow of hip. My legs are long in proportion to my trunk and are said to be shapely. My hair is grizzled gray [okay, mine is white], my eyes blue and my cheeks ruddy, a complexion inherited from my Irish mother. My face has not ignored the passage of time, but recorded it with scars, lines, furrows and erosions. I wear a beard and mustache but shave my cheeks...." I also read somewhere, perhaps in *America and Americans,* Steinbeck describing himself as having a barrel chest. I, too, am barrel-chested. This is not too surprising given that our ancestry is identical (German and Irish), but still, it is a little spooky. During the trip when Dimmie visited and saw that I was wearing the distinctive Steinbeck goatee (the mustache does not connect with the chin hairs), she said I had gone a little over the top. In truth, it started out as what some might call obsequious imitation, but resulted in a conscious choice. I found I liked the way that goatee looked and appreciated that the hairs did not touch the corners of my mouth, something that has always driven me nuts about facial hair. Plus, other women friends whose opinions I value have complimented me on it. Dimmie only wanted to know when I was going to shave off the "toilet brush."

The Green Mountain State presented sculpted rock faces, often in the median of the interstate, dense forests and quaint farms with covered bridges. I witnessed virtually no good old American Bs—billboards, box stores and blight. There were barns, however. I wondered how, without a super-box store, I was supposed to know I was *always* getting the cheapest stuff. Vermont does have really comfortable wayside/info centers offering free Wi-Fi, signs warning of "Moose Crossing" and, while I was there, brilliant color in the trees. As it turned out, I didn't get to St. Johnsbury. I took a call, which caused me to slip off I-91 and cross the Connecticut River to Woodsville, New Hampshire, onto US-302 northeast to Lisbon.

My detour into the knuckles (New Hampshire resembles a hand with the index finger pointing north) of the Live Free or Die State came after my brother, David, directed me to Bishop Farm Bed & Breakfast, just north of Lisbon, owned by his friend and co-worker, Heather Salter, and managed by Heather's sister, Annie, and mother, Maggie. I was given a cozy, wooden cottage tucked back in the trees. The best lodging of my trip, it turned out. The historic farm sits at the base of a hill covered by fields and forest. The shallow, rocky Ammonoosuc River, on its way to the Connecticut River and New Hampshire's western border with Vermont, runs just below.

The three single women, all with red-tinged brown hair, were warm and welcoming—impressive in their self-sufficiency. Maggie, in her seventies, is a carpenter. Heather is an entrepreneur and

a filmmaker. Annie is a jew-
elry artist. She has the lean,
strong look of a woman accustomed to handling and
hauling horses. She turned
my rig around in a very narrow space, somehow with-
out causing me any loss of
face. Later, when I was walk-

*The Bishop Farm Babes, from
left, Heather, Annie and Margaret.*

ing to the main farmhouse to take my three hosts out to dinner, I
observed Annie kicking a guinea rooster's butt, a clutch of eggs
pressed against her flat belly. "He may be the cock of the walk,
but I'm the alpha mama," she said with a grin, and explained the
miscreant had been pecking at a hen, which was being bred by a
rooster. "He goes wild when the rooster is breeding and just has
to get involved."

We drove Annie's '99 Caddie, which had one-hundred and
sixty-thousand miles on it, over several New Hampshire hills to a
bar with some pretty decent food and cold draft beer. I learned
that Margaret, married three times, had seven children with her
first husband. Annie is the oldest at fifty-one; Heather comes in
next-to-last at forty-five years of age.

Trees flashed by and arched above the car on the drive back
to the farm. Annie said she had talked her way out of a speeding
ticket on this same road. She had been pulled over by the local
deputy sheriff and explained to the officer (no doubt with a winning smile and an eyelash bat or two) that she was hurrying home
to see *American Idol.* As we drove, Heather, in the backseat with
her mom, bemoaned the fact that there were not many men
around the region, at least not many with teeth.

Speaking of males with no teeth, the next morning Max
made a new girlfriend, GiGi, Heather's Chihuahua. After he had

established dominance, he took an invigorating hike up a leaf-strewn path with her. GiGi was sporting a snazzy, red-and-white, fall sweater. As long as GiGi let Max lead, there was a perceptible spring in the old guy's step.

Max and Gigi go for a walk.

Heather and I had some history from a few summers back. We had worked together briefly on a Best Western commercial that my brother directed and produced in Jackson Hole. We laughed, remembering a time David had asked me on the walkie-talkie to go into a nearby garage and request that the mechanics close the large overhead door to reduce unwanted sound during an exterior shot. I went. They basically said, "Hell no." I reported that response over the radio to David and heard him shout, **"Heather!"** Heather strolled in the garage and subtly used her considerable assets as a means of persuasion. A few minutes later the door came down.

While Heather and I walked with the dogs, I mentioned the recession; Heather said it had had little impact on her lodging business. In fact, Bishop Farm had just completed its best year ever. I suggested that might be because people were staying closer to home for travel—the upside to the downturn.

During my stay, I pitched in by proofreading and rewriting Bishop Farm's website blurbs. Heather is very smart but spelling impaired, so I even helped her spell "frickin' dweeb" in a text message. It is so important to get these things right. When I asked Heather if she minded if I referred in my blog to the three Bishop women as the Bed and Breakfast Babes of Bishop Farm, she said in her scratchy, sexy voice, "Hell no, we don't get that enough."

Author's note to male readers: Guys, if you are single, heterosexual, have most of your teeth (or suitable replacements), and are between the ages of forty and seventy-five, I strongly recommend an invigorating weekend in the New Hampshire high country, stretching your legs, breathing country air and observing animal husbandry at Bishop Farm Bed and Breakfast.

I would have loved the time to explore Maine in a leisurely fashion, staying in the Bambi, but I was scheduled to meet Dimmie in Chicago in a few days, so I left the trailer at Bishop Farm. As one man I met on the trip said, when he heard I was going to be away from home for roughly nine weeks, "Buddy, if you're late to that date with your wife in Chicago, you might as well just keep right on driving."

The trip to Deer Isle from Lisbon, New Hampshire, consumed an entire spectacular New England fall day. The White Mountains flared with sun-drenched color. Towns were graced with quaint buildings, many of them small churches, predominantly painted white, just as Steinbeck described them in *Travels with Charley,* "The villages are the prettiest, I guess, in the whole nation, neat and white-painted and—not counting the motels and tourist courts—unchanged for a hundred years except for traffic and paved streets." Produce stands lined the road and were bursting with barrels and bins stacked high with colorful fall fruit and vegetables.

When Steinbeck was crossing the White Mountains, he stopped at a farm to buy eggs and asked for permission to camp there. He invited his host, the farmer, who was curious about Rocinante, in for a "touch of applejack." While sipping, Steinbeck asked if the man had heard any news from the United Nations that day. The farmer mentioned a report that Khrushchev had removed his shoe and pounded the table. The U.N. was also on the radio news the day I crossed the White Mountains, as President Obama sought sanctions against Iran for nuclear development.

U.S. 1, near the coast in the Bucksport and Searsport area, offered the first glorious views of Penobscot Bay, where blue water and blue sky appeared to be dueling to a draw. I

Room with a view above Penobscot Bay.

stopped at a cemetery overlooking the bay. I had noticed that all over New England headstones are, for the most part, tall, rectangular and cut from a thin sheet of pale, gray rock. As the monuments stand watch, they cast human-like shadows.

Steinbeck mentioned that he followed U.S. 2 across New Hampshire most of the way to Deer Isle. I veered south from that route at Bethel, Maine; I knew I would be catching U.S. 2 on my way back to New Hampshire. There was a distinct change in foliage somewhere around Bethel. The deciduous trees of New Hampshire had given over to the conifers of Maine. I followed at least a half-a-dozen state roads on a beeline to Deer Isle. After departing Deer Isle, I followed U.S. 1 all the way to Caribou, Maine, in Aroostock County.

On September 27, 1960, Steinbeck wrote to Elaine from Deer Isle:

> *Wherever I stop people look hungrily at Rocinante. They want to move on. Is this a symptom? They lust to move on. West—north, south—anywhere. Maybe it's their comment on their uneasiness. People are real restless.*

My experience was different from Steinbeck's. For example, in Danforth, Maine, I stopped for gas at Kinney Auto Center, where the costs for repairs were painted on the exterior wood wall. The gas pumps were the old-fashioned type that did not take credit cards and had to be cranked to start the flow of gas. The attendant came out and I knew immediately I had the genuine item. This stocky, strawberry-haired gentleman of-

Stonington Harbor.

fered directions to a customer, saying, "If you get to the bridge by the faahm, you've gone too faaah."

I went in to pay and saw a magazine on the desk that had something about cowboys and guns in the title. I asked the man if he'd ever been out west.

"Nah."

"Would you like to go?" I asked.

"Someday meybe—get rid of the wahife."

Not exactly an I-would-leave-this-afternoon-if-you've-got-the-space kind of answer. Everywhere I had encountered folks who said this trip was a great idea and a wonderful adventure, but not a single person had thus far expressed the wish to be elsewhere.

But, let's back up to Deer Isle. "It is a suckling that nestles against the breast of Maine...," was how Steinbeck described the island. Deer Isle lies on the eastern side of Penobscot Bay. Around 7:00 p.m. I crossed a high-arched iron bridge over Eggemoggin Reach and then followed a curving causeway to the island. It was getting dark and, although it was Saturday night, the few gas stations and stores I passed were closed. When I arrived in the town of Deer Isle, there did not appear to be any lodging. On the GPS I found an inn located nearby. Betty directed me to the Harbor Inn in Stonington, a few miles southeast of Deer Isle. The Harbor Inn is a weathered, brown-shingled building on a narrow, winding street by the water. I parked, got out and, while considering the pleasant-looking Harbor Inn, noticed a motel across Main Street. For some inexplicable reason, I went over and rang the bell at Boyce's Motel. I got the last room.

At a bayside café, I enjoyed a dinner of chowder

The Marlinspike Ship's Chandlery.

and clams washed down with a generous amount of local brew. Afterwards, I walked back to the motel. It was a cool, comfortable evening and I took my time, enjoying the sea air and the display of blinking lights out in the harbor. I wondered if I was seeing evidence of any of the eight lighthouses I had read were located on that part of the coast. As I neared my room, I saw something stuck to the door. It was a note saying that a woman named Charlotte had called the motel to invite me to Sunday brunch at her inn. I had not spoken to anyone on Deer Isle except for Barrett, the owner of Boyce's. Suddenly I had a mysterious invitation to breakfast. I could hardly wait for the morning to find out why.

I woke up early and walked Max. The light was flat as we climbed up a side street in a fine mist mixed with light rain. Foghorns on the bay moaned their forlorn warnings. Heavy cloud cover pressed down on the harbor when I drove up the hill toward the Victorian Prés du Port Bed and Breakfast. Below the clouds, I could see the nearby islands, each about one quarter of a mile apart. Church bells pealed across Stonington. Charlotte, the owner of the bed and breakfast, barely batted an eye when the wrong man showed up for breakfast. I gave her my card, she studied it, laughed and said, "You may be following Steinbeck's route, but you are not the man I met yesterday who is following Steinbeck's route." Charlotte graciously insisted I stay and eat.

Over breakfast Charlotte said she had met a man the day before whose name was Tom. He said he was retracing the Steinbeck route. I learned later Barrett had put the note on the wrong door. In fact, I realized I had seen Tom enter-

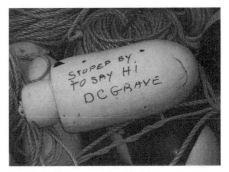

Maine's idea of a calling card.

ing his room when I returned from walking Max early that morning. Tom was tall and had white hair like me, and he was staying in the room right next to mine—strange coincidence. I never saw Tom again.

Charlotte was slender, elegant, and articulate, perhaps in her early seventies. She had severely arthritic hands, but a bright and quick mind. Over breakfast, as we looked out across the bay, she told me that lobstermen worry about kayaks in the fog because they are so low in the water they don't register on the radar. She said sometimes the tall, rainbow bridge onto Deer Isle sways as much as three feet in either direction in the wind, and that some people marvel at its construction, while others, with too much knowledge of engineering, are afraid to cross it. I said I was certain the rainbow bridge had been there at least fifty years because Steinbeck referred to crossing it in *Charley*.

When I mispronounced Acadia, the national park northeast of Deer Isle, by adding an *r*, Charlotte reminded me that there is no *r* in Maine—because the letter *r* is never pronounced. Think "paaak" for park. I asked Charlotte about the burned rubber tire tracks I had noticed all over Deer Isle's paved roads. She said that making elaborate designs with fast-spinning tires was a unique redneck art form that had sprung up in the region and had recently been celebrated in the premiere of an independent film at the Stonington Opera House. Charlotte was quick to point out that, if "peeling-out art" was not my taste, Stonington and other nearby towns were populated with many accomplished artists.

After "depaaating" the bed and breakfast, and while poking around Stonington, I discovered the Marlinspike Ship's Chandlery tucked among several three- and four-story frame buildings on the water. I surmised that it was where Steinbeck had shopped for a lantern and other supplies: "At a wonderful store in Stonington, half hardware store and half ship's chandler, I bought a kerosene lamp with a tin reflector for Rocinante." The Marlinspike was closed, but I noticed a tangle of lines in front of a stack of lobster traps beside the entrance. A pink float rested in the lines, inscribed with a hand-scrawled message, "Stoped [sic] by to say Hi, DC Grave"—Maine's idea of a calling card.

Stonington is aptly named. The town is built on a hill with exposed slabs of gray rock in places leading down to the harbor and even protruding out into the water, some supporting a growth of spruce trees. Granite has been quarried on Deer Isle for centuries. I walked Max on Main, packed the car and headed north, through the town of Deer Isle, en route to the mainland and U.S.1 at Ellsworth. Just north of Stonington, we passed two men loading lobster traps into the bed of a pickup.

I didn't see a single deer on Deer Isle, but I did see an oddly striped animal, larger than a house cat, dead by the road—a "coon cat" perhaps. Steinbeck described them as "huge tailless cats with gray coats barred with black, which is why they are called coon cats. They are wild; they live in the woods and are very fierce."

Steinbeck wrote of the quality of light on Deer Isle, "Everything stood out separate from everything else, a rock, a rounded rump of sea-polished driftwood on the beach, a roof line." I had a similar visual experience driving into Deer Isle for the first time at dusk. As I crossed the rainbow bridge, and then the causeway that links the mainland to Deer Isle, I noticed a solitary white dinghy on the gray water; the boat had an eerie fluorescence, as if lit from within.

Odd light, bizarre cats, tire-track art and weird coincidences—as Steinbeck wrote in *Charley,* "One doesn't have to be sensitive to feel the strangeness of Deer Isle."

It was raining the day I left, and U.S. 1 along the Maine coast east of Ellsworth was disappointing. Although it's called the Coastal Highway, it could have been Anywhere, USA. I realized that, as Steinbeck wrote in *Travels with Charley* about any part of this route, the person coming along ten minutes later would probably have a different experience. For me, however, the Coastal Highway was a letdown. There were few views of the bays and islands, and seafood joints were rare. The towns just looked like towns, and ugly towns at that—McDonald's, Family Dollar, mobile homes—rather typical American redundancy. I did pass a field of cheerful sunflowers and then barrens populated with low, rust-red blueberry bushes and that pleased me, until I saw Wild Blueberry Land, a building constructed to resemble a blueberry, surrounded by blue objects shaped like blueberries, and peddling all things blueberry.

Perhaps I was feeling frustrated that I had to pound out the miles and did not have time for a side-trip to the picturesque town of Bar Harbor and the beautiful and rugged Acadia National Park, which includes mountains that are the very first in the U.S. to be warmed by the morning sun. I did finally get a glimpse of a headland and bay, just beyond Hancock, and before turning north on State 191 toward the town of Meddybemps, I found a seafood restaurant in Machias called Helen's. I ordered lobster chowder, salad because I needed the greens, and Maine potatoes prepared the French way. While savoring my steamy chowder, I overheard a large woman with a round body, face, glasses and round hair speaking in the Maine vernacular, extolling the virtues of, what else—shopping at "Walmaaaat" (Curse you, Big Box! You are everywhere). But then, just outside of Machias, a rock face, an inlet, a church steeple—the sort of stereotypical New England-y stuff I had expected to see for much of this drive.

Max on *the box.*

Heading north away from the coast and through the timber was, by contrast, soothing and invigorating, even in the gentle rain. Timber and taters rule the Great North; the Maine-stays, I suppose you could say (if you dared). I drove up along a lazy river, saw a sign for a "canoe trail," and passed a little log cabin in the trees called "Gramps Camp." The forests were predominantly deciduous, as in New Hampshire. The tree-covered road wound through clusters of cottages and small, frame houses with tidy, little lawns.

About four-fifths of the way up the state, I made a wrong turn in Houlton, Maine, onto I-95 and headed east to the border of New Brunswick, Canada. I returned to Houlton and while trying to find a visitors' center, accidentally (or is it configured that way, eh?) turned into a Walmart parking lot. The visitor's center was across the street. There I learned that Houlton was the seat for Aroostock County. Maine's largest county is equal in size to Connecticut and Rhode Island combined. If you imagine that the often-chilly state of Maine wears a cap, then that cap is Aroostook County.

Max gave me a good laugh when I slid back in the car with my bag of visitor's information. Before the Steinbeck trip, he used to play a joke on me when he was riding shotgun. No matter how

comfortable I made his seat, when I left him in the car, he'd shift
to mine and there he'd be curled up when I returned. For this trip,
for his safety and my sanity, I blocked him in the back of the
4Runner. And, of course, he had devised a new prank. He would
climb up on the food box or kennel and sit in the items on top: a
package of paper towels, my duffle, whatever. Sometimes, when I
leaped into the car after a short stop and started out, a glance in
the rearview mirror revealed him standing on top of his kennel,
surfing in the back. That happened again in Houlton.

It was pouring and dark. I still had miles to go before
I...well, you get my gist. I found a safe place to park off the road,
and in the dim light of the car, studied the visitors' center flyer advertising local inns. I called Kate at the Old Iron Inn in Caribou.
She was a little prickly at first, but warmed when I explained my
Steinbeck mission. She invited me to stay. I wildly underestimated
how far it was to the inn and made a few hair-raising driving
choices in the reflected and refracting light on the rain-soaked
roads. But I made it to Caribou and soon met Caribou Kate (my
nickname).

Kate and I hit it off. She apologized for the initial chilliness
on the phone, explaining that she got a little burned out on people at the end of the season. Kate turned out to be a wonderful
hostess and guide to the area. She began the lesson by informing
me that there were no more caribou in or around Caribou. The
last one was killed in 1932. The animals were further south now
and attempts to reintroduce them near Caribou had been met with
disease and disaster. Kate also said the great western woods in
northern Maine had been a working forest for centuries with the
earliest demand being masts for ships. There was a recent move-
ment to try and turn the forests into a national park, but she felt
that, because of their history, such a plan was silly.

As to the recession, Kate said there had never been a big

boom in northern Maine and thus there was no bust. "This area is off the beaten path and sort of flies under the radar," she said. "Recently, more retirees are moving in, and I just hope they don't turn around and depart after their first six-month winter."

Kate told me what to look for when I rounded what Steinbeck called the "rooftree of Maine," before heading south. She said I would see evidence of a time when the population boomed, resulting in numerous large Catholic churches.

The Iron Inn was a three-story brick mansion filled with fascinating antiques, most of which were, well, old irons, as in for ironing shirts. My third-floor room was very comfortable, with a large, firm bed, private bath and delightful amenities. The rain had ceased. After Max's late-evening walk down a few Caribou city blocks in the cool, rain-washed air, I put him in the car for the night. Thank God, because just after closing the car door I turned to see four skunks emerge from the bushes onto the inn's driveway. I took the long way round to the front of the house. The skunks were the only wildlife I had seen in northern Maine. Not even a deer. I remembered noticing a front-page article in the Bangor paper, at Helen's Restaurant in Machias, indicating the hunt would be off that fall because the deer population was down.

I was feeling a bit down and lonely that night myself, but a call from my buddy, Dave, during which he said he was proud of me for imagining and initiating this adventure, lifted my spirits. He also told me a story about how he had once traveled the back roads in Maine looking for a put-in to canoe a river. He gambled on a direction at a fork in the road, but wasn't confident of his choice, so when he saw a man fishing he stopped and asked. The Mainer's response was classic, "Well, fo suah, you picked the best road, but it suah as hell ain't the right one."

I slept well. The next morning, the sky was still overcast, but the rain was holding off. While we enjoyed the sumptuous breakfast Kate had prepared, she explained that the current hot-button issue in Maine was gay marriage. She said, in northern Maine, a "mixed marriage" was considered to be one between a Protestant and a Catholic. She didn't get what the fuss was about. She supported gay marriage.

As I got to know this bespectacled, dark-haired woman, I learned she was a fugitive from a

Musée et Centre Culturel du Mont-Carmel in the Saint John Valley.

southern childhood, rife with alcoholism and excessive tobacco use in her home and peer abuse in her Atlanta high school. She had been teased mercilessly for "being smart and weird." Her mother died of lung cancer at the age of fifty-seven and her alcoholic father "took a short walk off a long building a few years later, putting everyone out of *his* misery." Kate loathed the South, a sentiment evident in where she had chosen to live.

When I informed her I would be skipping the New Orleans-to-Atlanta leg in my travels because Steinbeck had little to say about that stretch in his book, Kate said, "That's because there's nothing there worth seeing."

At Caribou Kate's suggestion, I stopped near the town of Lille and photographed the Musée et Centre Culturel du Mont-Carmel, an immense, restored Catholic church with two massive, gold bell towers flanking the central pitched roof. There were three large doors and a dozen windows on the side facing Highway 1. As I drove through the Saint John Valley, I heard "Valley French," a mixture of Old French and English, and saw ads for foods such as "ployes," yellow buckwheat pancakes. Acadians, people of French ancestry, were thrown out of Canada in the mid-

1700s when they refused to swear allegiance to the British Crown and the Anglican Church. Many settled in northern Maine, while others immigrated to Louisiana. According to a Cajun (corrupted from Acadian) myth, the lobsters tried to follow the Acadian boats on the trip to Louisiana, but the journey was so long and arduous they shrank in size to what are today known as crawfish, a staple in Cajun cooking.

I loved rereading the section of *Travels with Charley* in which Steinbeck shares an evening in Saint John Valley, and rare bottle of French cognac, with a family of French-Canadian migrant workers. Before departing the next morning, he reflected on the experience with the potato pickers, "There are times that one treasures for all one's life, and such times are burned clearly and sharply on the material of total recall. I felt very fortunate that morning." The joy Steinbeck experienced in the very human act of connecting and conversing with others is palpable in the retelling.

I had a similar experience in Kansas with the three gentlemen who took me catfish fishing. I remember feeling charged and exhilarated as I enjoyed that wonderful, memorable evening, made more so by the freely offered camaraderie of my new friends.

Unfortunately, such camaraderie was not to happen in the rolling Saint John Valley of northern Maine. Here's why. I had inquired in Caribou about migrant potato pickers and was told Hispanics had replaced the French-Canadians. Not a problem. I could adjust and had brought along a bottle of very nice sipping tequila in case of just such an eventuality. But when Mark Cyr, of the Cyr Potato Corporation of St. David, Maine, swung open the doors to his barn and introduced me to his picker, I could see the picker and I would not be sharing any drinks.

The picker was a huge machine, two actually, that work in

tandem—combined, they're about the size of a semi-truck and trailer. Mark said migrant pickers are a thing of the past, although some high school kids (school lets out for two weeks during the harvest) do work on the machines and in the potato houses.

Mark was an affable guy. If he hadn't been repairing his equipment after the harvest of one hundred and seventy-five acres of "early" potatoes, I would've offered *him* a drink. He spoke with the lyrical cadence of the Acadian patois. He sported a clean blue shirt with his farm's logo above the pocket. He was medium height, powerful in build, had blue eyes to match his shirt, and chiseled features. No doubt a heartthrob to potato groupies. When Mark saw Max, he quipped, "Traveling light, eh?"

I left, feeling grateful to Mark, but mindful of Steinbeck's concern for the universal plight of migrant workers. I'm certain he would not have been happy to learn machines have replaced them in northern Maine, which is, along with Idaho, one of the premier potato-growing regions in this country. (In 1960 Long Island would have been listed as competitive in potato production, but much of the available land for agriculture has been developed in the past few decades.) Nor would Steinbeck be happy to know that we are losing small farms at an alarming rate, that the number of people who claim farming as their profession in America is at less than one percent, and that "farmer" is no longer one of the choices for "occupation" on the U.S. census forms. "Other" has replaced it.

I had lunch at a little drive-in restaurant in Frenchville on the Saint John River, which defines the boundary with Canada.

At Fort Kent, Maine, I turned south on State 11 with my eventual goal being U.S. 2 back through New Hampshire. Just south of Fort Kent, the ground was still covered with puddles from rain the day before. The sky above the wooded hills was stuffed with bulging clouds, like sour cream piled on a baked po-

tato. I was circumnavigating
the great state of Maine,
which Steinbeck wrote is
"just as long coming down
as it is going up," on essen-
tially the same route the author took. Off to the west

Moose season in northern Maine.

were what appeared to be endless forests. Private logging roads
provided the only access for much of the Great North Woods. I
saw more trees than I believe exist in the entire state of Wyoming.
The sky began to clear. I passed acres of cut and stacked timber.
Then I got behind a semi-truck full of wood chips that eventually
pulled into a paper mill. I went through Eagle Lake, Winterville,
Portage, Ashland and Patten, where I stopped in the middle of the
afternoon for a roadside view of Mount Katahdin; a weakened
autumnal sun, partially concealed in haze, moved toward the
mountain. The temperature hit a pleasant sixty-eight degrees.

It was moose season and I saw signs of kills everywhere, including a bull strung up at a moose-cutting station in Ashland and
another strapped to a small flatbed trailer behind a gas station in
the town of Sherman Mills at the junction of State 11 and I-95. I
was still north of the highest point in New Hampshire and quite
a distance above the northernmost east-west route across Maine.
Steinbeck wrote in *Charley* that you should never ask Maine residents for directions because they delight in giving them incor-
rectly. I decided to test that caution. At the gas station in Sherman
Mills, I asked a middle-aged man for guidance. "Wait until my
boy comes out," he said with pride. "He knows northern Maine
like the back of his hand."

His "boy" was a ball-capped and mustached thirty-something man. When he came out of the gas station, I asked for help
choosing a southwestern route through the center of Maine that

would avoid the interstate and eventually connect with U.S. 2 to New Hampshire. Father and son studied my map spread on the hood of their pickup.

The dad said, "I've only been outta Maine twice." And "That's pretty faaah where yer tryin' to go." The myth of errant Maine directions was exploded. I was pretty certain by looking at the map that I was receiving good directions from native Mainers. I complained to the two men that my GPS kept insisting that I take interstates.

The son said, "Well, you should just reach in there and turn her off. If only that worked at home, eh?" We all roared. As I pulled away from these gentlemen, I felt a heartstring plucked with the longing to live close to both my boys someday.

Going further south on U.S. 11, I skirted several dark and glistening lakes near Millinocket, Brownville Junction (with American flags on every post) and Milo with its pretty stream down the center. I whisked under sun-dappled, flame-throwing trees and passed more lakes and camps and cottages tucked neatly in conifer groves. I owned the road; there was no one else out there. At one point I went five minutes without seeing another car.

Then I traveled State 150 to Dover-Foxcroft and, after night fell on the fall Maine day and a chill came in the air, State 7 to Dexter and Corina. I finally connected with U.S. 2 at Newport. The hour was late and the day had been long. I was resigned to turning into the first decent campground I could find on U.S. 2. But I also felt elated. It had been an exhilarating two days. I had reached my goals, on schedule, and had completed a successful, albeit whirlwind, tour of northern New England. When a trip combines the White Mountains of New Hampshire and the island-dotted coast and northern forests of Maine—with intermittent sunshine, warm temperatures, and buckets of fall color splashed in—the word *exquisite* comes to mind.

Near Canaan, Max and I got off U.S. 2 at a KOA Kampground. Since I had left Winnie at Bishop Farm, I was prepared to sleep outside on a pad. The lateness of the hour and lightning to the west dissuaded me from that plan. I booked a "Kamper Kabin." No kitchen, no linens, no bathroom, and it cost way too much money, but the "kabin" proved cozy and it sheltered us from the rain that came later that night. Dinner started with a cocktail, Laird's Applejack (a Steinbeck favorite), with water (no ice was available), in a large aluminum water bottle. My appetizer consisted of gas station cheddar crackers and nuts. My entrée was a sour, snappy Maine apple, and for dessert, I had a Snickers bar. Dinner, paired with more applejack, was consumed on a porch swing. I watched the lightning in the dark, swelling sky and counted the seconds before the ensuing rumble.

When I was a child, my father often took me out on our covered front porch to appreciate the power and beauty of electrical storms. Thunderstorms, enjoyed from a safe, warm spot, have always excited me. The storm in Canaan, Maine, did not disappoint. I sat on the porch swing beside Max and watched until it passed. We went inside.

Rain tapped out a cadence on the cabin roof. I read for a while on my bunk and, after a short, wet, walk for Max, turned in at 9:30. Max snored—loudly. I woke him, gently. He does not rouse easily and, when disturbed, can be pretty accurate with his few remaining teeth. He went back to sleep before I did, *and snored again.* I couldn't believe a seven-pound dog could make so much noise while sleeping. I didn't want to lock him in the car, so I popped in my earplugs and, somehow, we made it through the rainy night.

As for the KOA, with signs (including one about "tinkling" and one with POOP in large letters) and rules posted everywhere, it was too Kute for this Kamper by half. After we awoke, Max added his distain by "tinkling" on the cabin porch (He does the same thing on our deck. Hey, it's outside, right?), and we departed at first light.

The rain had moved off east. The sky was clear. It looked like it would be another glorious, color-infused crossing of western Maine and New Hampshire. I passed through Mexico,

Maine produce from a roadside stand.

Maine, (the naming of which was inspired by early nineteenth-century sympathy for Mexico's fight for independence from Spain), Ed McMahon's birthplace. There I won a thirty-five cent pack of Wrigley's gum from a scratch card at a Big Apple food store/gas station; it was not exactly Publishers Clearing House but still, even though I had to pay the two-cent tax, it was obviously my lucky day. I saw a woman in a red T-shirt that said, "Born to Party—Forced to Work," filling her car with gas.

Near Bethel, Maine, we pulled over at a farm's roadside stand. The stout, earthy, apron-wrapped proprietress chatted briefly, mentioning that her produce harvest was off by half because of too much rain. When she learned of my purpose, she warned, with characteristic dry New England humor, that the road ahead was under construction, "and it probably was when Steinbeck came through, too." We left with fresh corn, tomatoes, peppers and apples. Soon, after going across a stretch of torn-up highway, Maine was behind me.

I stopped near Shelburne, New Hampshire, for a view of the mountains just before the spot where the Appalachian Trail crosses U.S. 2, and met a most memorable character. I parked in a pull-off behind an older, boxy motorhome with Vermont plates. Just off the pavement, I saw a woman bent over, picking something from a grass-covered bank. I worked around in front of my car and leaned past the side of the RV, trying surreptitiously to

snag a humorous photo of the
woman's backside, a veritable field of
purple. I know, rude as hell. I didn't
get the shot and I almost got caught.
Around the other side of the RV came
her husband, a rail-thin, cigar-smok-
ing man in his mid-seventies. He introduced himself as Richard. I crossed
the road for a photo of the mountains

*Richard and I discuss
Obama while looking at
Mt. Washington.*

and when I returned, Richard and I chatted. I asked about
Obama.

"Between the wife and me, we've got ten kids—all Obama-
happy—not me," he replied.

He was a retired tool-and-die guy who was very concerned
about so much manufacturing being moved from New England to
China. "What if we have a war?" he asked. "I don't like Obama's
thinking or his spending." Then his eyes drifted to the skyline.
"Beautiful mountain," Richard said.

"Is that Washington?"

"Yup. In the middle."

"Have you driven it?" I asked.

"Nope. You?"

"No."

"You sure could in that. (He pointed to my car.) "I can't in
this old motorhome."

"Going back to Vermont?"

"Yup. Been over to the coast. I see your Wyoming plates.
Burned up five miles of your highway once. Near Cody."

"You must've been in a hurry."

"No, I *burned* it up. My boat (he pronounced it "bolt")
trailer blew a tire but I couldn't see it behind this old box and just
kept on driving with the metal dragging and the sparks flying. Five

and a third miles of roadside grass—burned. I even looked in the rearview at one point and said to the wife, 'There's a fire back there.' After the fire followed me for a while, I figured it out."

"You've got to be kidding. Were the authorities upset?"

"Well sure. I don't blame them. Wouldn't you be?"

"I guess I would be."

He shook his head. "It was an experience I shall never forget." He fixed me with his stare. "Ever tried to buy a "bolt" trailer in the middle of Wyoming?"

"No, I can't say as I have."

"Three hundred and eight-eight fence posts," Richard said, puffing and squinting up at Mt. Washington.

"How do you know that?"

He yanked his cigar out of his mouth. "They billed me for them."

I spent one more night with the Bed and Breakfast Babes of Bishop Farm. In the morning, Max gave the farm hens a good run for their money. There was a hint of winter in the air and I donned long johns and a down vest for the first time on the trip. After another wonderful breakfast, we said goodbye and were off, with Winnie once again in tow. Maine was behind me; I was feeling relaxed about the days ahead and happy to be heading west. I followed U.S. 302 north along the Amonoosuc River to Littleton, New Hampshire, and picked up I-93 for a short jaunt across the Connecticut River and into Vermont, where it was my intention to connect with U.S. 2 again.

Just south of St. Johnsbury, Vermont, on I-93, a sign said, "Moose 3000 Feet." I looked but I didn't see the moose. It must have been on a coffee break. The ramp for Exit 1 at St. Johnsbury appeared to rise right up through a cut in a rock escarpment and dump onto a red barn framed by two large, white silos. The off-ramp turned just before the farm and led to the Vermont section of U.S. 2, a stunning two-lane offering lovely views of rural Vermont. The local radio station transported me back in time by playing a song about a white sport coat and a pink carnation. I got the high school football report. "This is AM 1340, WSCJ, St. Johnsbury, celebrating sixty years as your hometown high school sports connection. Under the lights you get that big-game atmosphere. We are talking *high school football here.*" The announcer went on to describe the new uniforms, "Beautiful maroon pants and sky-blue top with easy-to-read numbers." He concluded by complimenting the high school administration for "outdoing themselves with the new broadcast booth with its excellent sightlines."

The bridge across Lake Champlain.

After following 2 through Danville and West Danville, I angled up through Vermont on State 15, the Grand Army of the Republic Highway, and went north on State 104. I felt pretty confident I was close to the route Steinbeck took to Rouses Point, New York, on Lake Champlain. My destination for that day was a campground near Watertown, New York, close to Lake Ontario. At the Swanton Access on Lake Champlain, I encountered the most deceptive pit toilet on the trip. A freshly painted privy near the parking lot, surrounded by boulders, grass and birch trees, turned out, behind the bright green door, to be revolting—and close to overflowing. A checklist posted on the interior wall for recording the dates of regular cleaning was blank. "I want you in my mouth" was scrawled over it with a black Sharpie.

I entered New York by bridge and, following U.S. 11 just above Adirondack Park, crossed the Great Chazy River several times. New York was not New England, not even with the few maple syrup places I saw. It was not as quaint, nor tree-covered, nor was the topography as interesting. It was, for the most part, flat and farmed.

It was raining off and on, hovering just around forty-two degrees, and low clouds were billowing to the west under a horizontal, gray sky. In Ellenburg I passed Lake Roxanne, doing a double take after mistakenly thinking the sign said "Lake Rocinante." In Potsdam, a larger Airstream approached me in the oncoming lane. The driver opened his window and gave me a double-pump thumbs up, flashing a big grin as he passed. A junction at Westville, New York, presented the chance to stop at a welcoming country café for lunch. I ordered a tuna salad sandwich and soup. I had noticed a town, Chateaugay, to the east and was curious about it. I pronounced it "Shat-toe-gay," but the owner corrected me, "Shat-a-gay," and told me a few things about it—none very remarkable. Not being one to pass up a bathroom opportunity, I visited the men's room and was delighted to see a note above the urinal that read, "Don't use this unless you have rubber boots" and, in a different ink and hand, "+ a lifejacket."

Home for the night was the Black River Bay Campground on the Black River near Watertown and the Thousand Islands area. The campground was deceptive. For starters, Betty had trouble finding it. When we finally located the park, I saw three deer (the first since Long Island) dodging among the huge trees that framed the entrance. That was promising, but the camping area itself was crowded and had the look of a place where folks had permanently lost their mobility—possibly by just running out of gas and/or ambition. The campsites were close together, offering no privacy. The bathrooms were marginal. The stalls had old, olive-colored, wool blankets hung for privacy—several with cigarette burn-holes at hand height.

I set up Winnie in a grassy spot, strolled down to the campground dock and watched six boats with fishermen, plying for salmon below a falls on the Black River, which flows west into Lake Ontario. Many of the fishermen wore day-glo lime pants. I wondered what marketing genius had convinced manly out- doorsmen to dress like neon signs.

A short, squat fellow in a flannel shirt and his young son, a chip off the old block, walked onto the dock. I asked why there were so many fishing boats right off the Black Bay dock. The dad said they were gathered there right below the dam, at the edge of the town of Dexter, because the salmon wanted to go upstream at that point and had to get over the dam to do it. "So the fish pause there, below the dam, to think and plan their next move and—like thinkin' does to me—it makes 'em hungry. So it's a great place to catch salmon," he said.

Just thinking about those ambitious salmon made me hun- gry. I returned to my trailer and enjoyed a grand dinner from sev- eral states: Maine corn, tomatoes and peppers; leftover Pennsylvania family farm double chocolate cake; with Lemoncello from Wyoming, as an aperitif. I was relieved, knowing that my next day was going to be relatively light in comparison to my blitz around Maine. Niagara Falls, a few hours to the west, was my goal. Before bed, I had a nice long cell phone catch-up with Dim- mie, but only after she landed a pretty good zinger. Being a little disoriented by constant travel, I began by asking her where I was the last time we talked.

Without missing a beat, and with her characteristic lack of vitriol, she said, "Jackson Hole, about two months before you left on your trip. Since then you have either been preoccupied or we've had a bad connection."

"Touché! Ya got me, Dim. Funny, I don't remember that con- versation," I said. We both laughed.

After crawling into bed, I thought about Steinbeck and how

he described having to call Elaine, at times, from crowded general store payphones with men tripping all over him. Cell phones are a pretty good defense against loneliness—when they work.

The next morning I settled up with Pam in the office. When I told her about my adventure, her whole de-

A lovely campsite at Niagara Falls North RV Park.

meanor changed. She was perhaps low thirties in age, and had a round, pretty face with heavily made-up eyes. She had a quick smile, and clean, flat, brown hair. Pam was ready to come along. She talked about how she had always wanted to take a trip like mine. I swear, if I had offered, she would have jumped aboard.

After packing up I had some reason, I've forgotten what, to drop in the office one last time before departing. Pam looked up, smiled and said, "You've come back for me haven't you? All I need is a shower and to throw a few things in a suitcase."

I had finally met someone who truly longed to be somewhere else. And I think she meant it. It pained me to disappoint Pam. She seemed like a nice gal. After departing Black Bay, I drifted through several miles of scenic New York farm and vineyard country and even saw a sign for Old MacDonald's Farm.

On the leg to Niagara Falls, I varied from what my '59 Rand McNally would suggest was Steinbeck's course, State 104, closer to Lake Ontario. It was my sixth straight day of driving; I gave in to my road weariness and to Betty who, as I said, being sort of an *a*-to-*b* gal always insisted on interstates. I took I-81 south to I-90 west to Buffalo, New York, and then veered north to Niagara Falls North RV Park in Lewiston, New York. When I was checking in at the office, I ran into a large man in coveralls wearing a full, scraggly, grayish beard and a stained hat that read, "Life's too short to dance with ugly women." A few minutes later, as I walked by his large pickup truck with Illinois plates and saw his large gal in the front seat, I concluded that he didn't dance with her much. The park had clean, shaded sites. I found mine and it was very private.

While in Lewiston, I thought about Steinbeck's prescient concern for the pollutants being dumped into our rivers:

> ...I do wonder whether there will come a time when we can no longer afford our wastefulness—chemical wastes in the river, metal wastes everywhere, and atomic wastes buried deep in the earth or sunk in the sea.

He was far ahead of his time on the fragility of the environment, and so many other critical American issues. I remembered how clueless I was in the early sixties, growing up near, and often swimming in, a dead river polluted by mine effluvium—never thinking or hearing about just how wrong that was. That river, the Kiskiminetas in western Pennsylvania, has almost fully recovered—a conservation victory Steinbeck would have heartily applauded.

Here is just a brief comment on my visit the next day to Niagara Falls—brief yes, but no match for Steinbeck's statement (no doubt with tongue firmly planted in cheek), "Niagara Falls is very nice," which begins a three-line paragraph about the falls in *Travels with Charley*. I went expecting, indeed planning, to be cynical, but that doesn't come easily to me and I was actually impressed. I have often been asked if Yellowstone National Park, with its predictable crush of people, is worth the trip. My answer is always, "Yes, it's well worth the effort." One of the reasons so many people from around the world visit Yellowstone is because Yellowstone is extraordinary, unlike any other place on this planet. I now feel that way about Niagara Falls.

Of course, just about every-thing surrounding the falls is tacky and ostentatious. Thank God, Yellowstone has been

Niagara Falls, well worth the visit.

spared that fate. But stand close to the absolute power of the water surging around Goat Island and blasting over the Niagara escarpment and block out all that is around you. Imagine you are seeing the falls for the first time three hundred years ago, and you will be impressed, and perhaps even moved, as was I. For every human travesty there is an offsetting triumph. According to an EPA website titled "Toxic Management in the Niagara River," until recently the river was laced with mercury, PCBs and pesti-cides. Then a management plan was formed between Canada, bordering the river to the west, and the U.S. that has resulted in an eighty percent reduction in pollution. Evidence of the recovery can be seen in the lake sturgeon's return to the upper reaches of the river. The website reported, however, that the Niagara River is still considered one of the Great Lakes "areas of concern."

On the third day, camped near Niagara Falls, I met Rodney. He was walking his male Maltese, named Harley Rodzilla. Rod-ney was a short, slightly paunchy man with thick, salt-and-pepper hair and a goatee. He was chewing tobacco—a high-energy, short-stab, finger-point-for-emphasis kind of guy—sometimes pointing into my chest. He was friendly—loved this country, loved the colored lights at night on Niagara Falls. "One of the prettiest things I've ever seen," he commented.

We compared male Maltese stories. I told him that early that morning I had clipped Max to his expandable leash, which was attached to the trailer. I had stepped inside to get some milk, when two dogs walked by. Max barked and ran the leash out to its end, jarring the trailer when he was stopped just short of the startled intruders. Rodney said Harley was exactly the same—great with people, terrible with all dogs. We also shared trailer tips, some resulting from mistakes we had made along the road. Rodney said if he is in a hurry and wants a short night of camping, he stays in Walmart parking lots.

Historic lighthouse on the Great Lakes at Old Fort Niagara.

Later that night I was joined for drinks in my trailer by Rodney and his wife, Donna, who had black hair, green eyes and a warm smile. They told me they both worked for casinos in Colorado. Rodney mentioned that he doesn't gamble. He doesn't see the wisdom in handing back the money the Casino pays him for being a floor boss. We discussed gambling, health care and the economy.

Rodney said the economy was strong in their hometown, but that wasn't indicative of national trends because people gambled more in tough times. "Not that that is a good thing," he was quick to add.

He was incredulous about the problem of universal health care. "We have to fix this health care situation. This has to be worked out. I spoke with a Canadian today and she said their system works. This is America, for chrissakes," Rodney said.

What was striking was how much these folks who, as Donna said, had been messing around since they were fourteen, still enjoyed each other. Not a critical word was exchanged between them. When the subject changed to families, Rodney said, "No matter how old your kids are, you should tell them you love them every day."

Donna commented on the Shaker village they had visited earlier on their trailer trip. They learned it was dying because of the ban on procreation, or as Donna said, "There ain't a whole lot a shakin' going on."

Rodney, Donna and I laughed a lot. When they said goodnight and left my trailer with a plan to depart early

Rodney, Donna and Harley Rodzilla—fellow trailer tramps.

the next morning, I had the strong feeling that I would see them again someday.

Before scrambling into bed, I got Gail Steinbeck on the phone and we had a nice conversation. She said some flattering things about my blog. Gail is Thomas Steinbeck's agent, as well as his wife and gatekeeper. When I tried to pin Gail down about an interview, she said, "Well, that's pretty far in the future, I don't even know if we will be in town. Plus, Thomas is really busy right now editing the manuscript for his new book. Call when you get close." I had no guarantees, but I felt good about my growing relationship with Gail and confident that an interview with Thomas was a strong possibility once I arrived in southern California.

Chapter Seven
The Cold Heartland with a Warm Heart

I drove this wide, eventless way called U.S. 90 which bypassed Buffalo and Erie to Madison, Ohio, and then found the equally wide and fast U.S. 20 past Cleveland and Toledo, and so into Michigan.

Travels with Charley

Judging by my 1959 Rand McNally, Steinbeck made a slight error in the quote above. U.S. 20 did not go "into Michigan," but it did go close to Michigan City, Indiana, on Lake Michigan, before heading on to Gary and Chicago. It was a setback and change of plans that put the author on U.S. 20 to Chicago. North of Buffalo, Steinbeck tried to enter Canada to traverse above Lake Erie to Detroit. Canadian authorities asked the author if he had a certificate of vaccination for Charley. He did not. He was informed that he would not be allowed to reenter the U.S. with a dog without proof of vaccination. Frustrated with bureaucracy, Steinbeck turned back and chose another way.

Regardless of route, Steinbeck and I had the same destination, Chicago, and the same powerful motivation, seeing our wives after several weeks on the road. On September 30, 1960, Steinbeck referred to midwestern cities in a letter to Elaine, "Now I'm about to hit the ragged centers, the Youngstowns, and Detroits, etc., crawling with production. I can't avoid them. There they are—right in the way." And he admitted they made him nervous. I admit they make *me* nervous—they always have. Not only was I going to go through Chicago pulling Winnie, but I needed to go all the way through and out the other side, ninety miles to Rockford, Illinois, where I planned to leave my trailer, turn right around the next morning, and drive back into "the ragged center" of Chicago.

I grew up a country mouse in Saltsburg, Pennsylvania, population less than one thousand then and now, and as an adult have usually lived in small towns or rural areas. Large arteries around cities and my own seem to work in sync—as the urban highways become more chaotic and clogged, my knuckles whiten and my blood pressure surges. Anticipating Chicago traffic while pulling a trailer filled me with trepidation.

I took the beltway south from Niagara Falls and around Buffalo to reconnect

Produce from Vermillion, Ohio.

with I-90. West of Buffalo, near Silver Creek, New York, I saw signs for the Seneca Nation including a thirty-to-forty-foot-high statue of an American Indian, presumably an Iroquois. That was followed by a billboard that said, "Break a Treaty; Break the Law."

I-90 was a toll road in New York, and I had been warned of a toll ahead in Ohio, so I got off the highway in Pennsylvania (no tolls) and got cash. Highway toll booths may well be the only remaining places in the U.S. that accept cash only, and God forbid you are caught without it. In Cleveland, Ohio, I veered off the Steinbeck route, leaving I-90 for U.S. 6. The highway soon left the city behind and evolved into a rural and pleasant, although flat (a midwesterner might say "flea-at"), drive along Lake Erie to Sandusky, east of Toledo.

Fall was now in full force and I savored violet and reddish-orange bushes and shrubs, level fields of rich brown grasses, produce stands bursting with pumpkins and corn stalks, and lake views forever. In Vermillion, Ohio, I bought tomatoes, onions, peppers, bread and a pumpkin to decorate Winnie. In the store I saw a heartrending sign for a missing nineteen-year-old that mentioned his family was praying for his return. I passed Ruggles

Beach, Huron and Sandusky. I left U.S. 6 and joined Ohio 2, crossing a causeway over Sandusky Bay of Lake Erie to Port Clinton.
Near Sandusky, I saw a sign for the Firelands Winery. I liked the
name.

Ohio 2 was ballyhooed as the Jackie Mayer Miss America
Highway. I speculated about what it must be like to have a road
named for you. I'd seen a lot of highways named for American
veterans. Does it help those still living feel more appreciated? Is
Jackie Mayer grateful for the recognition? I wondered. I imagine
it's sort of cool for Jackie to cruise Ohio 2 saying, "I'm just drivin' my road." I drove the last few miles northwest to Maumee
State Park, as storm clouds looking like stewed prunes congealed
over Lake Erie.

Inside the park, on the way to the campground, I passed a
lodge, rental cabins and a golf course. Just after I jackknifed back
into my chosen campsite, it started to rain. Max and I hunkered
down inside Winnie and listened to the raindrops pinging on the
aluminum skin. Max got his customary we've-survived-another-
day treat, and I got a fresh lime squeezed into straight tequila.
Steinbeck asserted in *Charley* that he never drank alone. I should
point out that I never drink alone either, but, like John, have found
that a dog can be perfectly acceptable company while imbibing.

After the rain and our treats, Maxie and I walked to the registration office under a layered raspberry frappé sky. There was no
attendant at the entrance booth. I helped a woman driving a red
sedan figure out the self-registration. She said I was really smart.
Her car had a bumper sticker that read, "I'm only speeding because I have to poop." On our walk back to the trailer, the sky appeared to have settled into a solid orange Creamsicle bar. I realized
I was hungry. I was feeling good, if a bit anxious about the co-
nundrum of a certain conurbation called Chicago that lay dead
ahead. I had covered fifty-five hundred miles and had been on the

road a month.

Perhaps because "rubber tramps" have their own special guardian angel, up to that point, large urban areas had not been a problem. I had been fortunate to hit many cities, such as Nashville and Cleveland, on weekends. But I was going to get to tour Chicago on a weekday (gulp!). The next morning—Chicago day—at least started out well with a beau-tiful morning moon to the west. A short

Morning moon over Ohio.

two-lane stretch (after skirting north around Toledo on the belt-way) on rural U.S. 20 took me through Assumption, Ohio, and brought red barns, tree-covered farmhouses, more produce stands and tractor dealers. I saw a hand-written sign by the turnoff to a small farm, "Pumpkins, rabbits—dead or alive." I passed Ever-green High, Home of the Vikings, and felt they had missed a great opportunity to choose Tree-Huggers as their mascot. After driv-ing through a short dip under a rusted railroad bridge (the only break in the topography all morning), and a delicate dance with a guy coming the other way pulling a huge piece of farm equip-ment that extended halfway into my lane, and then whistling past Our Lady of Fatima Cemetery near Lyons, I had pretty much knocked off Ohio.

It was back to I-90 for all of Indiana. Let's see, what nice thing can I say about Indiana? Oh yeah, Indiana has great uni-versities.

As soon as I-90 hits Illinois, you've hit Chicago, or Chicago's hit you. Steinbeck put it this way in *Charley*, "Knowing my ten-dency to panic in the roar and crush of traffic, I started into Chicago long before daylight. I wanted to end up at the Ambas-sador East where I had reservations, and, true to form, ended up lost. Finally, in a burst of invention, I hired an all-night taxi to lead me, and sure enough I had passed very near my hotel."

"An elegant and expensive pleasure dome."

Well I wasn't smart enough to get there well before daylight. It was closer to "noon-light." Just as I had feared, and just as Steinbeck had experienced, Chicago posed white-knuckle problems, both with traffic and constant tolls. I-90 was a crazy, chaotic blur, mitigated only by the occasional view of a very blue Lake Michigan. Insistent signs were ubiquitous (Got Milk? Got Leaks? Got God?). At least it wasn't raining. At one point I had no clue if I was in the correct toll lane and went through the toll area in a sea of traffic, without

The woman I danced with in Chicago in a nook of Ambassador East.

stopping. Immediately thereafter, signs began to appear, declaring that if I had blown off the toll, I had been videotaped. Only seven days to make it right online. Soon, I was drenched in sweat.

Ninety miles west of Chicago, I finally left I-90 at Rockford, Illinois. I found a large parking lot close to a bar. I had a beastly time accessing the bar's wireless internet, which had nothing to do with the one beer I had consumed, but, in time, I posted to my blog and drove on to the house belonging to my in-laws, Dimmis and Stuart Weller. The Wellers' house is on National Avenue, a pleasant tree-lined street paralleling the Rock River. Winnie would remain parked there, while I drove back to Chicago the next day and met Dimmie at the airport before our stay at the Ambassador East Hotel.

I was at the curb in the trailer on National Avenue, trailer-door open and Max inside, organizing my clothes for the trip to Chicago. A boy came by, walking his medium-sized

The Chicago skyline.

brown mutt on a leash. Max dove Superman-style out the door, ready to engage. I jumped out onto the wet grass in my socks and danced around on one foot trying to block Max from the intruder with the other foot. The boy was being turned in circles by his dog, which fancied a piece of Max. I finally got Max by the tail while his antagonist was dragged off, snarling and snapping. The next morning Max was moving slowly and favoring one leg. I got a baby aspirin cloaked in Swiss cheese down him and dropped him at the Airport Pet Lodge in Rockford on my way to pick up Dimmie at O'Hare. We had booked Max a "suite," a grooming and, as it turned out, a much-needed time to rest and recuperate. It won't surprise you to learn Charley had a similar appointment while in Chicago.

Dimmie and I were looking forward to our stay at the Ambassador East, "an elegant and expensive pleasure dome" as Steinbeck described it in *Charley*. But like Steinbeck, we got lost. The streets close to the hotel were narrow and, for the most part, one-way. Betty was no help. I finally knocked on the locked glass door of an office building and asked the too-busy-doing-nothing-to-be-bothered attendant where the Ambassador East was. He pointed over my shoulder. I was standing with my back to the side of the hotel.

John and Elaine chose the Ambassador East for their time in Chicago forty-nine years before our stay, almost to the day. According to *Historic Hotels of America*, the Ambassador East was built in 1926, and its "world famous" Pump Room restaurant was the place to be seen in the "prestigious Gold Coast" region of

Chicago. I found the Pump Room to be full of itself and its celebrity photos—of which there were twelve hundred total, with four hundred rotating up on the wood-panel walls. No staff member had a clue if there was a photograph of Steinbeck among them, but the restaurant seemed devoid of charm, and for that matter, people. The employees were jaded. I asked four of them if they had ever heard about Steinbeck's stay in 1960 and each time got the equivalent of a shoulder shrug in response. It cost twenty-five bucks, before tip, for a drink and a glass of wine. In my humble opinion, a high price to pay "to be seen." Plus, as I said, the joint was empty. How are you going to be seen if there is no one to see you? I wondered why John Steinbeck, who was reportedly traveling incognito, would choose the Ambassador East in the first place. But then, he was nothing if not paradoxical.

We checked in and, after exploring the rather interesting nooks and narrow hallways of the hotel, enjoyed a nice, sunny, chilly walk along the beach and concrete piers of Lake Michigan. The city skyline to the southeast was magnificent, and the lake flowed out to the horizon. We stopped for dinner at a nearby Irish pub, Butch McGuire's, and found our "peeps," great food, beverage and baseball on the flat screens. We also enjoyed a waiter who was everything you could ask for—funny, irreverent and well read. Back at the hotel, it took us several phone calls to get the non-allergenic pillows I had requested when I registered on-line, but I will admit our room was nicely appointed and quiet. Dimmie and I put on some sweet music and danced real slow. Turns out, I'm that guy who danced with his wife in Chicago. We had been together close to twenty-five years at that point, and like many old married folks were an amazing team and dear friends, but had forgotten some of the lyricism of lovemaking. That night in Chicago we remembered.

The next morning, when it was time to check out, I was

ruing the fact that I hadn't had a single significant conversation with an interesting stranger at the hotel. While waiting for my car to be brought around to the crowded street in front of the Ambassador East, I met a limo driver who looked and sounded like Morgan Freeman, the actor. Erroll Johnson wore a warm smile and reflector shades against the morning sun. After we talked for a while, he gave me a copy of an article indicating he had been recognized in February 2008 as "Go! Airport Express Driver of the Month." Erroll had been honored for, among other things, turning over fifteen hundred dollars in cash that he found on his bus. Accolades to him have been sent to the mayor and he has received invitations from folks from all over the world to visit their homes.

When Erroll learned I was from Jackson, he asked me if I knew his "homeboy, Harrison Ford." I told l him I had met Harrison years ago. Erroll said he had driven Harrison Ford to the airport many times. Wow! One degree of separation, I thought. Erroll greeted everyone who passed by, even those plugged into ear buds. I told him he reminded me of Freeman.

"I should call his bank and make a withdrawal," he replied with a grin.

"Yeah, they just might go for that," I said.

"I sure wouldn't want to do *Shawshank Redemption* [a prison film Freeman starred in] as reality TV," Erroll said. "I visited prison once for four hours. I *don't* want to go there. No sir." He nodded and smiled at a young black woman passing by. "Good morning, darling."

"I hear that. I watch too many crime shows."

"Used to think I got so mad at a guy I could murder him. Now it's 'send a nasty letter.'" He grinned at me and then greeted a middle-aged, tanned man in a camel-hair overcoat. "How are you this morning, sir?" He turned back to me. "Those guys in jail are all innocent. They say they caught a case like they caught a bad cold. Why'd you murder everybody? Uh, well, dunno, because they were home, I guess." I looked at him quizzically. "That's a Richard Pryor joke," he explained.

"Oh, okay. I get it."

"Yep, Harrison, Hilary, and the Hemingways—all from *Chi...ca...go*. It's a hell of a town." Our car was pulled to the curb; Erroll shook my hand, wished me a safe journey, and turned to greet a matron walking her Pomeranian.

Dimmie and I enjoyed the warm, clear, Illinois day with a drive around the campus of the University of Chicago, where both her great-grandfather and great-uncle once chaired the Geology Department, and with a visit to the Jane Addams Museum on the campus of the University of Illinois, Chicago. Jane Addams, a social reformer and Nobel Peace Prize winner, founded Hull House in 1889 for recently arrived immigrants. Hull House became a model for settlement houses in America. Dimmie's relative, Julia Lathrop, worked with Addams at Hull House in 1890. Later, equipped with lattes and scones, we enjoyed our time together in the car on the ninety-mile drive back to Rockford. This time, the drive through Chicago wasn't so bad. Of course it helped that Dim was driving.

Later that day, while getting my oil changed at a car dealership in Rockford, I spoke with a hefty blond guy with glasses named Howard. He paced back and forth in a salesroom that was as quiet as a mausoleum. There is nothing sadder than a bunch of car salesmen swimming around in slow circles waiting for someone to walk in the door. Howard seemed to know a lot about business in Rockford. I asked how the economy was.

"It sucks," he said and went on to explain why Rockford was so depressed, with twenty-five percent unemployment.

Many subdivisions and strip malls had been started but never finished. Car sales were flat. Howard explained that commercial properties all over the city were sitting boarded up and empty. "In the teens we were one of the largest furniture manufacturers in the country. From the forties through the sixties, when your buddy Steinbeck came through this area, we had the largest number of machine tool manufacturers in the country—we've lost them all." I asked why. Howard said that acquisitions, mergers, transfers of locale, outsourcing to foreign countries, and fam-

The Airport Pet Lodge decorated for Halloween.

ily members just being lazy and wanting out, so closing family businesses, were the main reasons. "Similar thing with banks," he said. "They're all merging and family banks are becoming a thing of the past." Howard reported business after business had sold, moved or closed. He said some family businesses simply couldn't compete with national chains like Home Depot. It was becoming a vicious cycle, public schools were in decline and even the police were controversial. "Support services suffer—everything, and everyone suffers—when the regional economy is in bad shape," Howard said.

Poor Howard. Not a single customer came in while we spoke.

The next morning I hooked up Winnie in the rain, said good-bye to my wife and her parents, and departed. (Dimmie was going to fly home to Wyoming in a few days.) My first stop was to pick up Max with his new "do." He looked good. We drove through a war zone of road construction, past boarded-up buildings with broken windows, on Kishwaukee Boulevard in Rockford.

On my way out of town on four-lane State 251, I passed numerous housing complexes and wondered why, as a nation, we didn't have the foresight to set four-lane corridors aside for industrial, agricultural or recreational uses exclusively. No one should have to live within sight, smell or earshot of a four-lane highway. I floated up 251 in a downpour and connected again with I-90 at the Wisconsin border. A Shell Oil station advertising cheese sat no more than one hundred yards inside the border of the "cheesehead" state. (Cheese is so much a part of Wisconsin's identity, it is the only state with an official state microbe. I read in *The Week* magazine that Lactococcus lactis, a bacterium used in the making of cheddar and Monterey Jack cheese, recently got the state honors.) I-90 took me northwest through Wisconsin and out of the pounding rain.

How did Steinbeck get out of Chicago? He didn't mention it, so it's anybody's guess. Even in 1960 there were many choices. He probably followed U.S. 14 from Chicago to Madison, Wisconsin, and then U.S. 12 to Mauston, Wisconsin, where he stayed. Mauston was my goal for the night.

After Chicago and Rockford, although feeling a little down, I was relieved to be in the country and finally heading back out to the West. To properly honor that fact, north of Madison, Wisconsin, I chose a country and western radio station. One of the songs grabbed my attention. It had something to do with a lovesick desperado being chased by the sheriff after running off with his daughter. Typical of the genre, with great economy, the lyrics said much about the human condition. "I knew that there would be hell to pay—just thought of it too late. I knew what I was feelin'. But what was I thinkin'?"

I was thinkin' it was a stinkin' dismal day, made more so by my miserable mood. And I know what I was feelin'. I was missin' my gal. Though the sky was still overcast, the rain had ceased by the time we reached Mauston. We drove north out of town to New Lisbon and took a right on State 58 to a campground tucked in a dense forest at Buckhorn State Park near Castle Rock Lake on the Wisconsin River.

There was not a soul around the registration station, and because the camping area seemed like it was miles from the entrance building, I ended up poaching the campsite. First a toll

Max at the beach on Castle Rock Lake.

in Chicago, and now this, I thought. I was beginning to feel like Clyde without Bonnie, but what the hell, Steinbeck admitted in an October 10 letter to Elaine that he stole an ashtray from the Ambassador East. After I got Winnie set up for the night, I sat at the table inside, checked the map and saw that south of Castle Rock Lake, the Wisconsin River hooked west and dumped into the Mississippi at Wyalusing, Wisconsin, just south of Prairie du Chien.

Max and I walked out over the wet, fallen leaves of the dimly lit forest to the water. He was delighted with a little stretch of beach, bounding up and down it several times. There were two small, heavily treed islands just off shore. As is usually the case with man-made lakes, the gray water appeared to be deep and sluggish. Max left the beach to poke about in the bushes and, I later learned, picked up some hitchhikers.

Night came in early, dark and damp, and I got a little spooked. I was camped in dense trees on a moonless night, far away from anything (cue the wolf howl), with no cell—and a mostly toothless and deaf seven-pound hound for a watchdog. Only one other site was occupied, and that was with a large white canvas tent. The men associated with it had ignored my wave when I arrived and, no doubt because of my frame of mind, looked sinister. And I still missed my wife. In *Charley*, Steinbeck wrote, "After the comfort and the company of Chicago, I had had to learn to be alone again. It takes a little time." I guess the same was true for me. My dinner consisted of cold leftovers from Rockford. Later, while lying on my bunk, I ripped open an envelope delivered to me by Dimmie in Chicago. It was filled with two-dozen letters from students in a ninth-grade English class Max and I had visited at Cumberland Valley High School in Carlisle, Pennsylvania. The kids' words reassured me and lifted my spirits. Here is one example.

Dear Mr. Zeigler,

Thank you so much for visiting us here at CV! I think your plan of taking a trip like Steinbeck's is brilliant, and I truly hope all goes well for you! I would love to hear about your progress in the future, and what conflicts you'll face, what issues you will be confronted with. Also, I am sure you'll encounter some amazing people and have some unusual experiences. We will be happy to hear about some of these!

Sincerely,
Marissa

Best wishes for you and Max!

After listening to the Phillies baseball game on the radio, I fell into a fitful sleep. In the middle of the night, I lay awake worrying about our son, Wil. He was living in a rough part of San Francisco and had just dropped out of college with no money and no job prospects. The previous year he had dropped out of high school and, while living on his own, had been arrested and placed on a year's probation for stealing a sandwich and a drink. Déjà vu. More worry. It doesn't get any easier the second time around. That night in Winnie, I was somewhat reassured thinking about

Wil's good heart and great mind. To borrow Alex's metaphor, Wil was simply not ready to write his own stories. I guess you could say he was still gathering his materials.

I carried three options for sleeping in Winnie, a fleece blanket and comforter combination, a light sleeping bag, and a heavy sleeping bag. I used all three at various times on the journey. That night near the Wisconsin River I had no electricity to operate the little heater in the ceiling of the Airstream and, when possible, I tried to avoid using the propane required to run the furnace. I like to sleep cool, but that chilly night was the first to require the heavy bag. In time, I fell back to sleep. It was cold in the morning when I got up—the coldest morning so far at thirty-six degrees. I walked Max in the dim pre-dawn light and packed up in a shivering hurry.

Back in Mauston at breakfast, I sat near a men's coffee klatch discussing the ballgame from the night before. After baseball was exhausted as a subject, I heard, "Walmart is better than K-Mart." On October 10, Steinbeck wrote in a letter to Elaine from Mauston (erroneously spelling it "Manston"), "Talk was all of baseball and little else. I heard the game on the radio and it was a fine one. No politics, just baseball." This is the same letter I referred to in Chapter One in which he justified his trip, "I'm still a man damn it. This may seem silly but to me it isn't. I've seen the creeping sickifying creep up on too many. But you married a man and I'm damn well going to keep him that way."

Wisconsin looked much more scenic in the light of a sunny day. "Why then was I unprepared for the beauty of this region, for its variety of field and hill, forest and lake?" Steinbeck wrote in *Travels with Charley*. I agree it is that combination of features that define Wisconsin's beauty. In addition, it may be states that preserve woodlots close to highways leave the most pleasant impression. Much of Wisconsin is wooded along the roads, and forests line streams and rivers as well. Wisconsin's sylvan beauty reminded me of Vermont and northern Maine. Mid-day, I pulled off the highway and took a hike up a hill to a viewpoint. I could see nothing but rolling hills covered with trees ignited by fall. At other times during the drive, it seemed Wisconsin consisted of silos dotting rolling green fields across valleys as far as far as the eye could see. I passed a gaggle of agitated wild turkeys huddled near the road, perhaps discussing Thanksgiving.

I-94 had joined I-90 in Madison and I-90 split off west at Tomah, Wisconsin. I followed I-94 to the state line. At a rest area, I read a sign that claimed Wisconsin was the "circus state" and later learned Ringling Brothers had been founded in 1884 in Baraboo, Wisconsin. Baraboo is now home to the Circus World Museum on Ringling's former wintering grounds.

I remember thinking as I drove that Wisconsin reminded me of a pretty, smart, popular girl. So I was delighted to rediscover in *Charley* that Steinbeck compared the state to a high-maintenance woman. "But this fact does not make her less lovely, if you can afford her," he wrote.

In Menomonie, just west of Eau Claire, I fueled up at a gas and dairy products emporium. I bought some milk and cheese, but I did not see any of the "cheese candy" that Steinbeck mentioned in *Charley*. I noticed an exterior phone booth with the phone removed—a sign of the times. I thought again of Steinbeck's constant search to find pay phones in order to hear Elaine's voice, assuming he reached her, and to check in with his boys at school. Now, of course, pay phones are quickly becoming a thing of the past.

According to *Steinbeck: A Life in Letters,* it was during one of these phone calls that Elaine told John she was enjoying his letters from the road. She said, "They remind me of *Travels with a Donkey*. I think of them as 'Travels with Charley'."

John replied, "You've just given me my title."

I got in the wrong lane at a red light while exiting the gas station and rolled down my window to appeal to a woman in a large, gray Suburban to let me into her lane. "I'm from Wyoming and I'm clueless," I said.

Mural at Sinclair Lewis Interpretive Center.

She smiled and waved me over, saying, "I'm from here and I still often get in the wrong lane."

After a fairly easy time around the Twin Cities, I entered rural Minnesota. With its rolling farmland and paucity of trees, it reminded me of a rugged, hard-working but comparatively plain brother to gorgeous Wisconsin. In Melrose, I saw a sign for Stearns Veterinary Outlet Service, "We do cows!"

I had followed my mentor's lead for five weeks. Mine was an act of admiration, and let's be honest, imitation. On rare occasions, I felt I'd improved slightly on what Steinbeck did, or observed, on his trip. In Sauk Centre, Minnesota, I got to do something *for* John Steinbeck. He wasted several hours lost in the Twin Cities and regretted not having the time to stop at the birthplace of his friend, Sinclair Lewis. I did. Because Betty was brilliant around the Twin Cities, I was able to spend a pleasant hour in the Sinclair Lewis Interpretive Center in Sauk Centre. "I had read *Main Street* when I was in high school, and I remember the violent hatred it aroused in the countryside of his nativity," wrote Steinbeck in *Charley*. As a result of writing about *his* hometown, Salinas, California, that "hatred" was painfully familiar to Steinbeck. Judging by the tribute to Lewis in the interpretative center, I'd say Sauk Centre got over it. Sure the display had the odd mannequin in period dress serving no apparent function, but, for a small town, this was a good exhibit, well maintained. I learned a

lot. For instance, I learned
Sinclair Lewis was America's
first winner of the Nobel
Prize for Literature—something else Steinbeck would
have in common with Lewis
just a few years after com-

A Minnesota montage of three eras.

pleting his trip with Charley. Another was that Lewis, like Steinbeck, chose his hometown as his final resting place.

U.S. 71 took me north from Sauk Centre. Soon I crossed
Spunk Creek and saw a billboard for an auto body shop named
"Wreck-a-mended." High, cirrus clouds formed chevrons, deco-
rating the remaining blue sky. The wind picked up and a chill
came into the air. I saw a montage of three eras; a couple on horse-
back rode next to an electrical pole that stood under a white, steel
power-generating windmill. I passed trucks sporting silhouettes
of ducks, and one black pickup passed me with "The Duckwacker
Rises and the Birds Fall" in large block letters on the rear window. (Freud would've had a field day with that one.) The sign at
Long Prairie High School encouraged the football team with the
words, "Go Thunder! Drain Lakers!" And then I left U.S. 71 and
headed west, bucking a headwind on U.S. 10 toward Detroit
Lakes, where Steinbeck had stayed. Along U.S. 10, I passed a
youthful Amish farmer sporting hat, beard and suspenders, standing on a flatbed wagon, driving a team of horses beside the road.

Nearing New York Mills, I noticed signs for lakes on both
sides of the highway. Around the time I reined in my rig in Detroit
Lakes, Minnesota, local radio reported a storm blowing in from
North Dakota promising snow, high winds, black ice and freezing
temperatures—twenty-three degrees was the predicted low. It was
October 9.

It had been a very long day. If, like Steinbeck, I had spent four hours lost, it would have been a day and drive from hell. I decided to stay an extra day at The Lodge at Detroit Lake to allow the weather to settle and the thirty-mile-an-hour head-

Early October snow on Detroit Lake.

winds to subside. Just after arriving, I walked to a nearby gas station for antifreeze to pour in Winnie's drains as a guard against frozen pipes.

Kathy, perhaps early fifties and blonde, worked the desk at the lodge. She was warm, welcoming and helpful. The Lodge at Detroit Lake offered the best combination of view, accommodations, service and price I had encountered in six thousand miles. Later that evening, I sat content by the lobby fireplace with wine and dinner, looking out over the choppy lake and enjoying the contrast to the previous night of cold and loneliness in Wisconsin. Familiar uplifting tunes emanated from the lobby player piano. My journal entry from that night captured some of my first impressions, "Ooh-kay. There ya goh. Youbetcha. Headlights flash like fireflies across the lake. The lake wrinkled now, whereas it was folded earlier with thirty-mile-an-hour winds. The thing about people is, although I love them, they are everywhere. Fickle of me, I know, to want you when I need you, but disdain you when you are too much with me. Detroit Lake, I expected you to be a wild northern outpost, but when you turned out to be a resort, I dove right into your luxurious lap."

The rooms had in-room recycling and "green" products and packaging. I snuck Max into the lodge the first night. He was quiet as a mouse, zipped inside my jacket, but delirious with gratitude once his paws hit the room's floor. He was not quite so happy the next morning when I performed a "tickectomy" on the hitchhiker on his head, because of his squirming, a botched job at best. Post-operation, Max looked like he had been cracked across the skull with a sharp object. I felt bad about the outcome, but kind of proud of the little guy. In his essay "Random Thoughts on Random Dogs," Steinbeck borrowed a quote from an early English treatise on dogs: "There been those smalle whyte dogges carried by ladys to draw the fleas away to theirselves." I had no ticks on me. Max obviously took one for the team. Of course, I wasn't the one who had poked around in the leaves and bushes beside the Wisconsin River.

When I went downstairs for breakfast, I overheard Kathy and another woman behind the lodge desk discussing the Minnesota Twins baseball game from the previous night. I didn't see a single dark face; even the chambermaids were white. The breakfast (included) was varied and delicious and far exceeded the typical motel fare. Max loved the hardboiled eggs.

I enjoyed a relaxing day of blogging in my room and hanging out and reading by the fire in the lobby. It was nice to be immobile and in a comfortable environment while riding out the storm that, for the second day, lashed the lake with wind and snow.

Early the next morning, Max and I were back at it, pounding toward North Dakota. Although the sky was still overcast, the winds had calmed. When Steinbeck wrote about this part of the country in *Travels with Charley,* he got philosophical about many subjects. He mused on the mystery inherent in Fargo, North Dakota, as well as the personal challenge of being alone on the road. He wrote about the agelessness of thespians after meeting an itinerant actor. He asked Charley if he felt the two of them were actually learning anything about their country, "Does all America so far smell alike?" Later Charley nosed around in some garbage, and Steinbeck found a note in it indicating a man was on the lam for not paying alimony. That discovery prompted Steinbeck to mention the danger of leaving a trail. Finally he relayed the eerie and disconcerting qualities he perceived in the Badlands and, after leaving them behind, fell head over heels for Montana, as expressed in a letter to Elaine written on Columbus Day, 1960, "Where the Badlands are naughty— Montana is grand. What grandeur!"

Geese in Flight (rear view). Welcome "relief" in North Dakota.

As for me, with the weather calm and the North Dakota skies gray but no longer threatening, I was happy to be back at the task of discovery. I immediately saw an example of my idea, formulated in Rockford, Illinois, regarding use of four-lane right-of-ways. Rolls of hay lined the North Dakota highway (I-94) just west of Fargo inside the limited-access fence. There was no housing in sight.

The Peace Garden State passed by uneventfully. I enjoyed local polka music by Peter and Paul and the Ring Dinger Band, tapping out the time on the steering wheel. The radio talked of the Fall Polka Festival at Long Lake, scheduled to run from 2:02 p.m. until 7:02 p.m. There were sales pitches for tractors and ads for co-ops and one message warned of smuggled poultry products. There is little to engage the eye in terms of topography and color in North Dakota, other than the occasional camel's hump hill adorned with antique farm equipment or sprouting a huge cutout of a cow. Stubble-covered fields stretched away for miles. I felt like I was swimming in a sea of brown on brown, fading to a brown horizon.

I don't remember where I purchased Max's North Dakota postcard for my sister's second graders, or where I mailed it, but

I wrote down what it said, "Hi Cool Kids! North Dakota has more horses than people. Very quiet here—that is, until I barked at the horses. Love, Max. c(-:" The front of the card depicted a collapsing prairie cabin, surrounded by tall grass, next to a windmill. Superimposed over the cabin was a map of the rectangular state, and superimposed over the map was a state seal and pictures of a western meadowlark, a wild prairie rose and an American elm tree.

What story do these items tell?

The Gladstone exit off I-94 provided whimsical "relief" and caused me to broaden my acceptable-use-of-land-lining-highways policy to include art installations. The Gladstone-to-Regent road is called the Enchanted Highway because of seven enormous metal sculptures created by a retired teacher, Gary Greff, who resides in Regent. The sculptures depict subjects ranging from Teddy Roosevelt on a bucking horse to a covey of pheasants in which the rooster is sixty feet long, and the hen fifty. I stopped to view the sculpture closest to the interstate, titled "Geese in Flight." Nine metal geese on a radiating egg-shaped, steel background encircle a central hole or sunburst. They are flying above hills fabricated from oil-well tanks. I later learned "Geese in Flight" is in the Guinness World Records as the "World's Largest Scrap Metal Sculpture." Perhaps the thing most indicative of the ethos of the region is that many local residents and organizations donated time and money to help Gary realize his dream. High school students did much of the welding. Ranchers lease the property for the sculptures to Gary for a song. Welcoming picnic areas and small parks accompany many of the massive works of art.

Walking back to the rig after viewing "Geese in Flight," I noticed a black plastic bag that had burst beside the on-ramp. The ground was littered with bottles and workmen's clothing in good condition:

The Badlands look pretty good in a dusting of snow.

boots, gloves, pants and shirt. I was reminded of the discarded plastic water bottles and shirts full of cactus spines that my brother and I have found in cactus patches around his property east of San Diego—items telling stories of migrant workers' desperate and painful attempts to enter the U.S. illegally. I wondered what dramatic events unfolded resulting in this costume being discarded in North Dakota.

In western North Dakota, the Badlands finally layered in some pink and blue rock for welcome variety. I camped in the Teddy Roosevelt National Park campground, in a grove of trees, on a terrace of land above the Little Missouri River. Because of my Golden Access Pass, my campsite cost $2.50. Temperatures dropped down during the night and we awoke to two inches of snow. I had to admit the Badlands looked rather good decorated in white. I hauled Winnie across packed snow for the first time ever; thankful I had sprung for new all-weather car tires before the trip. After a short drive, I got breakfast at a Flying J in Beach, North Dakota (where Steinbeck had spent the night). This was one of many Flying J visits en route. All could be uniformly relied on to provide internet connectivity (for a fee), friendly waitresses, decent food, dollar chocolate-chip cookies and the very latest in unbiased reporting from Fox News.

Snippets that I picked up from Fox News along the way gave me hope an Obama-led recovery from the recession was underway. Steinbeck put it best when writing of a similar phenomenon at the end of the Great Depression in his essay titled "A Primer on the '30s."

> *In Pacific Grove we heard that business was improving, but that hadn't much emphasis for us. One of the indices of improvement was that the men who had begged the Administration to take over and tell them what to do were now howling against Government control and calling Mr. Roosevelt highly colored names. This proved that they were on their feet again and was perfectly natural. You only tolerate help when you need it.*

It was twenty-one degrees and cloudy in Beach. There was no hope of lying outside and getting a tan.

Back on the road I saw the first Wyoming plates of the trip and honked, only then realizing that perhaps Wyoming plates were not that unusual in western North Dakota. At a gas station, a North Dakota rancher who was hauling his grown daughter's horses in a trailer behind his pickup asked me about the Bambi.

I got to thinking how easy it is to pass from place to place in this great country. I'm not referring to states, but to regions of team loyalty. It was the time of year when passions were split between baseball and football. I had been in Minnesota Twins country that morning and, judging by the presence of orange and blue sweatshirts, hats and bumper stickers, was clearly in Denver Broncos country that evening; to think such a passage is possible without a passport. I-94 took me on across the Montana border.

As I said, Steinbeck fell head over heels for Montana. He wrote in *Travels with Charley* that if Montana had been near an ocean, he would have chosen to live there. I resisted at first, convincing myself Montana was not that special. But I was not long in Montana before I had to concede that, although not without its flaws, it is spectacular for sure. As I bucketed through Wilbaux and by Glendive and Miles City, cruising beside the Yellowstone River, across the eastern plains south of the Big Sheep Mountains, I realized I *could* fall in love with Montana but, if I did, I would be cheating on my Wyoming.

Soon, I was neck-and-neck with a freight train for what seemed like an hour, and the sun burst out for the first time in three days as I crossed Rosebud County. I stopped at an overlook of the Yellowstone River near Rosebud Mountain. A bald eagle soared above the water. The interstate parallels the river from west of Billings to where the Yellowstone converges with the Missouri River in North Dakota.

In Forsyth for gas, I had to choose between the "Town Pump" on one side of the street and the "Kum and Go," on the other. You can't tell me that naming was accidental. I chose the Town Pump. I overheard a man in a red emergency vest, driving a car that runs on both rails and roads, say that he had been out fixing broken track. I left I-94 on State 47 to Hardin and found a nondescript RV park on the edge of town. I rang the bell on the office door several times before a gnarled, ancient woman wearing a black shawl shuffled slowly to the door.

I picked Hardin because of its proximity to the Little Bighorn Battlefield and, since I had left the road earlier than usual, I set up camp and immediately headed out to the national monument. The battlefield, a long, narrow, treeless ridge above the Little Bighorn River, is a charged and spiritual place. Steinbeck wrote in the Columbus Day letter to Elaine, "I shed a tear for Custer (the dumb bastard) at the field of Little Big Horn. And Charley peed a tear also." I had the same feeling of tragedy, futility and sheer stupidity. I had to ask myself, what part of the scenario—they know this country, we don't; they're rested, we're not; they have ten soldiers to our one—did Custer not understand? I was glad to learn that fallen soldiers on both sides of the fight have been honored with headstones at the battlefield.

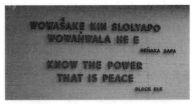

Wisdom on the wall of the Little Big Horn Visitors' Center.

The next morning, I explored Hardin while seeking out a suitable locals' café for breakfast. I have to say Hardin is not very impressive. The mixture of buildings, new and old, is lackluster and fungible western America. There is no apparent old town or city center. I drove past a large facility, set back from the main road and surrounded by gleaming chain-link fence and razor wire. The pristine building's parking lot was empty.

At breakfast at the Lariat Country Kitchen, I lucked into a men's coffee klatch. As I entered the café, I saw a pickup with a bumper sticker that read, "Only the Dummer Vote Obummer" and I thought, I want to talk to that guy, so I did. Tom Conroy, retired rancher and politician, was wearing a black cowboy hat, a black vest over a blue shirt, and jeans. Tom had four terms as a state legislator in the late seventies until the "liberals moved in from California and the governor at the time tossed me out." Tom was a tall, warm, articulate gentleman who appeared to be approaching eighty years of age. He was a weathered, handsome man with a dry sense of humor and a love of history. "Come to my ranch in the Pryor Mountains [near Billings] and we will talk history," he said. His beloved wife, Colleen, had died a decade earlier from breast cancer. Tom told me her headstone was adorned with a cross, fashioned out of welded horseshoes.

Colleen had a grandfather, a Crow Indian, who started a magazine, called *American Indian Journal*, aided by cowboy author Will James. Colleen's grandfather even sold James some of his

property in the Pryors. A
billionaire recently bought
the property, Tom said. I
brought up the bumper
sticker, which Tom said he
had custom made. He said,
"The current administration
is the worst thing to happen

*Last Stand Hill from the perspective of
a charging Sioux warrior.*

to America since 9/11/01. And we may never recover." Tom
showed me pictures of his ranch, including the outhouse he recently named for his "gold-digging" second wife, whom he di-
vorced after one year. He had painted his ex-wife's name in
brilliant blue above the outhouse door. He showed me pictures of
his "only family now"—hummingbirds by the dozen and bear
cubs playing on his porch and nuzzled up to his feet.

I asked Tom about a conversation I had overheard while eating breakfast. Tom tried to explain the situation with Hardin's
new twenty-seven million dollar, four hundred and sixty-four bed
prison, which stands empty "because of political red tape" and
why Hardin's mayor had been on national news offering the new
prison to Uncle Sam for housing Guantanamo Bay terrorists.
Everyone I spoke to seemed to agree on the subject of the prison.
They all felt the governor, who was, to say the least, spoken of in
unflattering terms, hated Hardin and was simply trying to hurt
the town any way he could. Several people said Hardin had become the laughing stock of the state. No one could explain to me
how it came about that Hardin, a town of less than four thousand, had funded and constructed Two Rivers Regional Correc-
tional Facility, without a firm plan as to how the prison would be
utilized to generate revenue. I got the sense the town had been the
victim of a smooth-talking, prison-peddling flimflammer.

Tom told me of tensions with young Crow Indians whose

"politics are crippling the town," and among whom alcohol and methamphetamine are taking a terrible toll. I told Tom I was looking for a certain type of hat, one that Steinbeck called a stockmen's hat, which he purchased in Billings. Tom directed me to Last Stand Western Wear on Main Street. Before departing, I accepted Tom's kind invitation to visit his ranch some day. With any luck, we can center the conversation on our mutual love of birds, animals and western history, and steer away from politics.

Brave men died on both sides.

I went straight from the restaurant to the western wear store. Sal, the solidly built, attractive owner, told me she loved *The Grapes of Wrath* and called me the Johnny Appleseed of Steinbeck. Sal promised to order me a hat similar to Steinbeck's in a week or two after she "cooked for the prison high school field trip and shipped some cattle."

I commented, as I walked out the door, "But I haven't given you any money."

"That's how we do things here, but there is one thing you can do for me. You can send me a copy of *The Grapes of Wrath*." And with Dimmie's help, I did.

Back at the RV Park, the old woman—whose deceased husband, I learned, had worked for the Bureau of Indian Affairs—ominously warned me, with a bony finger point and quavering voice, of the passes on I-90 that lay ahead.

I left Hardin on I-90, where it takes a sharp turn to the west and heads toward Billings. I was beginning to like Montana—like it a lot. And much of Montana was still to come.

Chapter Eight
Yellowstone: Critter Encounters Then and Now

I must confess to a laxness in the matter of National Parks.
Travels with Charley

Charley and his traveling companion, John Steinbeck, were ostensibly driven out of Yellowstone by bears. But Steinbeck didn't really want to go in the first place. "I am in love with Montana," he wrote in *Travels with Charley*. Yet he expressed disdain for national parks, declaring that Yellowstone was "no more representative of America than is Disneyland." Ultimately, Steinbeck went, only because he feared his friends would think him crazy for passing on the archetype of American natural wonders. Yellowstone overlaps slightly into Idaho to the west and Montana to the north, but the largest part of it lies within northwestern Wyoming.

Had Steinbeck stayed longer, Yellowstone's grandeur would likely have captivated him, and his description would remain with us today. Unfortunately, because of Charley, that was not to be. Steinbeck entered from Montana through the North Entrance, and paused for a chat with a ranger, who cautioned that bears and dogs don't mix. The author assured the official that Charley was a "dog of peace and tranquility," and drove a few miles into the park.

In 1960, bears were much more conditioned to human food and garbage. Several approached Steinbeck's truck to beg, sending Charley into paroxysms of barking, snapping and snarling. Today, thanks to the work of enlightened wildlife biologists, any human contact with bears is discouraged. A bear that develops a human food habit is likely to be drawn into conflicts and euthanized—"a fed bear is a dead bear." Perhaps Charley knew that bears are best appreciated from a respectful distance. Steinbeck left Yellowstone immediately after Charley's fit, and spent the night in Livingston, Montana—his loss as well as ours.

The truth is Yellowstone, the world's first national park, is worth a longer visit. I didn't want to feel similarly rushed while touring Yellowstone, so I spent several days there, one year before departing on my long journey. I invite you to step away from the tale of my trip around the country and join me in Yellowstone for a few days in September of 2008. As Charley knew, national parks can be risky for dogs, so Max was not along for this ride.

I parked the Bambi at the Madison Campground, where the Gibbon and Firehole rivers form the Madison River. When it was cocktail hour, I took a glass of wine to a bench on a bluff overlooking the confluence. A rocky butte paralleled the Firehole, coming from the south, directly across the valley from my perch, and to the east, the Gibbon cut through a small, flat valley. The two rivers merged to carve a peninsula in the center of a golden meadow. The autumn sun illuminated conifers that climbed the slopes of the butte. A few fly fishermen, casting their lines, etched arcs over the wind-wrinkled water. I sipped my wine.

An elderly woman by the name of Ellen joined me on the bench. Ellen had no teeth, an inconvenience that made her not the least bit self-conscious. Her chin, perfectly round at the tip, pointed straight out. Her skin was creased and weathered, and she wore tiny wire-rim glasses. A corncob pipe would have completed the effect nicely. We watched as four cow elk slowly entered the Gibbon River near the confluence.

Ellen had been camping at Madison for several days with her husband, "who had finally retired," and her son. She spoke enthusiastically of evening elk rituals witnessed from our spot. She reported a five-point bull elk, in rut, frantically rounding up six or seven cows on the peninsula. After all that hard work (I can only

imagine how exhausting rounding
up six or seven women would be),
a "royal" bull made his entrance,
chasing off the five-point and
stealing the cows for his harem.

Ellen's eyes widened behind
her glasses. She said that her son,

*Fascinating, yes, but Yellow-
stone's most dangerous animal.*

who used to hunt elk, made a sound imitating a bull elk, and she
was afraid "the royal would round him up or chase him off too."
We watched and waited but, alas, no bull.

After the cow elk worked their way gracefully up stream,
and as the sun set over the Madison flowing west, I said goodnight to Ellen and headed back to camp, glass and stomach empty
and wanting filling.

The second day at the campground dawned crisp and clear.
Sunlight slanted through the pines, and danced in the smoke from
campfires. I had a warm breakfast of coffee and steel-cut oats,
and then set out to explore the Yellowstone loop road.

On much of my route I saw dead lodgepole pine trees burned
in the passionately debated, seven-hundred-thousand-acre fires of
August 1988. The old spars spiked tall, straight and black above
the healthy green saplings—already over my head in height—
growing up around them.

I encountered animal jams everywhere. Huge RVs were
stopped in the middle of the road, completely blocking traffic.
People were out of their vehicles, gawking at and photographing
animals. Many people approached bison to photograph them.
Bison may seem like your grandfather's cow. They may seem like
they want to pose for a family portrait, but bison, not bears, kill
more people than any other animal in Yellowstone.

As for animal jams, I've learned how to gauge the cause for
the excitement. Two to four cars mean elk or bison have been

spotted, four to six mean a moose, six to ten equal big horn sheep, and for bears or wolves—gridlock. I was tempted to pick a nondescript spot, get out of my car and stare off into the trees at nothing, to see how many vehicles would stop. I saw about a dozen animal jams on my tour that day. According to a friend who is a seasonal ranger, over seven hundred bear jams were reported in the summer of 2008. When asked about the dumbest thing he witnessed, he said, "The park recommends maintaining a distance from bears of one hundred yards. I've seen people surrounding a sow and cubs within thirty yards." As I drove, I tried to be patient and remind myself that, in Yellowstone, animal jams are part of the excitement. I returned to the trailer for a dinner of chili and beer (a camping favorite), and a pleasant evening bundled up by the fire.

Day three was damp and chilly, perfect for a longer tour of the region. Hoping to see wolves, I drove out to the Lamar Valley in the northeast corner of the park. The valley offers wide vistas above a flat valley floor, stitched by the sinuous meanders of the Lamar River. Suddenly ahead of me—gridlock. I jammed the car onto the shoulder, grabbed my binoculars and jogged up the road. A kind fellow, gripping a high-speed camera with a huge lens, pointed a finger toward the foothills.

A sleek black wolf with yellow eyes played and hunted on a ridge above the river. She seemed to delight in trotting, sniffing and occasionally pouncing on prey, her enthusiasm not dampened by lack of success. Behind her, the mountain slopes shimmered with a composite of gray-green sage, soft-brown grasses and splashes of golden aspens interspersed with evergreens. A line from Steinbeck's *East of Eden,* referring to his beloved Gavilan Mountains, came to mind, "They were beckoning mountains with a brown grass love." The wolves of Yellowstone were eradicated in the 1920s—*eradicated,* in a national park. When John Steinbeck visited in 1960 not a single wolf roamed the region. They were reintroduced in 1995. This was my first wolf sighting ever, so I lingered, relishing a sense of righteousness and timelessness. A bald eagle soared above my wolf.

I exited the park through the rocky terrain of the northeast entrance and immediately needed to hunt up a burger. I stopped at the Buns and Beds in Cooke City, sniffed the smell of meat grilling on the porch and pounced on the special, The Bomb, Sirloin Steak Burger. The owner, a short, grizzled

Yellowstone reminds us awe is relative.

man wearing a Steelers football jersey, delivered my meal.

"Who's from Pittsburgh?" I asked, taking in the Pittsburgh memorabilia plastered about the log and plank building.

"You're lookin' at 'im," the owner said. He pointed out the flat-screen TV, the fanciest object in this room of exposed pipes and duct-taped conduit. The TV was tuned to the Red Zone, a cable channel that changes NFL games automatically every few minutes, relieving the American male from even having to ride the remote. "Course when the Pixburg Stillers comes on, the channel don't change," he said.

I informed him I was from Pittsburgh originally, and was a Steelers fan myself. When I left, he insisted I take two shrink-wrapped brownies to sustain me through the mountain pass ahead.

Just past Cooke City, Beartooth Pass topped out at eleven thousand feet and bottomed at thirty-one degrees. At one point, the road actually traversed *above* a ski and snowboard area. The rocky and wind-swept tundra just below the pass was dotted with lakes. In that harsh environment, no living thing around the lakes grew taller than two feet. As I neared the top, I wound up through a dense, bitter fog, but emerged to a view of long, sunlit, distant ranges and valleys. Below me a series of tight, hairpin turns snaked down the exposed mountainside; I saw a sign:

Welcome to Montana
Speed Limit 70

As if!

I held my speed to well under seventy during the steep, switching descent into Red Lodge, which gave me time to enjoy the views. Red Lodge, known for its arts and spectacular views, sits at the northern foot of the Beartooth Range. Rock Creek, after tumbling down from the mountains, meanders through the middle of town. I filled my tank at a shiny convenience store and then, having no map of Montana, got lost trying to find the way to Cody, Wyoming, ending up in the little town of Roberts, Montana. I love maps and don't like feeling disoriented, but I was somewhat reassured to remember that Steinbeck touted getting lost as one of the better ways to meet people.

I saw a faded-white clapboard gas station on a corner with tomato vines growing under the bargain signs plastering the exterior wall. Inside, I asked the blonde, middle-aged proprietress if she would sell me a map of Montana.

"Nope," she replied, pausing for effect, "but I'll give you one." She smiled and began to dig through a pile of papers on the cluttered counter.

"I see you're growing tomatoes out front."

"Yep. Like tomatoes?"

"I lust for tomatoes. If I ever move again, I'm going to be able to grow tomatoes. Can't grow them in Jackson."

"From Jackson, huh? Pick some," she said. "They don't have but a few more weeks."

She accompanied me outside and I chose a few tomatoes from her vines splayed in a raised, weathered-wood box. Her name was Roxy (like a nickname for Steinbeck's truck). Roxy said

Kayakers on Yellowstone Lake.

that she and her husband had just moved out from Georgia three years prior. Both had worked for Georgia Power. Roxy liked the mild Montana summers and easy access to winter sports.

I told Roxy I had lived in north Georgia and we reminisced about the region's amazing produce, especially the tomatoes and strawberries. Her secret for growing tomatoes in Montana was tons of Miracle-Gro. When I asked her the price of the tomatoes, she said they were on the house.

"But the map was free and the tomatoes are free, and I don't need gas. I'm not buying anything."

"That's how you grow neighbors," she said grinning. And then, when I thanked her and turned to go, Roxy said, "Y'all come back now, ya hear." It was good to hear that again. I told her I would, and I will, and next time I'll fill up at Roxy's.

Heading south toward Cody on an isolated two-lane road that ran flat and straight and roughly parallel to the Beartooths, I sailed through an ocean of green sage and sepia grass—waves of bobbing and swaying seed heads. Trees occasionally peeked out from odd, low, wet places behind rounded, bald hills. Several abandoned coal-mining operations dotted the countryside. More contemporary energy icons, praying mantis-like oilrigs, bowed to and rose from the parched earth. West above the Beartooths, the late afternoon sky was a mosaic of pale light. Striated, gray clouds, backlit by the sun, were punctuated by puffy, white clouds. The rock strata of the Beartooths pointed toward the sky in a cuneiform pattern, like the bear's teeth for which they are named.

A log gate with a sign indicated the entrance to the Two Dot Ranch, the ranch road winding away through low hills. I envisioned the ranchers and hands sitting down to a bountiful dinner and thought of the "bindlestiffs" in Steinbeck's *Of Mice and Men.* If I dropped in, would I be welcomed and offered a seat at the table, my probing questions graciously answered, the mashed potatoes humbly passed?

I went by a turnoff for the Chief Joseph All American Highway. Chief Joseph lead his people, the Nez Perce, on the run through Yellowstone in 1877, five years after it was declared a national park. That was a little over seventy years after the Nez Perce saved the men of the Lewis and Clark expedition, in what is now northern Idaho. Although the Nez Perce traveled through Yellowstone with their families, they were not there to see the sights. They had been pushed off their ancestral lands, treaties had been broken, and they were fighting their way to Canada and the dream of better treatment.

There were several bloody encounters with soldiers, and even with tourists ("You're not gonna believe what we did on our trip to Yellowstone!"). Ultimately, the Nez Perce failed because the warriors, although fierce fighters, wouldn't abandon their families and were slowed by them. I could imagine the tribal meeting, in which the question must surely have been posed, "Wait—run that oral history by me again. You say we *saved* these white folks' bacon seventy years ago?" I recalled seeing a bumper sticker on an older RV, "Sure you can trust the government—just ask an Indian."

An increase in the number of trees along the road, many draped in brilliant yellow, orange, rust and gold, were a sign that Cody was close. In 1896, Colonel William F. (Buffalo Bill) Cody established his eponymous town as a way of supporting the government's attempts to turn Yellowstone into a tourist destination and make a few bucks himself. Buffalo Bill built a luxurious western hotel, the Irma, named for his daughter. I entered the hotel through the huge wrap-around porch and was seated at a table in the bar, below the steer skull adorning the rock and fossil fireplace. The hostess placed me amidst one table with two trim cowboys in boots and Stetsons, a second with a young sophisticated couple who could barely speak enough English to order their buffalo burgers, and a third table with three grimy beer guzzlers totally decked out in camo. The bar was all smoke, faded velvet, burnished wood and dusty stone. Except for the football game on the flat screen, and perhaps the post-modern camo garb, Buffalo Bill himself could have strolled, or for that matter ridden, into the room.

The next leg of the journey took me from Cody to Yellowstone's East Entrance. There was no moon; the night was clear. The road passed through several tunnels carved out of bedrock left in its natural chiseled state, not covered with concrete. My headlights reflected off the flat planes in the rock. Next the route followed the shore of the massive Buffalo Bill Cody Reservoir, where the separation of water and sky was evident only by the shimmering of stars above. The Yellowstone region is often referred to as the Serengeti of North America because of the abundant wildlife. Although on this trip I had already seen plenty of "charismatic megafauna," as some charismatic resource managers like to call them—I like to call them bison, big horn sheep, antelope, elk and wolf—I had never seen as many animals on one drive as I saw that night.

Near Yellowstone, in the Wapiti Wilderness area, deer bounded into the headlights, lots of deer, on at least six occasions. And I spotted deer along the road, large bucks and does, another two or three times. I'm not exaggerating; I lost count. It was like a video game. Not that I've ever played one.

A magnificent bull elk lumbered into my lane, thankfully traveling in the same direction. His antlers were as long as my arm. The bull (was he a "royal?") refused to move off the road, bugling as he went and eyeing my car as he might a contender for his harem, which was no doubt sheltered nearby, demurely cheering the big guy on. I thought of the fellow I had overheard at the Yellowstone Visitors' Center telling everyone that his car had been attacked by a bull elk, declaring proudly, "I'm just like the guy in the movie." He was referring to the videos shown all over the park depicting bulls, head down and antlers brandished, attacking SUVs. I conceded this bull his space and slowly followed him, with the windows down to listen to his bugling, marveling at how such a delicate, flute-like sound can come out of such a huge animal with such a huge need—the rut. In time, he gave way and headed into the trees beside the road.

I was back up to speed, but driving on extreme alert, when I again braked hard, spotting two bearded monsters with horns right in front of the car. Imagine something out of *Where the Wild Things Are*. Two bull bison crossed the road in slow motion. Both paused midway and turned their massive, spiky heads toward me as if to inquire, "You got a problem with this?" I wondered how Charley would have reacted to these atavistic dudes. Eventually the bulls cleared the road, and on I went into the Yellowstone night.

The ranger booth at the east entrance was empty and there were few cars on the road. For mile after mile the only illumination was my headlights. There were no lights on buildings, no streetlights. Total darkness. I thought about how accustomed we are to artificial illumination. In the vast darkness of Yellowstone, car lights seem meager, and I felt, well, small and vulnerable. Add to that a winding mountain road, no cell service, and the fresh memory of four tons of bison giving you the hairy eye (not to mention that, even though you haven't yet seen a grizzly bear, you know they are out there), and you have a unique adventure that keeps your hands gripped on the wheel and eyes darting from roadside to fuel gauge.

Geyser gazers.

Soon I saw an expansive circle of light, indicating I was approaching my campground. I was drawn to the light and, at the same time, repelled by it. Why do we assume light equals safety? I wondered. Nevertheless, I was home. I crawled into the Bambi and, after donning a mask to block the light streaming through the white curtains, fell into a deep sleep.

The next day was dripping and damp, but perfect for a visit to the geyser basins, with their mud pots and fumaroles. Yellowstone has more geysers than any other place on the planet. I was reminded of Julianne, our recent German exchange student, who returned from her first trip to Yellowstone full of enthusiasm for the "geezers." During the summer, volunteer retirees note every burp and sputter from the popular thermal features. These "geyser gazer geezers," as a friend of mine calls them, provide important data for tracking the frequency of geyser eruptions. Julianne was not that far off.

Yellowstone is a large active volcano. Several major eruptions have occurred over the last two million years. In fact, "present time" is a mere geologic hiatus between big blowouts. The center of the park is a large caldera, and subsurface magmatic heat powers the park's thermal features, causing geysers to burst and steam. The basins are a fantastical witch's brew of shimmering pools, gurgling mud pots and spouting geysers. Because of the rising steam, the basins are visible from miles away. And these babies are hot. Domestic animals and people have literally been boiled alive in Yellowstone's thermal features. But they are so cool!

I learned a new term at one of the geyser basin displays that could well describe a few of my friends—"extremophiles"— microorganisms that live in conditions once thought too extreme to support life. Sure enough, these tiny, sausage-shaped critters live right near boiling water, in multicolored mats that work in ways very similar to dense forests, with photosynthesis and nutrient sharing.

At midday, cold and wet, I stopped at Old Faithful Inn for bison stew and a warm read by the lodge fire. If the reliable "old boy" blew while I sat by the fire, so much the better. It did and was reliably spectacular viewed through the lodge window. A squirrel in the hotel lobby was equally entertaining. He sat on his haunches, atop my coffee table, and worked over a muffin paper left by an earlier visitor whose mother hadn't raised him right. The round paper twirled like a tiny umbrella in the skillful forepaws of this cute little opportunist, who was content picking every crumb from the wrapper.

I overheard this exchange between a burly father and his sandy-haired boy of three or four, while they departed the lodge hand in hand.

"Well, we had a pretty good day, bud." Dad said. "We saw a moose, a bear and we saw Old Faithful erupt."

"And we saw a chipmunk, Dad! Don't forget the chipmunk!"

I was reminded of the gift of wonder—and how awe is relative. Sometimes we simply need to look at the miraculous through the eyes of others. I made a silent promise that a car stopped on the road in Yellowstone would never irritate me again. The animal jammers are experiencing awe in the presence of something new and exciting to them—be it a bear or a butterfly.

Somehow lunch at the lodge blended seamlessly into dinner. It was my last night; I decided to indulge myself and not do a single camp chore.

After dinner I was driving to the campground, feeling that my trip was perfect and thinking about what I had to do to break camp the next day. Suddenly, in my headlights I saw two grizzly bears wrestling by the side of the road. The larger of the two reared up on his hind legs and, in a blur of fur and fury, charged my car. His head filled up the entire passenger-side window. I swerved; the bear missed. Stunned, I watched in my rearview mirror as he turned back toward the shoulder and got hit by the car behind me. I pulled off the road and jumped out (what was I thinking?). The car that had collided with the bear stopped and a man appearing to be in his fifties got out (what was he thinking?). We peered into the darkness in the direction of the bear impact and chattered excitedly. I checked his broken headlight and was relieved to see no blood or hair. A third car pulled over and the woman driving rolled down her window (at least she was thinking!) and asked if we were all right. She said she had seen two bears go off into the night. One, no doubt, was sore as hell and a whole lot smarter.

The speed of the grizzly's charge had been stunning. It was an impressive animal. If I had been carrying bear repellent pepper spray on my belt, as I always do when hiking in bear country, I doubt I would've had time to get my hand to my waist before being overtaken—a sobering thought as I stared into the darkness.

Back at my campsite, my neighbor of a few days, an older gentleman clad in battered ball cap and jeans with back pockets almost drooping to the knees, got very chatty. The starter on his Suburban had died and he had been towed fourteen miles to the town of West Yellowstone to "get 'er fixed." I told him about my bear encounter. He whistled, scratched his jaw and said, "It's a wilderness out there." Then he hooked up his trailer and was gone. I have this theory that, just as passengers on planes begin conversations right before disembarking, people in campgrounds get more talkative just prior to leaving. In case they regret ever starting up a conversation, they know it will be short. I was disappointed to see him go, I was looking forward to telling him about my prostate problems. (Just kidding. I don't have a prostate problem...and I wouldn't tell the guy about it even if I did.)

I had trouble falling asleep in Winnie that night. When I closed my eyes, I saw the bear's massive head in the headlights. All I could think about was what my friend, Clint, had said when I told him one of my reasons for buying an Airstream was for greater security in bear country: "Bears know where the doors are and they know how to get 'em off."

The next morning dawned cool again, but clear and sunny. I packed up the Bambi and drove south to Jackson Hole. I knew I would return to Yellowstone soon. Yellowstone has a palpable pull, a magnetism and mysticism that makes me regret John Steinbeck did not delve into it in more depth. Yellowstone is definitely *not* a theme park; the water is hot, the animals are wild and the drivers are wilder. Millions of people from all over the world have fallen in love with Yellowstone. Yet somehow Yellowstone has survived this love, and the park continues to deliver large and small surprises, both human and natural. Yellowstone resists change when possible, renews itself when change is inevitable and goes on in a timeless way, never failing to delight. Yellowstone is and, until it blows up again, will remain one of the most amazing places on this planet. We can always find inspiration there—if not from the geysers and bears, then certainly from the chipmunks.

Chapter Nine
West by Northwest

*The next passage in my journey is a love affair.
I am in love with Montana.*

Travels with Charley

Now we can rejoin the trip around America, and I'll kick it back into gear with a confession: I succumbed to Montana's unrelenting allure. I, like Steinbeck, fell in love

Montana mountains—gorgeous landscape.

with Montana. So much so, that I really did feel guilty, like I was sneaking around to the north, behind Wyoming's back. I had to admit I'd been treating neighboring Montana like the proverbial neighbor's wife—stunning but unseemly to covet—and so I overtly ignored and secretly admired her. One can't ignore Montana while driving across her; she *is* lovely.

West of Livingston, the light was unlike any I had ever experienced. It was as if it had texture, a golden viscosity; it felt as though I were looking through amber. Every object stood out distinct from the next, just as Steinbeck had described the scene in Deer Isle, Maine. On one mountain pass, the colorful surfaces of the bands of rock appeared as if an artist had chosen them. The distant mountains were draped in a blue-gray haze and fluffy white clouds floated above in a pale, *pale* blue sky. In the foreground, the autumnal browns and oranges of the grasslands and the intense green of the conifers made for an amazing palette. It was a gorgeous landscape.

Typically, Montana displays a scene of which any western

state would be proud, fertile fields un-
dulating up to tree-covered slopes
capped by a snowy mountain, but
then Montana throws in flourishes,
such as a meandering stream, a few
picturesque cattle, a train laboring up
a valley, and an even taller and cloud-
covered distant peak—all as acces-
sories. Are there flaws? Of course
there are. Butte, with its copper min-

*Montana is generally
sublime, but occasionally
ridiculous.*

ing history, is a scar, and there are way too many tacky casinos
across the state, some with gaudy exterior plastic palms the size
of telephone poles ("A Taste of the Tropics," the sign above the
door said). On balance, however, Montana is a paradise and I
thoroughly enjoyed my time there. And there was still the exotic,
world-famous festival held in Clinton, Montana, to anticipate. I
had been looking forward to that for quite some time.

But I'm getting ahead of myself. Let's back up to Billings and
my second day in Montana. Even when a guy's head-over-heels
in love, he still has to eat. In Billings, I wanted to get Max and me
our Arby's fix. I went around the side of a combination Arby's
and Exxon station, thinking there might be large-vehicle parking;
there wasn't. I kept going around the back, through a gauntlet of
parked cars and pickups, and suddenly realized I was in trouble;
I was being funneled down into a single lane. It was way past the
point where backing up was an option. Rounding the third corner, I realized I was heading the wrong way in the Arby's drive-
through lane. There were actually three fortunate aspects to this
experience: (a) no one was coming in the proper direction, (b) the
lane was wide enough and the clearance high enough for me to get
the trailer through unscathed and (c) as I inched past the window
in the wrong direction, judging by the looks I saw on the faces of

the three Arby's employees, I would say I gave them the best laugh they had all day.

I found a suitable place to park, swallowed my pride and walked inside, hoping not to be recognized. I didn't linger. While driving again on I-90, I ate my Arby's sandwich, even adding horsey sauce. I saw several deer along the Yellowstone River, with a rainbow arching above them. Rain and sunshine were coming in alternating shifts, roughly ten minutes apart.

During a break in the rain, near Big Timber, Montana, which is roughly half way across the state, I stopped at a rest area that looked north, toward the mist-enshrouded Crazy Mountains. I met a man named Frank Koshere, a tall, lean, fellow in a camo hunting cap, wearing a trim moustache. He drove a recent-model 4Runner, brown like mine, pulling a low trailer covered with a tarp. We began our conversation by favorably comparing Toyotas. Frank hailed from Superior, Wisconsin. He worked as a water resources biologist for the Wisconsin Department of Natural Resources. He was also a black-powder elk hunter heading to Salmon, Idaho, for the hunt. Turns out we had been on the same route for several days. Frank said he had made this pilgrimage every fall for many years. Each time he set up a remote, primitive camp and hunted within five or six miles of it until he got his elk. Now that he was fifty-eight years old, he had dubbed his trip the "over-the-hill hunt."

I commented that Frank could not possibly be that far over the hill if he was still humping an elk carcass, even a field-butchered elk carcass, for that many miles over the hills of Idaho while the meat was fresh and before the kill was claimed by bears. He just smiled, obviously relishing the challenge.

A mud-spattered, black pickup truck, with huge tires and an ATV riding in the bed, pulled into the rest area. It had a bumper sticker that said, "No Guns—No Service."

"Now there's a guy with a little different style than yours," I said.

Frank shook his head and replied, "To each his own...I guess."

The road between Livingston and Bozeman traversed high, snow-covered passes, offering spectacular views of both the Absaroka and Madison ranges. I stopped in Bozeman for gas at a Gulf station and made a contribution to a food bank. I signed, "John Steinbeck" and tacked the yellow paper ribbon up on a board that displayed all the contributors.

My long-anticipated arrival in Clinton, Montana, was met with disappointment. I'd missed the event I alluded to earlier, the World's Largest Testicle Festival, held every fall at the Rock Creek Lodge. According to the website (www.testyfesty.com), "The festival attracts more than fifteen thousand fans annually to its five-day event. Tossing around the motto, 'I had a ball at the Testicle Festival,' the festival feeds over two and one half tons of bull balls [at two per, that's a lot of bulls] to its many hungry revelers. Not only can you get a taste of these yummy, delicious, deep-fried bull's testicles, but while you're there, you'll no doubt want to participate in the bull-chip throwing contest, the wet T-shirt or hairy chest competitions ['I coulda been a contendah'], and bull-shit bingo."

I'd planned to stop at the festival but had never exactly figured out the dates. (Later, I dropped a ballsy hint to Dimmie, telling her that two tickets to the Testicle Festival would be a great idea for my August 2010 birthday.) Oh well, it was on to Missoula, my goal for the night.

My hope was to camp for what would be the third night in a row. It was getting late in the season for RV parks that far north and I was even finding some KOAs closed for the winter. I saw a sign for one in western Missoula I hoped was still open and exited the interstate. At first I was convinced I had taken the wrong exit; the frontage road looked way more chain-store urban than any place I had ever camped. I drove several blocks with no sign of the KOA. At last I found the park, on a relatively quiet street a block off the frontage road, next to a subdivision of small homes.

During the check-in process, Kevin, in the prerequisite yellow KOA shirt, asked me if I wanted cable.

"No, no thanks, no TV on board," I said.

"Oh, roughing it," he said.

Kevin, the KOA klerk, gave me the off-season rate because the water and sewer hook-ups were shut off for the winter. Three straight nights of camping in Winnie had cost a total of $59.50 or approximately twenty dollars a night.

It turned out missing the Testicle Festival may have been fortuitous. My schedule was pretty tight, with two speaking engagements in Washington. I was forced to hurry through this lovely country on interstates. Coincidentally, because Charley was sick, Steinbeck had to rush across western Montana and northern Idaho to Spokane, to find a veterinarian. He wrote:

> *In the middle of the night Charley awakened me with a soft apologetic whining, and since he is not a whining dog, I got up immediately. He was in trouble, his abdomen extended and his nose and ears hot. I took him out and stayed with him but he could not relieve the pressure.*

Hurried as I was, I still saw an impressive expanse of Big Sky Country from the highway. I officially declared I-90 across western Montana as the runner-up in the most beautiful stretch of U.S. interstate contest—second only to I-70 near Glenwood Springs, Colorado. In western Montana, I-90 follows precipitous canyons with steep, conifer-covered slopes. It crosses and re-crosses the graceful, twisting Clark's Fork of the Yellowstone River. The pièce de résistance is the steep climb to Lookout Pass and the Montana/Idaho border. I ascended in the rain and fog behind a loaded horse trailer going forty miles an hour. Near the top, I shivered, remembering the warning about this pass in Hardin, Montana. The old gal, no doubt, had my best interests at heart but, still, it felt spooky (bony finger point, scratchy

The Oasis Bordello Museum in Wallace, Idaho.

wavering voice, parting blessing), so I was grateful that the temperature was a few degrees above freezing and it was raining but not snowing when I (literally) dropped into Idaho mountain and mining country. Snow or freezing rain would have been bad, "veeerrry baaaaad" (scratchy voice).

It was still raining when I braked into Wallace, Idaho, for a taste of the other Idaho (no mention of potatoes or Mormons there). Wallace, a quirky western town tucked up against the slopes of the northern Idaho Bitterroot Mountains, claims to be the silver capital of the world, and is still producing silver today for a total of 1.8 billion ounces of silver since 1884. I was chagrined to find the Oasis Bordello Museum closed for the season ("Ask us about our bordello tours," read a sign in the window), but did catch a tasty lunch at the 1313 Saloon.

According to the brief history on the back of the menu, the historic and cavernous 1313 Saloon was established as the thirteenth bar and brothel in Wallace. On that same informative menu, there were some interesting highs, lows, firsts and lasts about Idaho. Idaho has the highest waterfall in the U.S., Shoshone Falls. Idaho has the deepest canyon, Hell's Canyon. According to the menu, Idaho has the largest designated wilderness area in the contiguous United States, the Frank Church River of No Return Wilderness Area. Also, Idaho has the first city powered by atomic energy, Atomic City. And finally, Idaho was the last place in the contiguous U.S.

John Rowland and his wife, Margret.

to be explored by Europeans, and their names were...Lewis and Clark.

That night I stayed with an old school chum, John Rowland, and his wife, Margret, in their cozy bungalow high in the hills north of downtown Spokane, Washington. John grew up in Ohio, and attended Kiski School in the mid-sixties as a boarding student. He was a champion one-hundred-and-eighteen-pound wrestler at Kiski, coached by my father. Unlike me, John has had the discipline to maintain his high school weight, though he was slowly losing his sight and hearing to Usher's disease. He wore very thick glasses and two hearing aids, yet he refused to give in to the disease. John told me he worked out seven days a week at his downtown club to keep depression at bay. Margret drove him. My old friend joked about his disability; he worries he will enter the club's sauna naked and accidentally sit on another man's lap.

We had dinner with John and Margret's twenty-eight-year-old daughter, Marissa, who was unemployed and living at home since being laid off from her job in Seattle. After we ate and the two women departed, John poured a rare Bushmills, a single-malt Irish whiskey that, if I may say so, was the elixir of the gods. I asked John over our whiskeys what he had liked about wrestling in high school. He said, "Well, I loved the coach; your father had a stronger influence on me than my own. Jake was demanding. We learned a lot about denial. That same discipline is serving me well today. If I let one thing get in the way, I will let something else." After graduating from Kiski, John was an All-American East Coast rugby player at Williams College. All John's athletic accomplishments might have been excellent preparation, but they certainly pale beside what he faces every single waking moment now. John demonstrated his practiced technique for consuming the Bushmills. He sniffed before sipping and inhaled through the mouth after swallowing. John drank his Bushmills slowly, while maximizing its taste and smell.

John would never forgive me if I didn't say a word about his adopted home, the Lilac City. Although Spokane, the largest city between Minneapolis and Seattle, is often overlooked, John had nothing but good things to say about it. He likes the size and small-town feel; he said everything you need is close and there are no traffic concerns. John said Spokane has one hundred lakes within fifty miles, and unlike places west of the Cascade Mountains, enjoys the four seasons. That includes snow in winter and hot days in summer. Annual rainfall is seventeen inches.

"Compare that to Seattle." John hooted, with civic pride. "And Spokane has excellent colleges and medical facilities."

After a short, one-night-stay, I left John's neighborhood early in the morning, passing several beautifully landscaped city parks tucked under towering timber.

I experienced a sense of continuity, accomplishment and anticipation driving I-90 across the grasslands and massive agricultural fields of eastern Washington. It felt good to be so close to the Pacific Ocean. I was elated and wired. Perhaps I had consumed too much of John's strong, aromatic coffee. Or perhaps I felt fortunate to be able to perform the simple act of driving while viewing the countryside.

I opened my window. "Good Morning, Monster America!" I shouted into the sunshine-charged air. Near Moses Lake, it was time to do the tank thing. Full tank—car. Empty tank—me. Once again, I had pushed a little too hard and a little too long, and I entered the men's room as a man on a mission.

I pulled in at an overlook of the Columbia River near Vantage, Washington. The terrain on either side of

The Columbia River near Vantage, Washington.

that massive flow was brown, barren and dotted with low scrubs and grasses. The Cascade Mountains form a remarkable and distinct demarcation in the Northwest—rain forest to the west—grasslands and high desert, in the rain shadow, to the east. The volcanic Cascades, running from southern British Columbia to northern California, delineate the boundary right down the center. Since I was still a few hours drive from the Cascades, the terrain at the Vantage "vantage point" was rock-strewn high desert.

When I finally reached the Cascades east of Seattle, I climbed up to Snoqualmie Pass. It was every bit as beautiful as Lookout Pass between Montana and Idaho, and even displayed some lovely fall colors. The rain forests sprung up on the western side, thick, majestic, towering. Cascade forests offer some of the most impressive timber in this country, including, among other species, redwoods, Douglas firs and mixed evergreens.

I spoke at two schools—one in Kirkland, a suburb of Seattle, and one in Vancouver, Washington, in the south, connecting the two with I-405 and I-5. At the Kirkland school, I received special permission from the principal to take Max on school grounds. When I pulled him out of his kennel in the gym where I was speaking, he was greeted with "oohs" and "ahhs" and "cuuuuuutes!" What would I have done without that guy? He stole the show as usual. As I always do when addressing elementary students, at the end of my comments and Keynote slides, I challenged them to stump me with their questions. One very smart girl at the Kirkland school succeeded. She asked me how far I had driven. That's easy, I thought, and rattled off the miles and started to move on to the next raised hand, when she said. "Wait please. I'm not finished. How many inches is that?"

I stayed with a good friend who had insisted that I not drive through the Northwest without stopping at her new home. Harriette, a slender blonde, and her handsome, towheaded, six-year-old son, Alex, had just moved to Kirkland. They had a lovely two-story English Tudor house on a tree-lined cul-de-sac, relatively close to Lake Washington. It started to rain just as I backed Winnie into Harriette's driveway. I organized a few things and then, at his request, Alex and I shared a bottle of water and some crackers at the Bambi's table and listened to the rain on the roof.

Two guests joined us for dinner in the house. One was Jim, Harriette's boyfriend, a former NBA player who worked as a basketball coach. Jim mentioned that his daughter, Sherry, age thirty-six, had been living with him for the two years since receiving her doctor's degree. Jim said the arrangement was temporary, and mostly to save money, while his daughter paid off student loans and sold her Pasadena condominium. His daughter did a lot of house sitting for other people, he said, so their time living together was sporadic. Still, in the recession, the condo was not selling, and the life of a single dad sharing his home with an adult child brought both challenges and advantages.

The other guest was Mary, a tall, attractive woman in her early forties, also a newcomer to Kirkland. She had just left *Playboy* magazine to come to Washington and work for Nintendo. As a paralegal, her job was to track down and legally pursue pirates operating in cyberspace. Mary was enthusiastic about my trip, but secretive about her work, for reasons one can imagine. No doubt the milieu of cyber-pirating—stealing and duplicating copyrighted material—has its sleazy characters and dangerous situations, perhaps every bit as many as the milieu of reprehensible robbers on the high seas.

A Kirkland, Washington, rose at nose height.

We spent one comfortable night at Harriette's house in Kirkland. We had to be in Vancouver, a four-hour drive to the south, the next afternoon. Before departing in the morning, I walked Max around the block. The pavement was wet, but the rain had ceased. The red maples and yellow oaks, combined with the long, green leaves of the banana trees and roses glistening with moisture, made for a lovely mosaic. I discovered a convenient yellow rose arching over the sidewalk at nose height, requiring not the least bit of effort to stop and smell it.

And then the rains came again. It seemed like I was experiencing the weather each region was known for: snowy and cold in North Dakota, sunny and moderate in Montana, pounding rain in Seattle and all down the western side of Washington. I was a bit down myself during that particular drive—going without caffeine to aid in the Battle of the Bladder; and it seemed to help, a little. But, combined with driving in the rain, caffeine withdrawal played hell with my mood. My talk at the Vancouver school was brief and successful, I thought. Soon I was heading to Oregon.

Fortunately, Oregon broke the weather stereotype as the skies cleared and the sun broke through. Oregon has it all, by the way. From an environmentally oriented and culturally rich city (Portland) to Shakespeare (Ashland)—from sunny, rugged desert to rainy, rugged coastline—with some of the most significant geography and flora in this nation in between. Not to mention the Columbia River Gorge (and other important rivers), volcanic peaks, a green philosophy including cage-free eggs at fast food restaurants, free public transportation (in places), progressive towns, and endless outdoor recreation. And, if you are worried about the rain, you can live east of the Cascade Mountains in dry mountain foothills or high desert.

Some time ago, friends, originally from the East, asked my advice about where to retire in the West. I suggested they start in central Oregon. Without looking any further, they bought a house. Because they love film, the opera and fine dining, and because both of their sons lived in the city, they subsequently acquired a small apartment in Portland as well. I know what you are thinking, and I agree. In the have-your-cake-and-eat-it department, these folks pretty much take the cake.

"Why don't you live there?" you ask. I have—twice, in the late eighties near Bend, in central Oregon, and again years later, in Portland. That's why I sound like the Chamber of Commerce. If we hadn't discovered Wyoming before Oregon, Oregon would probably be our home today. Call it, if you will, my second favorite state. Or, considering my nascent love for Montana, perhaps it has been bumped to third.

As I indicated, the weather had cleared and a startling Mt. Hood was visible to the east when I crossed the Columbia River on the beltway around Portland.

It was in this region that Steinbeck had his only mechanical problem with Rocinante the entire trip. He wrote that he had the truck way overloaded, and had begun to take her reliability for granted, when this incident took place. "And in Oregon on a rainy Sunday, moving through an endless muddy puddle, a right rear tire blew out with a damp explosion." While changing the blown tire in the rain, he noticed the other rear tire was in very bad shape also. In a small Oregon town Steinbeck didn't name, an "evil looking service station man" went way out of his way to find truck tires and get the vagabond author back on the road. Steinbeck was very grateful. "I could have knelt in the mud and kissed the man's hands, but I didn't."

Because of the kindness I had enjoyed all across the country, I sensed that if I'd found myself in similar straits, I would have had a similar experience—perhaps even met a similar saint. Fortunately for me, I never had to put that feeling to the test.

The Airstream performed beautifully in northern Oregon, tracking my Toyota 4Runner as if they were one unit, up and down passes and through brief rain showers. California lay ahead. I was expecting two long days of driving and one night camping en route to Salinas, California, but I was already getting anxious to see Dimmie and our son, Wil, in San Francisco. And I was eager to explore John Steinbeck's roots in Steinbeck country.

Chapter Ten
Steinbeck Country, Part One-Where's the Stink?

"I find it difficult to write about my native place, northern California. What it is is warped with memory of what it was and that with what happened there to me, the whole bundle wracked until objectiveness is nigh impossible."

Travels with Charley

If Oregon has it all—California *had* it all. The old expression "California or bust" has become "California *is* bust." The beauty and sheer expansiveness of California has become marred with litter, **traffic,** graffiti, gangs, **traffic,** poor roads, **traffic** and people—people everywhere—twelve percent of whom were unemployed in 2009. The California prison system was at double capacity. The state was running a twenty billion dollar deficit.

As one Californian put it, "We are just putting on a front. Things are very bad." She went on to say the state parks were only open because vendors with contracts threatened lawsuits if the parks had been closed as planned. Cathy worked in an optometrist's office in Santa Cruz. She had an "Elvira" sort of shapeliness and beauty, with long, straight, raven hair and black eye shadow, and was kind enough to help me understand what was happening *vis á vis* the recession in Santa Cruz and Silicon Valley. It was not pretty. Unemployment was high. Businesses were hurting. People were still being laid off. Meth use among the middle class was rising and destroying families. Another woman, a young clerk in a Santa Cruz shop, whose name I did not get, spoke of a recent random and senseless gang-related murder at a party.

I learned at the National Steinbeck Center in Salinas that, at times, Steinbeck didn't want to get out of the truck when he visited his home state in 1960, because it had changed so much. "My return caused only confusion and uneasiness," he wrote in

Charley. Among other affronts were the mobile homes, "...California spawns them like herrings." I can't imagine how he would feel today. (I saw many jammed mobile home parks in California. My choice for most ironic moniker was Cavalier Mobile Estates.) What is going to happen when we experience a reverse migration and California's residents flee to the East? Refugee camps in Arizona and Nevada come to mind.

But California *is* Steinbeck, or at least it is early Steinbeck. Just about everywhere, from San Francisco to the bottom of the Baja peninsula, has the Steinbeck stamp on it. *Tortilla Flat, The Grapes of Wrath, Of Mice and Men, Cannery Row, The Sea of Cortez, East of Eden, The Red Pony* and *The Pearl,* among others, were rooted in this region.

California's unfortunate downside notwithstanding, my three days in Salinas, Santa Cruz, Monterey and San Francisco were distinctive, invigorating and peppered with colorful characters, including my son, Wil, with his ten-inch Mohawk. One afternoon, Dimmie and I were walking with Wil in the Tenderloin district in San Francisco when a short, tattered, homeless man shuffled toward us, bent over, with his eyes down. When he neared, looked up, and saw Wil, he jolted upright and asked, "Whoa, what kind of bird are you?"

Wil and Dimmie discovered Max had actually taken *two* ticks for the team. They uncovered another imbedded hitchhiker, looking contented, gray and bloated on Max's forehead. Because there were two strong people, one to pin him and one to wield the tweezers, the operation was much more successful than the one I had performed alone in northern Minnesota. That little guy could put up a fight. Our groomer in Jackson once said grooming Max was like trying to give a mosquito a haircut.

The three of us ate dinner at the historic John's Grill on Ellis Street, known as the setting for Dashiell Hammett's *The Maltese*

Falcon. Sam Spade lunched often at John's, and understandably so. The grill, established in 1908, had an old San Francisco wood-panel décor and style, combined with a new San Francisco sense of fun and informality. And the food was delicious.

We went on to Salinas, "the salad bowl for the

The National Steinbeck Center in Salinas, California.

world." Dimmie, a foodie and would-be organic farmer, marveled at the dark richness of the soil, long ago reclaimed from swampland. We whizzed by endless fields of washboard-like dirt mounds, perfectly aligned. In places, beautifully restored older homes, surrounded by trees and small yards, occupied the center of those fields. And, of course, we saw migrant workers bending and gathering onions and other late-season crops. The outskirts of Salinas had an agriculture-meets-small-industry feel, with railroad yards figuring prominently. The city center projected a modern, orderly, brick-and-glass look, perhaps because of the prominence of the National Steinbeck Center. Restored buildings, housing businesses and restaurants, lined the street leading up to the center.

The National Steinbeck Center is impressive—helpful and knowledgeable people and excellent exhibits. I had my second hour-long conversation with Herb Behrens, the volunteer archivist at the center. This time it was in person. It is always stimulating when one aficionado meets another. Herb was, once again, very helpful and giving. One of the exhibits featured the original Rocinante, restored. She was looking sharp, if a bit dated—dark green paint, gleaming white camper shell. Okay, the stuffed standard poodle (*white*, no less) in the cab was a little over the top; but all in all, Roxy looked as ready to rock and roll as she had forty-nine years ago. Above her were the words, "We do not take a trip; a trip takes us."

Roxy's refurbished and ready to rock and roll.

I visited John Steinbeck's boyhood home on Central Avenue, an attractively restored, tan Victorian with blue and gray trim, and then paid my respects at the Hamilton and Steinbeck plots in Salinas's Garden of Memories, where John and Elaine are buried. Then we headed to Monterey to visit Cannery Row. Steinbeck described it this way:

> *Cannery Row in Monterey in California is a poem, a stink, a grating noise, a quality of light, a tone, a habit, a nostalgia, a dream. Cannery Row is the gathered and scattered, tin and iron and rust and splintered wood, chipped pavement and weedy lots and junk heaps, sardine canneries of corrugated iron, honky tonks, restaurants and whorehouses, and little crowded groceries, and laboratories and flophouses.*

Well, let's see, I saw some restaurants. Seriously, I'm sorry to say that Cannery Row no longer comes even close to fitting Steinbeck's lyrical description, except perhaps for the quality of light over Monterey Bay, because no one has figured out how to sell "quality of light" to tourists. Cannery Row doesn't even stink. While writing this book, I read an article in *The New York Times* that said America's last sardine cannery, in Prospect Harbor, Maine, closed its doors in April 2010. The article went on to say that, at one time, America had fifty such plants, several of which used to be on Cannery Row.

At the Monterey Bay Aquarium, housed in restored canneries and warehouses, I met Merilyn, a sparkly, bespectacled doyenne and volunteer, who said she had known Ed Ricketts, Steinbeck's Cannery Row soulmate, and the

Rocinante's refurbished interior looking sharp.

person upon whom the character "Doc," in both *Cannery Row* and *Sweet Thursday,* is based. Ricketts was a philosopher and an ecologist; he and John Steinbeck were very close. Merilyn shared stories of visiting Ricketts' laboratory as a young woman. She was twenty at the time and working for the Stanford Research Center in Monterey. One summer evening, Merilyn and a friend climbed through Ricketts' laboratory window and waited for him to return from collecting marine samples. She said he was famous for his collecting—some of which was done with Steinbeck and reported in *The Sea of Cortez.* Merilyn said Ricketts was very handsome, intelligent and popular with the ladies. As far as they were concerned, he was a perfect gentleman that night. He played Gregorian chants on the phonograph and they chatted for several hours. Apparently, this sort of visit became commonplace for Ricketts after the success of *Cannery Row.* Steinbeck's book turned the scientist and his laboratory into tourist attractions. A train hit Ed Ricketts's car on May 8, 1948; he died three days later, at the age of fifty. Steinbeck was devastated.

From the deck of the aquarium, we looked out across the half-moon shoreline of Monterey Bay. Waves washed over black rock ledges, leaving the sort of tide pools and potholes that attracted Ricketts and Steinbeck. Seabirds and sea lions clung to the occasional boulder outcrop.

Just up the tourist-attraction-lined street from the aquarium, I popped into Ms. Laurie's Palm and Card Readings to have my Tarot cards read. I figured the psychic might be the sort of threatened and endangered Cannery Row character Steinbeck revered. Ms. Laurie's was a little grotto of faux-velvet, glass beads and fringe-on-fringe in mustard hues. Two chairs faced a small table. Amber, an aging, fading, spreading blonde and former actress, who was standing in for Ms. Laurie, did my reading. I asked for information regarding my Steinbeck projects.

John's boyhood home in Salinas.

Grave in the Hamilton and Steinbeck plot in the Garden of Memories in Salinas.

"We ask for guidance and seek the highest wisdom, Divine Mother," Amber chanted several times over the cards with her eyes closed. After dealing, she said that, according to the cards, I had a green light on all my creative en-

A green light from Ms. Laurie's on Cannery Row.

deavors. I would work in synergy with at least two other people, and an older woman would play an important role.

After the reading was concluded, I interviewed the seer. Amber was reluctant to discuss politics or the economy, but she did say something that I found noteworthy. She sensed people in this country were finally waking up and could tell when they are being lied to. She felt that the Obama administration was lying to us *less* than previous administrations. As to whether Amber was lying to me about knowing something about my future, I always try to keep an open mind. Only time will tell.

The little Steinbeck cottage in Pacific Grove.

I visited the little cottage in Pacific Grove, now slated for much-needed historic preservation, where Steinbeck lived and wrote as a struggling young author. It sits a few blocks from the ocean and has dark, clapboard siding, a shake-shingle roof and stained-glass windows. I photographed an overgrown brick barbeque in the back yard that John and his father, John

The barbeque built by John and his father, John Ernst.

Ernst, had built, and upon which John had scratched a Latin phrase while the cement was still wet. Herb Behrens had suggested I look for the barbeque, and said the hand-etched words had something to do with "feeding the masses."

After a difficult visit in his hometown, Steinbeck wanted out of California by the shortest route. But first he drove to Fremont Peak in the Gavilan Mountains east of Salinas and, after climbing the mountain, looked out over the Salinas Valley. This is a turning point for the author and, ultimately, for *Travels with Charley.* "High on these rocks my memory myth repaired itself." On Fremont Peak, John Steinbeck reconciled the duality of past and present, youth and adulthood, California and New York; he even appeared to be comfortable with the inevitability of death, which we now know, was eight short years away. He remembered a family story of his father burning his mother's name into the bark of a tree, and shared that and other memories with Charley:

In the spring, Charley, when the valley is carpeted with blue lupines like a flowery sea, there's the smell of heaven up here, the smell of heaven. I printed it once more with my eyes, south, west and, north and then we hurried away from the permanent and changeless past where my mother is always shooting a wildcat and my father is always burning her name with his love.

There was at least one humorous moment in the emotional tumult of Steinbeck's failed attempt to come home again. He was, reportedly, upset to learn about an unauthorized movie theater in Monterey named the "John Steinbeck Theater." It was not the sort of attention he welcomed. Steinbeck and a companion approached the theater and the friend said to the ticket seller in the booth, "This is John Steinbeck."

The seller looked Steinbeck over and said, "Yeah, right, and I'm the King of Africa."

Steinbeck headed inland to Fresno, and then south and east to Barstow. I went off the Steinbeck route because I wanted to see Big Sur for the first time and was still hoping for an interview with Thomas Steinbeck in Santa Barbara. Big Sur was everything I had imagined, squared—slamming surf, slanting rock, tall timber. Big Sur is a magical place. Henry Miller described it in *Big Sur and the Oranges of Hieronymus Bosch* as "…an inviting land, but hard to conquer. It seeks to remain unspoiled, uninhabited by man."

Not far south of Carmel Highlands on Highway One, I passed the Henry Miller Memorial Library, "where nothing happens." I parked at the next pull-off and walked back along the road to the library, where I purchased two Steinbeck novels and conversed under the towering redwoods with redheaded Susanna Williams. Susanna's grandmother was the first white baby born in Jackson Hole, (or so her relatives claim; she admits to a family tendency to make a good yarn better). Her parents were beekeepers in Dillard, Georgia, for a time and she attended college in Utah. When I told her all those places were fixed firmly in my peripatetic history, she accused me of making it up. Then Susanna pointed to her lip stud and

The Henry Miller Library under the redwood trees at Big Sur.

said that she had had her piercing done in San Francisco at Mom's Body Shop. I was wearing a Mom's T-shirt because I got my tattoo there. I accused Susanna of making *that* up.

I walked the one hundred yards or so back to the rig and let Max out of the car. We slipped off into the cavernous forest to perform a Charley-inspired ritual—peeing on a redwood tree. For some reason it was very important to John Steinbeck that Charley fire away on a redwood, for he wrote, "I dragged him to the trunk and rubbed his nose against it." Recognizing that no amount of nose rubbing would do, what with Max being a squatter, not a lifter, it fell to me to do the honors. After completing the Charley ritual, I leaned back, craned my neck, and turned in a slow circle. The sun-infused tops of the giants swirled above me, their entwined limbs embracing the sky. For the first time I understood how it was that in battles over redwood forests, environmentalists were willing to risk death so redwoods could live on and on. As Steinbeck wrote:

> *The redwoods, once seen, leave a mark or create a vision that stays with you always. No one has ever successfully painted or photographed a redwood tree. The feeling they produce is not transferable. From them comes silence and awe...they are ambassadors from another time.*

What followed was approxi-
mately sixty-plus miles of cliffhang-
ing driving above the foaming
breakers and turquoise sea. Then
the terrain flattened. I was surprised at what I saw south of Big
Sur. The Santa Lucia Mountains

Yes, sir! Big Sur.

pull back from the ocean. The topography is rolling, treeless and
arid, a little like high desert on the coast, or how I imagine the
Baja peninsula. The herd of zebra wandering unfettered on the
grounds of the Hearst San Simeon Historical Monument, which
includes the magnificent Hearst Castle, north of the town of Cam-
bria, added to the exotic feel of the land. A car approached from
the south at a point where the road runs close to the breakers and
was inundated by sun-sparkled rainbows of seawater arching over
both lanes of the highway.

I camped on a bluff above the ocean at El Capitan State Park,
twenty minutes north of Santa Barbara. After dinner, I hauled a
folding chair and cocktail to a grassy viewpoint, high over the
waves. A searing band of reflected light knifed across the sea from
horizon to breakers. The strip narrowed as the sun descended.
The surf was calm, not pounding but tapping a liquid tempo on
the sand. I watched the sun dissolve into the water, casting the
rounded contours of the planet into stark relief. The campground
had quieted. Back at the trailer, before turning in for the night, I
called Gail Steinbeck and left a voicemail message indicating I was
in the area and hoped to meet with Thomas.

The next morning, Friday, October 23, at 10:30 a.m., I got
a call from Gail Steinbeck. She wondered if I could have lunch
with Thomas in Santa Barbara that day. Gail chatted on about
houseguests and her cherished nieces and nephews and even an
impending marriage. She was very pleasant, but I was frantically

looking at the clock and calculating what I needed to do before I met Thomas. After thanking Gail and ending the call, I scurried around to get a camp shower, shave and dress. With Betty's help, I arrived at the appointed place at the appointed hour.

I saw a man in a felt fedora sitting alone at a table on the café's patio. Based on his visage, there was no doubt who he was—John Steinbeck's son. Thomas was wearing a brown fly fishermen's vest over a black T-shirt with white letters that said "I'm not dead yet," the hilarious line from *Monty*

Thomas Steinbeck, looking very much alive.

Python and the Holy Grail. Soon after we introduced ourselves, I commented on his shirt as emblematic of his dad's interest in King Arthur; Thomas chuckled and told me a story. He said a few years ago he was eating lunch in a restaurant in Salinas, close to the Steinbeck Center, when he noticed an elderly couple at a nearby table. The woman was holding a cane. She was talking; her husband was eating. Periodically, the lady would give the old fellow a shot to the ankle with her cane and say, "Are you listening to me?" When Thomas got up to leave and walked past the couple, the matron rapped her husband on the leg and said, "I told you John Steinbeck was still alive."

Thomas and I spent a leisurely hour and a half over lunch. Thomas was kind enough to give me a signed copy of his first book, *Down to a Soundless Sea*, which captures some of the intriguing stories about early life along the rugged and beautiful central California coast. He also spoke about his work-in-progress, his first serious attempt at fiction, *In the Shadow of the Cypress*. He said he had avoided fiction previously for fear of being compared to his father. (In my view, Thomas's foray into the realm of fiction is an admirable act of courage.) As I said, Thomas looks like his father. And like his dad, is a raconteur.

"Dad was a hardware store addict. He loved Barry's store in Sag Harbor for gadgets and fix-it materials."

"He was also an avid gardener, right?"

"Yes, but he didn't really have a green thumb. He was so obsessed with driving away all the pests that feasted on his garden that our backyard looked like a Buddhist temple. There were so many twirling and glittering things; it was like a neon sign inviting the critters to dine."

"I can just imagine."

"Oh, and rabbits, he had a special enmity for rabbits. One day he got so enraged with the rabbits he said, 'Boys, load up.' We all marched out with shotguns, prepared to slaughter the critters, and we were successful beyond our wildest imagining. We shot eighteen rabbits."

"I would love to have seen *that* hunting expedition."

"But, do you know who would have no part of it?"

"Elaine?"

"No, Charley. Charley was a very sensitive dog and he loved to pal up with all creatures, especially cats. Charley loved cats. And he hated loud noises. When the shooting started, he got very distraught and then disappeared. We realized when the smoke cleared, at the conclusion of the rabbit war, that Charley was still missing. He didn't come when we called. He was gone for three days; we assumed he was without food, since he wouldn't hurt a fly."

"That had to be a little scary, being surrounded by so much water." I said.

"It was. I got really worried about him and spent much of my day calling and searching. Then Dad saw Charley lying down in the reeds by the water. When he went up to him, Charley growled really menacingly. Dad was stunned at Charley's un-characteristic behavior, but he backed off and sent me in to try and reason with him."

"And did Charley listen to reason?"

"Well, that and he accepted a bribe of some steak I had wrapped up in my pocket in case I found him. When he got up reluctantly to take the meat, I noticed something furry and squirming beneath him. It was three baby rabbits. Charley was looking after three refugees from the rabbit war."

"That's amazing. How'd your dad react to that?"

"He felt the only civilized thing to do was raise those rabbits. And we did."

Thomas is neither overly modest about his heritage, nor smug about it. He treats his patrilineage, as all things, with humor. He has fond memories of his father. After lunch Thomas asked to meet Max and gave him, and my rig, his blessing. He said, paraphrasing his father, "You don't take a trip, a trip takes you." It is about the experience not the vehicle, he added. He asked me to stay in touch.

Tucked in Winnie, within sound of the breakers that night, I curled up with a book, *John Steinbeck: America and Americans and Selected Nonfiction*. The sea breeze ruffled the Bambi's curtains. Max snored gently under the table. Herb at the Steinbeck Center had recommended the compendium as "some of Steinbeck's best essays." I wasn't disappointed. In fact, I was particularly delighted to read, "My War with the Ospreys," first published in *Holiday* magazine. In the essay, Steinbeck professes his love for all creatures. He even wrote, "The baby rabbits skitter through my vegetable garden and, since I like the rabbits better than my scrawny vegetables, I permit them not only to live, but to pursue happiness on my land."

I concluded that John wasn't intentionally dissembling in this essay. When he wrote it, he was relatively new to his two acres in Sag Harbor and, being predisposed from childhood to love most birds and animals, was still feeling magnanimous toward the rabbits. It is my guess that, a few years after the end of hostilities in the osprey war, the rabbits had so taken advantage of Steinbeck's largesse that they had strained his generosity to the breaking point, resulting in a declaration of war. In fact, if you want to hear a menacing growl, just tell my wife, the animal lover and gardener, you think Uinta ground squirrels are cute.

If you are not familiar with "My War with the Ospreys," and if you are a bird lover, you will be relieved to know the title of this humorous essay is ironic. Steinbeck was "at war" with the birds to try and get them to nest in his oaks rather than across the bay on a utility pole.

Reading "My War with the Ospreys" delighted me in another way. I realized by referring to his story as the "rabbit war," Thomas was inviting me to listen in on the family vernacular. In the Steinbeck family, mundane tasks were obviously made more entertaining by the application of weighty titles. My father used to do the same thing. For example, the routine job of putting in a small concrete wall in the basement of his cottage became the "big pour."

Reflecting back on my time with Thomas, while being lulled to sleep by the sound of the surf, I reckoned I had just had the very best day of the trip. The next day was the very worst.

Steinbeck Country, Part Two—Fathers and Sons

Then Cain went away from the presence of the Lord, and settled in the land of Nod, east of Eden.

The Book of Genesis, 4:16

Before I relay the details of the worst day of the trip, allow me to slip out of the time continuum of this narrative one final time and address the subject of John Steinbeck and his sons.

Although I was reluctant to do so at first, as my research took me deeper and deeper into Steinbeck's personal life and into his relationship with his two sons, Thomas and John (IV), and the boys' relationship to *East of Eden*, it became all the more imperative that I comment on Steinbeck's two boys. Steinbeck was often criticized for being overly sentimental and emotional in his work. I, for one, admire that element in his writing. Although I have tried to be objective and unsentimental about the conclusions I arrived at in this chapter, I must admit my observations may have been influenced somewhat by the fact that I liked Thomas Steinbeck, and that, like Steinbeck, I am familiar with the complexities of ending a marriage, which included a much-loved child, and with the challenges of raising two boys.

Thom and Johnny Steinbeck were two years apart, born in 1944 and 1946 respectively. Johnny died in 1991. It is said he struggled with drugs and alcohol most of his life. Gwyn, the boys' mother, was thought to have had similar problems. It is a matter of record that she made Steinbeck's life hell after their separation. "Gwyn had decided to cut him off completely, knowing that to withhold information about the boys would amount to torture," Jay Parini wrote in *John Steinbeck, a Biography*. Both boys struggled in school. Thomas had a learning disability. As I have mentioned, Johnny, just before his death in 1991, wrote an exposé about his father and mother. In short, there was a great deal of tumult in the Steinbeck family. After all, Thom and Johnny were children of divorce and the sons of a world-famous writer growing up in the sixties.

Steinbeck was, at times, a heavy drinker prone to hypochondria, serious mood swings and a tendency to blame others for his problems. He often wrote in his letters how hard it was to get work done when the boys were visiting and constantly interrupting him. John Steinbeck's third wife, Elaine, was thrown into the mix as the boys' stepmother (and tutor), and thus undertook one of the hardest jobs in the difficult realm of parenting. Gwyn worked constantly at poisoning the boys' view of their father and stepmother.

That all made for a pretty volatile domestic situation, but it does not mean John Steinbeck did not love his sons or would have wanted to see them disinherited. In fact, his letters and personal essays are rife with evidence that he adored his children and intended to provide for them after he was gone. Jackson Benson wrote in his biography, *John Steinbeck, Writer,* that he felt Steinbeck loved his boys and desperately wanted to be a good father, but he simply did not know how. Benson wrote, "Despite his failures, however, John cared, cared deeply about them, and no matter what happened—and many things did—never gave up hope for them or stopped trying, in his erratic way, to help them."

Thomas Steinbeck speaks very highly of his father, saying he feels he was a pretty good dad for "someone who was sort of backed into fatherhood and just wanted to write."

Thom's wife, Gail, told me, "Thom's father adored him."

Johnny was quoted in an interview from 1986 as saying, "He didn't want us to be rich kids of a famous father. He got what he wanted. We're both well cultured. I think he wanted stevedores who could read Greek." But as you will read below, Johnny made this statement just five years after he and Thom sued Elaine for what they felt was owed them.

Thomas and Gail Steinbeck are involved in a long and bitter lawsuit to insure that Johnny's only daughter, Blake Smyle, and Thomas (John Steinbeck's two remaining blood heirs), obtain legal rights to several of Steinbeck's works. Although many of the books show that Elaine, Thom, and John IV renewed the copyright, it is not clear what money the sons received. When Elaine died in 2003, those rights were left to Elaine Steinbeck's sister and Elaine's heirs. None of the beneficiaries are direct descendants of John Steinbeck. The lawsuit has caused much enmity between the two branches of the family.

In the interest of full disclosure, in the fall of 2009, when I posted on my blog a piece about meeting with Thomas in Santa Barbara and an open letter to Gail Steinbeck prior to that meeting, I was accused, in a blog comment, of pandering to Thomas and Gail Steinbeck to curry favor. That same respondent wrote, "She (Gail) is only relaying what she and her husband would like the world to believe: that John Steinbeck cared a great deal for Tom [sic]. According to all historical and contemporary accounts the opposite is true. Tom has sued his family members several times, including his father, in a misguided effort to obtain that which his father never gave: his love. In fact, his father effectively disinherited Tom. It is unfortunate that Tom must live with that legacy but no amount of revisionist history will alter the facts of Tom and John's dysfunctional relationship."

This comment, above all, made me want to be as objective as possible in making any assumptions about this complex and private matter.

Here are my conclusions: There is no doubt that, at times, the going was very rocky with John, Elaine, Thom and Johnny. Yet, from everything I have read and heard, I cannot believe that when John Steinbeck left his estate to Elaine, he did not intend to have his sons share in that estate upon her death. A loving parent would wish that, and John Steinbeck was a loving parent. I believe that John Steinbeck, being somewhat careless in business matters, and apparently never having addressed copyrights in his will, acted thoughtlessly.

According to Michelle O'Donnell, in an article published on August 2, 2004, in *The New York Times,* and titled, "Steinbeck Heirs Entangled In an Epic Family Lawsuit," Steinbeck left each of his sons $50,000 in 1968 when he died, totaling close to ten percent of the worth of his entire estate—so much for the "disinherited" argument. Also according to the article, the boys sued Elaine for what they felt was still due them in 1981, and the suit was settled in 1983. Although the terms of the settlement are sealed, it is safe to assume Steinbeck's sons got something significant at that juncture, or at least were promised something significant. As for suing his father, according to Jackson Benson, Thom was pulled into a support case brought against his father by his mother, Gwyn, in 1964 when Thom was nineteen years old. The judge, for all intents and purposes, ruled in favor of John and, although hurt and upset by their actions, John subsequently forgave his sons. Thom was only twenty-four when his father died in December 1968 and was present at the burial of his father's ashes in California.

The question that remains is why Elaine, said to be a loving person who tried to do her best for her stepsons, would leave Thomas and Johnny's daughter completely out of the will when she died in 2003? In so doing, was she fulfilling her husband's wishes? Here, I'm moving into the realm of pure speculation. I believe Elaine was so deeply estranged from Steinbeck's sons and so hurt by that estrangement, including the lawsuit brought by the boys in the early eighties, that she acted without appropriate attention to their interests. I also believe that Steinbeck would have wanted to see his legacy and estate equitably divided to favor his blood heirs more, and distant relatives, like his sister-in-law by his third wife, less. Perhaps if he could have called the shots, anticipating all this family turmoil—and here I'm speculating wildly—he might have said in his gruff voice, "Give the whole goddamn lot to a charity to support the homeless and be done with it." As is the case in all private family matters, no one on the outside can—or should, for that matter—know all the details.

Then there is the most astounding piece of the whole Steinbeck family saga. John Steinbeck admitted freely and openly that he wanted *East of Eden* to be a sort of legacy and lesson to his boys. "I have chosen to write this work to my sons," Steinbeck wrote to Pascal Covici, his editor and close friend. *East of Eden* is, among many other things, a modern allegory, retelling the Cain and Abel story from the Bible, except the novel chronicles two generations of brothers, Charles and Adam, and Adam's twin sons, Caleb and Aron. Charles brutalizes his brother, Adam, and Cal torments his brother, Aron, just as Cain destroyed Abel in the original. Jealousy is the common catalyst in these sibling rivalries. The flip side of the coin is the love of sons for their fathers, and of fathers for their sons.

The descriptions of Cal and Aron in *East of Eden* are said to bear a very close resemblance to Thomas and Johnny as boys. Would it not then be logical to arrive at the conclusion that Cathy in *East of Eden,* mother to Cal and Aron, and one of the most thoroughly evil characters in modern literature, was influenced by Steinbeck's second wife, Gwyn, Thom and John's mother? That had to be a heavy burden for Johnny and Thomas to bear. And here's the saddest part—what with life reflecting art in this perverse self-fulfilling prophesy—brothers Johnny and Thomas ended up, as adults, feuding with each other. I know you are way ahead of me in recognizing the sad irony. This is a tragic tale Steinbeck could have written. And, I guess, in a way, he did.

But now I have to get you out of Steinbeck country and south to San Diego, where I spent a few relaxing days at my brother's rural retreat, Rocky Pines, in Jamul (Ha-Mule). Getting there was anything but relaxing.

I awoke at my campsite above the beach north of Santa Barbara; the sun was on the trailer. It was a beautiful day. I walked Max out to the bluff that overlooks the surf and was warmed, not only by the sun but also by my memories of time spent with Thomas Steinbeck the day before. Cormorants bobbed on the light surf.

Weather was obviously not the problem. Traffic was not the problem either. Yes, I was scheduled to drive through Los Angeles, and you're already aware of my city-averse driving mindset, but it was Sunday, so although I later encountered way too much traffic for this timorous titmouse from Teton County, Wyoming, I can't really blame L.A. traffic. The screw-ups of the day were all on me. Were I a baseball player, I would've been touching my cap brim and tapping my chest all morning in the universal signal that says "my bad."

I kicked off this doozy of a day by doing something I had never done before with my Toyota, and, as much as I'd like to, I can't even blame Toyota. Positioning the car to hook it to the trailer, I intended to go forward, but inadvertently put it in reverse and slammed backward, knocking the Bambi's hitch post off her plastic blocks and causing a screeching metal-on-asphalt sound loud enough to wake up the entire campground. Embarrassing, but no real harm done. My second attempt to hook up was successful.

Just beyond Santa Barbara, I needed fuel and a bathroom and was having problems determining from the freeway where the gas stations were. I got off U.S. 101 near Carpentaria and found no service stations; however, returning to 101 was extremely confusing and difficult, made more so by Betty barking orders at me. I ended up crossing back and forth over the highway several times before finding an on-ramp. That, of course, was a relief, but failing to find a gas station was not.

It seemed that the gas stations along 101, when I saw them at all, were very small and cramped. Jamming Winnie into a tight space around gas pumps had resulted in an expensive accident just prior to my trip, so yes, I was gun-shy. I saw no truck stops. I wondered what trucks did for gasoline along that stretch of highway. My paranoia was rising, along with my blood pressure. I threw the dice again somewhere around Ventura, got off the highway and was fortunate to find a gas station. It was cramped and crowded, but I managed to corkscrew my rig in beside a pump. By now, of course, internal water pressure was building as well.

I've never been a guy who can relax when people are waiting for him to get out of their way. I started to rush. I leaped out of the car and discovered that the station only accepted debit cards—no credit cards, no cash. I had a debit card with me, but it was locked in my trailer. I jerked the trailer keys from the glove compartment and they flew out of my hand and landed somewhere behind me in the crowded car. I frantically searched the floor of the car for the keys. No luck. I now had three cars in line waiting for my pump.

At least I can use the men's room, I thought. I hate it when other drivers do this, but I left my rig at the pump and ran inside. The men's room was locked and in use. I ran back outside, jumped in the car and got back on the freeway. I had exited U.S. 101 for a second time and accomplished nothing except to add a new complication: I was temporarily unable to unlock my trailer to use my own bathroom.

Have you heard the expression, "It doesn't rain but it pours"? Hard to believe it has applicability in sunny southern California. In my urgency, somewhere near Oxnard, I exited from 101 a third time, only to be dumped onto a major four-lane highway going somewhere I did not want to go, with no sign of a gas station. I finally managed to find a light for a left turn that took me into the large parking lot of an office complex. Luckily, because it was Sunday, there was no one around. After another brief, frantic search, I could not locate my trailer keys. In desperation, I took care of problem number one, side-by-side with Max, right there in broad daylight in the parking lot. But still, there was the little gasoline problem. My tank was low, but fortunately not yet on reserve. I got back on 101 and resumed the frantic search for any sign of a gas station. My knuckles were white, my throat was dry, and, as far as I could tell, I hadn't even gotten to L.A. yet.

Soon I found a rest area. I pulled in, determined to regroup and get it together. I sat in the car and took several deep breaths. After a visit to the restroom, I calmly walked Max and then pulled everything out of the front half of the car and found the missing keys. Now all I needed to do was maintain my newly regained equanimity (breathe, breathe), and find some damn gas before I ran out of it on some damn freeway near L.A! I did, at last, find gas at a large, RV-friendly gas station near Thousand Oaks, right off 101. That was on my fifth stop. Now you see what I mean, a comedy of screw-ups, all mine.

By comparison to the morning, the afternoon, including what I guessed was actually driving through Los Angeles (where does that city begin and end?) and Anaheim, was actually pretty tame. Oh, there was way too much traffic, especially for the weekend, and traffic slowed to a near standstill around every major city and town, but at least I was moving and making progress. I really don't remember much from the afternoon drive (no memories are good memories), except

Winnie in Jamul, California.

for one surreal experience.

Now on "the 5" (Californians always give highways the definite article), I was traveling in the middle of seven lanes of vehicles when a police car, lights flashing, started to weave back and forth in front of us from the shoulder to the median. The officer driving had his arm out the window alerting people to slow down. We all stayed behind him and slowed dutifully. After about half a mile of playing follow-the-cop, the police car turned sideways in the middle of the highway and all seven lanes stopped on command. Then the cop car swung over to the median and led another car, which appeared to be stranded there, across the highway to an exit. Now that is power, I thought.

Still on the road, somewhere between Los Angeles and San Diego, I called my brother, David, and lamented to him about my day. "Way too many people and only one road," he said, referring to I-5. Oh sorry, *the 5.*

For the rest of that crazy drive, I tried to relax and imagine the view from my brother's property (twenty-five miles east of San Diego), down verdant valleys and across boulder-strewn granite peaks to Otay Mountain just north of the Mexican border. I could almost taste David's salubrious Ruby Red grapefruits, eaten poolside, right off the tree, and washed down with cold Mexican brew. It helped to pass the time.

I made it to Jamul in time for cocktails and a late dinner with a grapefruit appetizer. During my visit, it hit ninety-three degrees under a cloudless sky. My stay (mostly by the pool) was akin to cooling my heels at a shady oasis before entering the fiery desert kiln ahead.

Chapter Eleven
Desert Opus

Across the Colorado River from Needles, the dark and jagged ramparts of Arizona stood up against the sky, and behind them the huge tilted plain rising toward the backbone of the continent again.

Travels with Charley

Steinbeck hammered out of California via Los Banos, Fresno, Bakersfield and Barstow, and then camped in the Mojave Desert. He followed Route 66 across Arizona to the Continental Divide in New Mexico, where he spent the next night. My 1959 Rand McNally indicates only thirty miles of I-40 was completed anywhere in the U.S. in 1959 and that was near Santa Rosa, New Mexico, still to the east of Steinbeck's camping spot on the divide.

The author only wrote one paragraph about Arizona in *Travels with Charley,* commenting briefly on the cities, "I know this way so well from many crossings—Kingman, Ash Fork, Flagstaff with its mountain peak behind it, then Winslow, Holbrook, Sanders, down hill and up again, and then Arizona passed."

In New Mexico, he realized he was no longer assimilating his experience. "And I sat in the seat and faced what I had concealed from myself. I was driving myself, pounding out the miles because I was no longer hearing or seeing." After a heart-to-heart talk with Charley (and in this case he has Charley vocalizing his replies), Steinbeck made his companion a "birthday cake" of pancakes and syrup and poured himself some "straight whiskey." He wrote that they both felt better and went to sleep early in the camper.

I wonder if ghosts haunted John along this stretch of highway. Although he made no reference to it in *Travels with Charley,* U.S. 66 is the route followed by the Joad family in *The Grapes of*

Wrath from Oklahoma to southern California. Steinbeck wrote in *Grapes,* "Highway 66 is the main migrant road. 66 is the path of a people in flight, refugees from dust and shrinking land…66 is the mother road, the road of flight." Two riveting pages begin the twelfth chapter of the book, summarizing the importance of Route 66 to the great migrations of the 1930s. Steinbeck ended this tribute with words that captured the emotions of the migrants when they arrived in western California after the arduous trip, culminating with crossing the Mojave Desert: "And, oh, my God, it's over." Perhaps Steinbeck felt he had nothing more to say about U.S. 66. The Joads still had to face the harsh reality of survival in a state overrun by desperate migrant workers who were often spurned and brutalized.

It is likely that Steinbeck was fighting his recurring battle with loneliness and depression, exacerbated by concern for his health. What I find most intriguing is comparing what I read in *Travels with Charley* with what was actually going on in Steinbeck's life at the time of the trip. His departure was delayed for several days in September of 1960 because of Hurricane Donna. In the first few pages of *Charley,* Steinbeck describes saving his boat, the *Fayre Eleyne.* She was being shoved against a pier by other storm-driven boats in a ninety-five-mile-an-hour wind and certain to be sunk. Steinbeck jumped into her and motored out to the middle of the bay to safe anchor. Then he dove into the water and swam to shore, fully clothed.

As described in the book, this is impressive, especially for a fifty-eight year-old man. But it is incredible when you realize that Steinbeck was still recovering from a probable stroke—during which a cigarette set fire to his bed—worrying about losing his dignity and independence as a man, and fighting for his life as an author under heavy criticism that he had never equaled *The Grapes of Wrath.* He had also recently failed to complete the arduous project of crafting a modern-language version of Malory's *Le Morte d'Arthur,* a compilation of Arthurian romances that Steinbeck had loved and been influenced by all his reading and writing life. While recovering from this health episode, which had temporarily resulted in slurred speech and shaky hands, Steinbeck wrote in a letter on December 30, 1959, to his agent, Elizabeth Otis, expressing his fear of being treated like an invalid, "It's not taking it easy that matters but taking it right and true." He added for emphasis, "I will not take it easy. That would be sick." John Steinbeck was being tossed about in his own personal tempest, no hurricane required. In June of 1960, four months prior to departing on his drive around the country, he wrote to Otis, "Between us, what I'm proposing is not a little trip or reporting, but a frantic last attempt to save my life and the integrity of my creative pulse."

Are there any more common and provocative metaphors in classic literature (not to mention popular culture) than storms and journeys? It seems every family has to weather its tempests, some of which rage in the middle of odysseys.

I had a speaking engagement at the Menaul School in Albuquerque, so I sailed I-8 from Jamul to El Centro and then State 78 across the Imperial Sand Dunes Recreation Area, where trucks on the road plowed blowing sand as fine as sugar, and finally took U.S. 95 along the Colorado River north to Needles, California, where I camped. I was stopped twice en route, north of El Centro, at Border Patrol checkpoints. Once I was asked to roll down my rear window. Fortunately the little white dog in the back did not get profiled and retained for further inspection. After Imperial Dunes, I passed miles and miles of razor-wire-topped, chain-link fence. Inside the fence was what appeared to be an open pit mine. A sign touted "The New Gold Company." Near the settlement of Palo Verde, pale green Palo Verde trees sprung up from pebbly sand the color of cinnamon. And believe it or not, the little town of Ripley, near the Colorado River, offered about a million bales of hay and a few falling-down shacks on flat, dry, treeless lots ringed by junk. The

Imperial Sand Dunes Recreation Area.

next day, I pushed from Needles to Albuquerque, New Mexico, in one long day on I-40.

Over lunch, Thomas Steinbeck had mentioned to me that his father wanted his "Twainian" voice to shine through in *Travels with Charley.* Thomas said that Steinbeck had decided that humor was the best teacher and instrument for change. I reminded him that both Twain's *Roughing It* and *Charley* had pivotal desert scenes with coyotes. He indicated I'd made an important connection.

Steinbeck had pulled over in the Mojave to give a very thirsty Charley some water when he noticed two coyotes, watching him, about fifty yards away. He sighted them in with his rifle, "I moved the crosshairs to the breast of the right-hand animal, and pushed the safety. There was no question of missing with the rifle at that range. I owned both animals." All his training growing up on a ranch shouted at him to kill. "Coyotes are vermin. They steal chickens." But he couldn't pull the trigger. In fact, before driving away, he put out a can of dog food for the animals. He felt that since he had saved their lives, he was now responsible for them. This was a pivotal moment in Steinbeck's life and in his relationship with all living things.

I encounter coyotes often in Jackson Hole, and I'm always pleased when I do. A few years ago at mid-day, I spotted a big bushy-tailed coyote right in front of my house. He was yipping at another coyote, which was answering from on top of the cliffs behind our lot. It was a thrilling sight and sound. Hearing unseen coyotes sing in the distance is almost as pleasurable. Admittedly, coyote sightings are not that unusual. After all, a rather wily coyote recently made his way to Central Park in New York City. They are smart and opportunistic, and yes, they occasionally steal chickens; can you blame them? Steinbeck wrote some lovely lines about coyotes in *East of Eden,* "The coyotes nuzzled along the slopes and, torn with sorrow-joy, raised their heads and shouted their feeling, half keen, half laughter, at their goddess moon."

I sought my own coyote moment in the Steinbeck tradition. Once I passed Vital Junction on U.S. 95, I assumed I had entered the Mojave and began my vigil. On that hot, brilliant day, as I passed crumbling rock hillocks and sparse tufts of desiccated grass sprouting from the sand, I was totally focused on seeing coyotes. The only real disappointment in my trip had been the paucity of wildlife. I suppose you could say I'm spoiled, living in the Yellowstone ecosystem where wildlife is abundant, but I felt several deer, a few dozen wild turkeys, four skunks, two dead moose and one squashed coon cat were pretty slim pickins, considering how far I had driven around this great and bountiful land. And I had not seen a single coyote. On U.S. 95 in southeastern California specifically, I surmised that the lack of wild animals was due to too little desert solitude and too much traffic and roadside development. One humble homeowner's sign made me smile, however; the mailbox read, "Casa not so Grande."

It was getting late. It was still hot. The sun was drilling in my driver's side window. Max's tongue was dragging. I stopped at several Bureau of Land Management pull-offs looking both for places to camp and for any evidence of "song dog." I saw puddles of broken glass and roadside signs with sunlight shooting through bullet holes, but no animals.

As a family, we make a point of never feeding wildlife. Feeding habituates wild animals to humans and human food and ultimately deprives them of their wildness. Still, I was seriously considering putting a raw steak out by my trailer that night if that was what it took. I *wanted* my Mojave coyote moment. Hey, at least I wasn't considering staking out Max as bait.

Nothing appropriate presented itself for camping and no animals were to be seen. In time, I saw a sign that indicated I was six miles from Needles, California. I felt drained from the heat and disappointed about my failed quest. At a junction, I came upon a second sign that pointed west to Needles and east to I-40 and Arizona. I reluctantly chose to turn east in defeat. Soon California and the Mojave would be behind me. Worse yet, I would be on an interstate, again. Small consolation was a marker indicating that, by pure chance, I had turned onto a short stretch of the original Route 66 that was not on my map. I got a kick—knowing that once again my tracks were covering Steinbeck's—on Route 66. The asphalt looked like it could have been there forty-nine years ago. I thought of asphalt as archeological dig. If I bored down in the layers of the "mother road" was there any chance I might find microscopic traces of Rocinante's tires? The strip of Highway 66 was disappointingly short and soon I was dumped onto I-40 heading to the border. The bridge over the Colorado River to Topock, Arizona, was dead ahead.

And then I saw him. He had a short, slick, ocher coat and alert, pointed ears. He was making his way down a sparsely grassed hill inside the fence to the interstate. He appeared to be trying to cross. I wrenched my rig to the shoulder of the highway and, while braking, shouted with glee. My abrupt arrival caused him to retreat partway back up the hill. He stopped and turned. We locked eyes. He appeared young and a bit tentative. Certainly his size indicated youth. I remember this moment almost as if it were in freeze frame. I forgot all about the busy highway behind me. I'd like to say my Mojave coyote moment seemed like an eternity, but I would be lying. A trucker blasted by and laid on his air horn. The young coyote and I both jumped and he bolted up through a hole in the fence and disappeared over the top of the hill. I pulled back on the highway, at first miffed at the trucker, and wondering what prompted his rudeness. Was he angry with me for parking on the shoulder or was he just being obnoxious and trying to scare away the animal? But within a few miles I realized the truck driver might have done the animal and me a favor. I was reminded that no amount of enthusiasm for something sighted from a busy highway warrants creating a safety hazard. More importantly, perhaps the coyote learned that trying to cross a busy highway is a very bad idea. Coyotes are smart and quick to master new situations. Perhaps the lesson even saved his life. I remember wishing there was a way I could turn around, park safely, scramble up the hill and leave my steak for the young coyote.

I camped that night at Moabi Park, next to the Colorado River, on the California side. The park was built on a flat gravel flood plain for the river, and I got one of the few sites shaded by cottonwood trees. The heat of the day had subsided. Outside the trailer at my picnic table, I caught up with Dimmie in an hour-and-twenty-minute hands-free cell call, during which I grilled the coyote's steak, ate and cleaned up my dinner, and toasted my "song dog" with some red wine. Just after saying goodnight to Dimmie, I walked Max across the campground to the pebbly beach and enjoyed an autumnal sunset, blazing orange on the silt-red river.

I've been interested in the Colorado River since kayaking as a teenager through the white water of Cataract Canyon, below the confluence of the Green and the Colorado, in southern Utah. As an adult I've explored, researched and written extensively about the Colorado.

The *Jackson Hole Daily* recently reported on the status of the Colorado River and Lake Mead, a man-made lake mostly in Nevada about one hundred miles north of where I was camped on the Colorado. Tim Barnett at the Scripps Institute of Oceanography published a study a few years ago stating there is a fifty percent chance that Lake Mead, now much depleted as the West continues to heat up and dry out, could run completely dry by 2021. Much of the water that supplies Las Vegas is siphoned out of Lake Mead with tunnels, or "straws" as they are called. Imagine Las Vegas as a ghost town. Interesting thought. Seriously, 27 million people in seven states and Mexico, according to the article, rely on the Colorado to irrigate, run businesses, produce drinking water and water lawns. Things could get really parched and very nasty. Mark Twain allegedly put it well, saying, in the American West, "whiskey is for drinking; water is for fighting over."

I walked Max back to our camp; a breeze came off the river. The cottonwoods' leaves rustled above the trailer. I noticed two kids close to the water kicking a ragged soccer ball near an older, sagging, brown cabin tent and a small, decrepit, green trailer. I was packing up my gear outside the trailer in preparation for an early getaway the next morning when a stocky, fiftyish man dropped in. He had reddish-brown hair, wore shorts and a sleeveless athletic shirt, and carried a beer in a cozy. He said his name was Rick, remarking on my Wyoming plates. I pulled a beer out of the trailer fridge and Rick pulled up a camp chair.

Rick told me he lived in Verde Valley, a few hours north of Phoenix. He had come to California to attend truck-driving school after being laid off from his job of twenty-plus years at a machine shop. Rick figured he was one of the lucky ones. "Kid's grown, mortgage is doable," he said, sipping. Rick had an interesting perspective on how "it had all gone south." He mentioned that he

had to "jump through all kinds of hoops" when he was just starting out, including getting his father to cosign for a thousand-dol-
lar loan to buy a car. He figured that was a good thing. It had all
gotten too easy, and then the "friggin' house of cards came down,
big time." He was pretty certain things would get worse before
they got better. Rick mentioned that his truck drivers' class was
made up of lots of skilled out-of-work guys: carpenters, tile layers, even restaurant owners.

We crossed the campground to check out Rick's huge, white,
fifth-wheel trailer to see the cargo hold for motorized toys. After
the tour, he said. "I'm planning to qualify for the full deal: semis,
haz-mat, the long trucks. Hey, I'm too young to retire—gotta do
something. But for now we're okay—for starters, my wife's still
got her job." He sipped his beer. "In Arizona, veteran teachers
with twenty-five to thirty years in are getting 'riffed.' And look at
those guys over there. A park employee I spoke to earlier said that
group's been here for weeks. Shit! That's a trailer park night-
mare."

Rick was referring to the cluttered campsite where I had seen
the kids kicking a ball. He said it contained eight people of three
generations, ranging from a matriarch to small children. They had
a pit bull and were all living in a small, dingy trailer and an aging
tent. I thought of the Joad family from *The Grapes of Wrath*. I
told Rick I wanted to speak with some of those folks and get their
story. Rick said he had tried and failed to get any of them to talk.
We polished off our beers and shook hands. I said I hoped to see
him on the road someday.

Night was coming in and the campground lights had clicked
on. I watched for the people from the crowded campsite to go to
the restroom. In time, three young men headed that way. I hur-
riedly gathered up my toiletries and towel and went over. My attempts to start a conversation in the bathroom with the men were

shunned. Rick had said their two older cars, both with New Hampshire plates, were their living rooms. That's how they escaped for a little privacy to converse or listen to music. I couldn't imagine living under such cramped conditions, especially with young children; yet, in the time I was camped there, I never heard a harsh word or loud noise from the crowded campsite. The quiet was actually disconcerting, like they were trying desperately not to be noticed.

The next morning I kicked it into gear early. Albuquerque was a long way away. What I took to be the eponymous needles of Needles, California, in a nearby rock formation, were interesting, jagged and columnar, but they looked no more like needles than the Tetons look like breasts. The mountains further east in Arizona, however, resembled "ramparts," just as Steinbeck had described them in *Charley*. They appeared to be a solid black wall, lacking detail in the deceptive light of dawn. I crossed Holy Moses Wash near Kingman. It was forty degrees and cloudy. To my dismay, I soon discovered all the rest areas in Arizona along I-40 were closed, possibly due to the recession.

In order to pass the time on the road, I searched unsuccessfully for saguaro cactus along the four-lane. I've always felt the saguaro, with their human-like appendages—some shadow boxing, others praying—are remarkable. Their only habitat in the world, the Sonoran desert, continues well north of Phoenix, and for miles giant cacti line the roads, waving from the rocky *bajadas*, gently sloping plains or slopes of unconsolidated sediment. An average mature saguaro—they can grow as old as two hundred years—has five arms and is thirty feet tall. Their spines are two inches long. I played golf once on a challenging course near Tucson. Saguaro grew close to the tees and wild hitters like me had slammed drives into their green flesh. Some were studded with several balls, like buttons on a stout man's vest. No one seemed anxious to try retrieving the balls. The cacti are so popular as landscaping elements that, to reduce theft, many have been implanted with microchips.

Saguaro can't tolerate cold and don't exist much above two thousand feet in elevation, so I knew better than to expect them anywhere near Flagstaff. It made me wonder where the closest one to I-40 was. And if that individual can survive, why can't one grow ten more feet to the north? It turned out saguaro do not grow as far north as I-40. I did a search later on Google Earth for that northernmost saguaro, but alas, the poor resolution in the pictures resulted in no resolution to my quest. However, further research revealed that the northernmost saguaro in the world, and the closest to Interstate 40, is just east of Lake Havasu, Arizona, a mere twenty miles below where I-40 passes through Topock. The Sonoran and Mojave deserts meet in northwestern Arizona. Near Lake Havasu, it is possible to see the iconic Sonoran saguaro and the iconic Mojave Joshua tree, the largest yucca species, with gigantic green "bottle-washers" spiraling around the ends of its branches, within a few hundred yards of each other.

Here is my first (and only) impression of Kingman, Arizona. It is a crossroads—a place on the way to more interesting places. Some towns try to capitalize on that fact. I saw a sign in Winnemucca, Nevada, that read, "Winnemucca, Halfway To Everywhere." Kingman claims to be "The Heart Of Route 66," and indeed, Arizona does have the longest intact stretch of the mother road, which once covered twenty-four hundred miles from Chicago to Los Angeles, much of the way along the thirty-fifth parallel. However, it's hard to sense the history of a road while stuck in what is proclaimed to be its heart and, after doing a little research, my initial impression was confirmed. Kingman began as a siding for the Atlantic and Pacific Railroad, located at a freshwater spring, and today provides access and amenities to I-40 travelers who are headed elsewhere.

Before I joined those travelers, I had some business to attend to. Standing in the men's room of the Conoco station, reading the sports page on the wall, I felt like I was being watched. A glance down the row revealed a stocky man in a ball cap and dark glasses. When I looked up, he averted his gaze, not from me, but from something behind me. A quick head swivel revealed a condom machine that I had somehow missed when I entered. No wonder the gentleman was staring. The machine offered a veritable smorgasbord of choices. There were your typical extenders, ticklers and even the glow-in-the-dark variety, but to my amazement there was one that, in case the sex was not hot enough, got, well, hot with applied friction.

I decided to save my quarters for some iced tea. I waited in line behind a woman in yellow shorts, fighting middle age spread and sporting a barbed-wire tattoo on her ankle. She called in a flat midwestern tone to a man wandering through the shelves, "Whatcha doin' beack there. I got you a Mountain Dew, now keatch up!" A few minutes later as I walked by a fire engine-red convertible, I noticed the same woman in the passenger seat, feeding Cheetos to a Chihuahua puppy.

In a parking lot for large rigs behind the gas station, I sat at Winnie's table and consumed a lunch of pretzels, cheese and nuts with, what else, a large can of ice cold AriZona Tea. No surprise it's a big seller in Arizona. Folks don't seem to know or care that AriZona Tea is made in Brooklyn, New York, by a guy named Don Vultaggio. It's kind of like Canada Dry Ginger Ale, which is made all over the globe. I noticed my straw cowboy hat had fallen off its hook and something pink was peeking out of the hatband. I plucked out a heart-shaped sticky note that had long since lost its stick, covered with x's and o's. For six months or so my wife and I had been hiding that note for each other in unlikely places.

This one really caught me by surprise because I had worn the hat several times on the trip and had not noticed the heart in the hatband. It was good timing. It made me smile and miss home—and ponder how *o* came to represent a hug and *x* came to represent a kiss—arms and lips, perhaps.

Driving toward the on-ramp for I-40, I swerved around a large bale of hay that had tumbled off the back of a flatbed trailer towed by a pickup with two cowboys inside, and passed a Toyota Prius pulled over by the highway patrol. I wanted to believe the hybrid had been speeding. I headed out of town on the freeway that replaced Route 66. Notice, no one sings about getting "kicks" on Interstate 40. The four-lane climbed up through fractured rock cliffs and brown bluffs with houses tucked on every ledge and in every crevice. The country around Kingman is rugged, rocky and, well, ugly. The flats were covered with creosote bushes and yellow-headed rabbit brush. The foliage was spare and resembled stubble on bad skin. I passed several exits simply named "Ranch Road," and saw a sign that said, "No Services for 57 miles." In time, I whisked over Rattlesnake Wash. It looked to be aptly named.

Crossing Arizona on I-40 is like attending an opera. Act One—after a very slow start in the form of Kingman, the western section of the highway builds to a dramatic ponderosa-pine-covered crescendo at seventy-three hundred feet in Flagstaff. Act Two—with the snowcapped San Francisco Peaks as a backdrop, provides exciting twists and turns as the highway begins its descent. Act Three—the route gets a bit flat and bland with the occasional gaudy flourish in the form of a Navajo trading center, but the climax, in the Painted Cliffs south of Window Rock, sends one away exhilarated.

I noticed I was already at five thousand feet in elevation with one hundred miles yet to go to Flagstaff. Because of its elevation,

Flagstaff is more mountain/foothill than desert. The first impression ones gets is of the dense ponderosa pines, both the sight and smell. Flagstaff sits in the largest contiguous ponderosa pine forest in the country. Ponderosa bark looks like nutty milk chocolate poured and cracking over dark chocolate. It smells like vanilla. The second impression is of the snowcapped San Francisco Peaks that tower over the city, and the third is the realization that one cannot get the "ding, da da ding, da da ding, da da ding, ding, ding—**ding!**" theme from the vintage TV show, *Bonanza*, featuring the Ponderosa Ranch, out of one's head. The fourth, possible only while driving with the windows open to clear the head of unwanted jingles, is that of the crisp, dry, high mountain air. And my final impression, formed while being almost blown over at a brief stop at a gas-and-goodies emporium, is that it can get windy as hell in Flagstaff and that the people, many of whom are Hispanic, are very pleasant.

It is for a ponderosa pine that the town was named. In 1855, Lieutenant Edward Beale was surveying a road from New Mexico to California. In what is now Flagstaff, he ordered his men to cut the limbs from a tree so that it could be used to fly the American flag. By 1886, Flagstaff was the largest city on the railroad line from Albuquerque to the West Coast. Flagstaff is notable for two other events. It is home to the Lowell Observatory, from which Pluto was discovered in 1930. (I'll bet the city mourned Pluto's recent demotion from planet to orbiting ball of ice.) In 1958, Flagstaff became the first municipality in the world to pass an ordinance to curtail outdoor lighting and preserve dark skies.

In Winslow, I met a really cool lady. Well, I can't say I actually met her, or even saw her, but we spoke and I know she was cool. I was fighting and losing my daily battle with the bladder and, with the rest areas closed and gated, couldn't find a convenient place to pull off and use the head in Winnie. By the time I bucketed into Winslow and found a Gulf station, I was, you might say, extremely ill at ease. I slammed into the station, found the men's room closed for cleaning and without hesitation pushed into the women's room thinking it was a small bathroom I could lock. It was not. It had several stalls. I shoved the door on the first one and stood with my back to the entrance, stall door open. My relief was short-lived. I heard someone enter and pause. I said, obviously without turning around, "I'm really sorry, forgive me. The men's room was closed and I was desperate."

"If you're desperate, you're desperate," this really cool woman said and immediately went into the stall next to me and closed the door. I finished, flushed and left after thanking the mystery woman for her understanding.

After that close encounter in Winslow, Arizona, with an awesome member of the female gender, I asked myself, as I drove out of town, who are the "seven women on my mind"? I thought of Dimmie, and six others who were colleagues, confidantes and/or just really good friends. Not one, to my knowledge, ever wanted to "own me." But all, I admire (and some, desire), respect and appreciate.

And, okay, I also thought about one guy as I drove across Arizona, my friend, Clint, who grew up on a ranch near the heart of present-day Scottsdale, Arizona. His father sold the ranch and the family moved to Jackson Hole in 1962 when Clint was a teenager. Clint has never worked for another person and equates interviewing for a job to begging. My friend has owned several businesses, from clothing stores to river rafting companies and currently runs a non-profit, providing western tours to mobility-impaired folks.

Clint often talks about change in the West and rails against lost freedoms. I remembered a conversation we had once in his pickup truck, pulling a trailer load of hay for his horses across an open rolling stretch of rural Wyoming. He was driving and had just reached behind his seat, pulled out two small bottles of red wine and, after handing me one, ripped the cap off the other.

"I like to drink while driving," Clint said. "Until a few years ago there was no open container law in Wyoming. People used to judge distance by beers, not miles. Casper was three—if you made it five and got tipsy, you were breakin' the law. It *was* against the law to drive drunk. If a cop saw or smelled booze and suspected you were blitzed, you did the walk. If you were fine, he'd say, 'be careful. Have a good day.'"

"Is there a downside to not allowing drinking while driving?" I asked.

"Yep. Causes people to chug-a-lug at closing time. It hasn't reduced drunk driving one iota. There are just too many people now—we are losing the rural lifestyle—and there's too many rules and regs to inhibit the few violators and protect the many." Clint said, polishing off his wine and tossing the empty behind my seat.

I noticed in passing that the Holbrook, Arizona, high school mascot is the Roadrunner. You gotta love the roadrunner. According to a website called DesertUSA, roadrunners are perfectly adapted to desert living and thrive in all the southwestern states. They are the size of a small chicken and quick enough to catch and eat rattlesnakes—by snatching the snake by the tail and cracking it like a whip—and they only fly for short bursts when in danger or traveling downhill. The birds prefer walking or running at speeds up to seventeen miles per hour. In fact, since they can only digest a snake a few inches at a time, they are often observed hurrying about, with a partially digested snake hanging out of their mouths. Members of the cuckoo family, roadrunners are also New Mexico's state bird. I wondered if Holbrook High School's football coach eschews going to the air and prefers the running game.

My first stop in New Mexico was at the visitors' center just across the border. Native Americans ran the clean, spacious facility at Manulito, west of Gallup. The soft American Indian flute music that permeated the building was welcoming and relaxing. It also reminded

A building at historic Menaul School in Albuquerque, New Mexico.

me I hadn't yet touched the wooden flute I was planning to master while on my trip.

Soon, "the Land of Enchantment" delivered an enchanting, unseasonal and, fortunately, brief snowstorm. The distant rock buttes, backlit in the snowy mist, were draped in gentle pastels. Visibility deteriorated; my wipers slapped slush off the windshield. I clung to the right lane, risking as little as possible.

After the snowstorm, as I was driving up and down the rolling desert hills of western New Mexico, I got a call from my daughter, Jamie. She shared the wonderful news that she was going to be a mother, and I was going to be a grandfather, both of us for the first time. The remaining miles to Albuquerque were consumed with happy thoughts of what wisdom I, the venerable granddad, would impart to my grandson. He was going to be raised in New York City and in southern France; clearly the very important wilderness component of his upbringing would default to me. I tried to recall if I had ever seen a pair of really small snowshoes.

I stayed with my friends, Lindsey and Laurie Gilbert, at the Presbyterian Menaul School in Albuquerque. Lindsey is the head of school and an old friend and colleague. Menaul is in the heart of the city, on seventeen acres of prime real estate. The salmon adobe buildings, though a little shopworn, are neat and functional, sitting beneath mature cottonwood, elm and mulberry trees. Founded in 1896, Menaul has a long history of racial tolerance and of serving Hispanic and American Indian students. Sixty percent of Menaul's students today identify themselves as belonging to a racial and ethnic minority. I taught a few classes and spoke at a school-wide chapel. The students were, for the most

A friendly Pumpkin on Halloween.

part, pleasant and interested. Several junior high kids expressed the strong desire to stow away in Winnie.

The next morning was Saturday and it was Halloween. My sister, Jeanne, flew in to Albuquerque to join me for the drive to Austin, Texas. The Gilberts drove us an hour west to tour the Acoma Pueblo. The ancient village, founded in the twelfth century and perched on top of a four-hundred-foot-high sandstone mesa, was chosen for its defenses against raiders. Acoma Pueblo is considered to be one of the oldest continually inhabited communities in America.

An Acoma native employee drove us up the steep mesa road in a van. Our first stop on the walking tour of the mesa top was the Catholic mission, San Esteban Rey, established in 1641. It was a clear day; the dazzling sun warmed us. From our lofty perch, we could see several other sheer-sided, sandstone buttes poking up into the indigo New Mexico sky. Our short, round, native tour guide, Conran, told us he was a member of the Pumpkin Clan. Conran was a warm and enthusiastic teacher. He spoke of several battles over the centuries that always seemed to result in some enemy or other—and sometimes vanquished Acoma warriors themselves—being tossed over the side of the butte. At one point, Conran pointed down to the flat terrain below the pueblo and said that his people once grew cotton there. He concluded by saying, "The Pueblo people no longer grow cotton, we just shop at Walmart."

At the conclusion of the tour, we thanked Conran and scrambled down the chiseled steps in the natural vertical crack dividing the face of the butte. Our last stop was in the nearby visitors' center admiring the display of delicate and intricate Acoma Pueblo pottery. That was

Kiva for religious rituals on Acoma Pueblo.

one Halloween with friends I shall always remember, both for the stunning location and for our animated and knowledgeable "Pumpkin." Jeanne and I returned to the Menaul School campus and prepared the Winnie, including converting the dinette into a second bed, for our impending exploration of the Lone Star State, Texas.

Chapter Twelve
Texas: Where West Meets South

I have said that Texas is a state of mind, but I think it is more than that. It is a mystique closely approximating a religion.

Travels with Charley

Except for the brief stretch of recently constructed I-40 that I mentioned, Steinbeck followed Route 66 from the Continental Divide, between Gallup and Grants in western New Mexico, to Amarillo, Texas. Once there, he spent several days getting Rocinante's window fixed; pebbles on a gravel road thrown up from a passing car had broken it. Poor Charley spent four days at a vet's office, while being treated for his recurring prostate problem. Elaine flew down and joined her husband. Elaine and John visited the ranch of a "rich friend" (Elaine's ex-brother-in-law). There they went quail hunting and celebrated Thanksgiving. After Amarillo, Steinbeck must have taken U.S. 87 to Lubbock, Texas, and U.S. 84 to Sweetwater.

Jeanne and I followed I-40 out of New Mexico and into Texas. The last little town in New Mexico, heading east, is Endee, a ghost town of collapsed adobe shops and shacks. Endee was not named for being the last town in New Mexico, but for the large ranch nearby called the ND. Even before Route 66 put it on the map, cowboys relied on Endee to slake their thirst in several saloons, as well as attend to other recreational requirements. After Highway 66 was routed through, Endee thrived. But with the advent of I-40 and demise of 66, Endee met its end.

We entered the Texas panhandle and lost an hour to the Central Time Zone. The terrain had that one-cow-per-ten-acre look with ranches stretching out to low mesas in the distance. A roadside billboard advertised "Rodeopia—a Cowboy's Utopia." We

passed the Jesus Christ is Lord
Travel Center and the town of
Happy, Texas. The scent in the air
was eau de bovine. Not a bad
smell, really. Whereas flat terrain
covered with brown grasses
stretching to distant juniper and

Palo Duro State Park.

pinion-covered pink rock buttes had seemed wrong, or disen-
chanting, for eastern New Mexico, it seemed right for western
Texas. Perhaps that's because western Texas doesn't make pre-
tenses about being anything but cow-and-horse country. I read of
one Texas panhandle ranch, the Capital Freehold Land and In-
vestment Company, whose boundaries in 1885 stretched forty-
five by one hundred and ninety-five miles, encompassing three
million acres of Deaf Smith County.

We camped at Palo Duro State Park, near the town of
Canyon, south of Amarillo. A brown-and-white longhorn steer
lounged near the entrance to the park. Palo Duro is a rugged and
deep gouge cut by the Red River with several scrub-dotted tiers of
rock leading down to the cottonwood-lined stream—a welcome
break from the relatively monotonous ranch and farm country
surrounding the canyon. We crawled down a steep, winding road
to the bottom of the gorge. Although the trip had gone off without a hitch thus far, I managed to turn so tightly into our campground that I damaged my trailer hitch. Fortunately, it turned out
to be a part that is important, but not critical, which we later had
fixed near Austin.

The next morning in Amarillo, Jeanne and I had a packed
agenda, especially considering we needed to get to Abilene that
evening. We had breakfast at a Starbucks. I asked a rather incon-
gruous, flamboyantly dressed, non-fat male barista ("Don't say
skinny latte, that's not correct—we say non-fat.") for directions to

the main library in Amarillo. As we were leaving, a man I had not spoken with, or even noticed, got up from his table and clarified the barista's rather hazy directions. That was taking "nice" to a whole new level. On the way to the library, we saw the Church of the

A steer guards the entrance to Palo Duro State Park.

Cowboy—The Arena, a large, white structure with a cross on the roof, surrounded by red-metal corrals.

Steinbeck's description of Texas in *Travels with Charley* is brilliant. Because of his wife, Steinbeck came to know the state and its inhabitants very well. Elaine was born in Texas, as was her first husband, the Hollywood actor Zachary Scott. Steinbeck joked about the Lone Star State's singular right to secede at will, and how Texans love to threaten to do so, but are offended at the slightest suggestion that they should. Gayle, the reference librarian at the main branch of the Amarillo Public Library, laughed when I read her that passage from *Travels with Charley*. She said it is still true today. I learned later that Texas Governor Rick Perry had recently threatened to secede from the union at a "Tea Party" gathering in his state.

Steinbeck wrote about the intense personal energy of Texans in the 1960s, and the importance of football and politics. He claimed a Texan couldn't get elected to public office if he didn't own a ranch and wear the appropriate boots and hat. He commented on the paradoxical and varied nature of Texas, writing in *Charley,* "Everything in Texas is likely to be cancelled by something else." And later, "I have moved over a great part of Texas and I know that within its borders I have seen just about as many kinds of country, contour, climate and conformation as there are in the world, saving only the Arctic, and a good north wind can even bring the icy breath down."

In the reference section of the library, I searched 1960 phone books looking for glass repair shops, as well as indexes of newspaper articles. (The advertisement for the Princess phone on the back of the book claimed, "It's little, it's lovely, it lights.") Steinbeck was apparently very successful at maintaining anonymity in the Amarillo area. I found no media evidence of his extended stay in November 1960.

Starting the fire that Max later walked into.

I did find an ironic statement by Zachary Scott, in an earlier newspaper article, about the enduring strength of his marriage to Elaine Scott (later Elaine Steinbeck).

Let me begin this part of the Texas tale by saying no animals were harmed in the following events. Max had his worst day of the trip at Palo Duro. First, he fell out of the car at a nearby gas station. Often, when I left him in the car, he would stand on his hind legs and put his forepaws on the back door so he could see out the window. Sometimes, in my haste, I would not notice him through the tinted glass and, when I opened the door, he would scramble to regain his balance. This time he fell out—straight to the pavement. Fortunately, I broke his fall with my foot, scooped him up and checked him over. He was fine, for the time being. But Max's terrible, horrible, very bad day was far from over.

That night, camped at Palo Duro, Jeanne and I were enjoying my first fire of the entire journey. While I went to the trailer for supplies, I handed Jeanne Max's expandable leash and Max did a crazy thing. He walked right into the fire, slightly singeing his beautiful white coat on the side, before Jeanne could reel him in. While I observed Max's trial by fire in helpless horror, the accusations of my ex-wife rushed back. Fortunately, he did not burst into flames and wasn't hurt a bit. His little feet didn't even seem burned or tender afterwards. He did, however, smell smoky for several days. Jeanne, a former blonde herself, pronounced

Max after his very bad day—singed side down.

Max the "blonde" of the dog set. I had to admit it was a pretty doggone dumb dog thing to do. Later that night, perhaps out of relief, or a deep sense of connection with our canine brethren, Jeanne and I sat by the fire and howled at the full moon. Max just stared at us like we were the lunatics.

The country south of Amarillo was more of the same, ranch meadows and farm fields with the occasional high promontory or low riparian area. We chose U.S. 70 and 62 to avoid I-27 south of Amarillo and bypass Lubbock. Near Floydada, there was so much cotton from nearby fields covering the roads that, when we stopped, we noticed the car's mud flaps were adorned with a row of cotton tassels. Trees were sparse. We saw the occasional house and attendant barn. The roads were straight, flat and well maintained, and there was rarely a car in sight. The sky was clear, the winds were mild and the temperatures, though it had been cold the night before, were in the mid-seventies. On State 207, between Ralls and Post, a mill town for Post Cereal, we saw a sign for a viewpoint for Duffy's Peak. Jeanne and I stopped and jumped out of the rig for a look. All we could make out was a tree-covered uplift, a bump really. "Where's the peak?" I asked. Jeanne shrugged and squinted, as if squinting might lift the uplift a bit more.

Several minutes went by, without a single car passing. Then, a white pickup approached from the north. As it passed, a cowboy hat visible above the driver's seat, Jeanne waved and called out, "Howdy!" And as it disappeared over the next bump, she hollered, "Woo hoo, that was exciting!"

Near Snyder, we saw the Texas version of a wind

Worst Little RV Park in Texas.

farm. Legions of the gangling, long-limbed devices stretched on for miles, above cultivated fields. I commented that had Don Quixote encountered such a phalanx of "outrageous giants" marching off to the horizon, he would have been compelled by honor to engage them in battle, and the overwhelming number of windmills would have no doubt driven him from his normal condition of pleasantly deranged to completely bonkers.

Below Sweetwater, Steinbeck drove through Balinger, Austin and, after bypassing Houston, Beaumont. As was often the case when he crossed a state from north to south on the bias, he followed country roads, as did we. Although too numerous to mention, such roads are a fine way to see the land. I appreciated having my sister to pass the time with, making small talk as we drove the seemingly endless state of Texas. As Steinbeck wrote in *Charley*, "Once you are in Texas it seems to take forever to get out, and some people never make it."

"Man, its flat out in these parts," Jeanne said.

"Where the hell are we?" I asked.

"Beats me. Oh look, a Stuckey's. There are still Stuckey's around. How 'bout that?"

"Maybe we should stop for a pecan log roll," I suggested. "Remember how Jim (a family friend we often accompanied on western ski trips) could drive all night and hated to stop?"

"Yeah, no pecan rolls for Jim, a few saltines and some gamey cheese, and he would just keep going," Jeanne said, smiling and looking out the window.

We cruised through Sweetwater. A large billboard for a western wear store shouted, "Where fit happens!" Just beyond Sweetwater, we passed Stink Creek Road. The terrain around Sweetwater is rolling and tree-covered. We pulled in at a TA Truck Stop. After

Driving the high road.

the usual needs were taken care of for man, woman, beast and machine, we visited the gift shop and Jeanne considered purchasing the Elvis Birdhouse and the Armadillo on a Plank. She settled for a really neat pen. A huge harvest moon was rising, and we reined in for the day just short of Abilene in Tye. I had discovered the Tye RV Park in Betty's database. I expected interstate traffic noise in RV parks, and trains near highways and thus near RV parks are pretty commonplace, but the manager of the Tye park failed to mention we would be camped right under an ear-splitting and trailer-rattling flight path for Tye Air Force Base. Fortunately for us, the Tye flyboys (and girls) don't fly much past 9:00 p.m.

It was in Abilene that I sensed we had passed from the West into the South. Typical of the South, religious zeal was much more overt. After the night in the worst little RV park in Texas, we went to a Flying J in Abilene for breakfast. We saw a motor home with Texas plates, sporting a cross made from tiny white lights on the bumper. Churches, mostly Baptist and/or varying degrees of fundamentalist, were once again ubiquitous. We were back in the Bible Belt.

Often during our time together, especially while I was driving, I'd ask Jeanne to jot down interesting things she observed or that I pointed out. That proved to be much safer than my shaky method of writing while steering. This is her entry in my journal from that morning, "Flying J—Abilene, Nov. 3rd, BIG ASS breakfast (enough for GZ, JZ, and Max Z—and then some), great service."

Jeanne included, I'm pleased to say, a report from the ladies room—a rich area for observation sadly lacking in my logs (with the exception, of course, of my bold infiltration in Winslow, Arizona). Her journal entry continued, "This exchange between a prisoner and her guard in the ladies room, as guard removed handcuffs so prisoner could sit down. 'I didn't scratch you, did I, honey?' the guard asked. 'No, no thanks very much....'" The journal entry was signed Cub Reporter—J. Zeigler.

I found two post cards in the truck stop gift store that said, "Don't Mess with Texas," a slogan that apparently began as an anti-litter campaign and then won wider appeal. As we were paying for breakfast and my post cards, Minnie—petite, middle-aged and not to be messed with—who worked the cash register said, "Ah know that some people who ask for the senior discount ain't seniors. Ah tell them to take their dang discount right out the door." Guess "ah" passed Minnie's scrutiny. "Ah" got the discount.

On the move again, we saw a sign that read, "Big Rigs Lube: Change is Good." The only hills around Abilene were man-made, where the freeway was humped up to allow a road to pass underneath. It was overcast and in the low fifties. We explored Abilene a bit and on Pine Street passed a misspelled sign tacked to a pile of bucked up logs, "Far Wood Fer Sale."

I learned this about Texas: just as soon as you feel you have her pegged, she changes. In general, the state is more lush and tree-covered, often with pin oaks, than expected. In terms of landscape, there are many faces to Texas, but the people present only one—exceptionally friendly and helpful. After a stop at a convenience store outside of Abilene, where I was warmly greeted by all on my way in and out, I mentioned to Jeanne that Texans are almost disarmingly friendly. Texans don't just say, "Hi," when they greet you, they sincerely want to know how you're doing. Texans give the impression that, after first meeting, a brief chat could lead directly into an invitation to dinner in their homes. Jeanne was driving now, so I read a *Travels with Charley* quote that indicated Steinbeck had a similar notion: "...I know no place where hospitality is practiced so fervently as in Texas."

Then my sis and I had one of those moments that can only transpire between close members of the same family. She asked why the panel on the front of the Bambi had been replaced in Salt Lake City just prior to the long trip. I began, "We were planning to camp at a lake and I stopped for gas near Pinedale, Wyoming and..."

I was obviously using a very familiar cadence because Jeanne filled in my sentence without missing a beat, "...and some—dumb—S.O.B.," exactly as Dad would have said it. We looked at each other and cracked up.

"It's true, some—dumb—S.O.B. pulled in after me at an adjacent gas pump and parked his Volvo so close that his rear driver's-side door was open in my trailer's line of travel. I was preoccupied by the S.O.B.'s kids running in front of my car, and failed to check to see if I had the clearance to proceed. Crunch—*cha-ching*, a twenty-six hundred dollar ding on the Bambi," I said.

The terrain south of Abilene was green, hilly country, with wet lowlands—lush for Texas. Deciduous trees surrounded fields of round hay bales and pastures full of horses. About halfway between Abilene and Austin, we were approaching Goldwaite while listening to the Lucinda Williams song "If Wishes Were Horses" on a CD. Jeanne improvised, crooning, "If wishes were horses, I'd have me a ranch in Goldwaite, Texas." We were out of beer, so I went in a small store, Oliver's Place, to buy a six-pack. The proprietor was thin, sported a goatee and looked to be in his mid-forties. He had blue eyes and wore a Texas Longhorns ball cap. When I inquired about beer, he informed me, in a wry tone, that it was a "dry county." He obviously was not pleased about that fact. "The Baptists around here drive me nuts," he said.

I told him an old joke that can be applied to any teetotaler sect. "Do you know the best way to insure that your Baptist buddy doesn't drink your beer on a fishing trip? Take two Baptists with you."

"That's the truth," he said emphatically. "Baptists around here will drive fifty miles to Walmart to avoid being seen buying their beer and wine."

"Wow. That's wanting it pretty bad. Can't get beer and alcohol sales passed here?" I asked.

"My mom is my partner in this store." He pointed to a woman behind the counter in a yellow sweatshirt, with her back to us, talking on the phone. "Her recent petition to become a wet county lost by seven votes. I know every one of those seven—and they all drink! Guy wrote a letter to the editor of the paper attacking my mother. His wife was secretly photographed recently on someone's cell phone. She was buying wine at Walmart."

"Do you think it's about underage drinking?"

"Well, that's what they claim. But kids are going to get it somehow. I know I did when I was seventeen. I tell my seventeen-year-old daughter to drink at home. I like a few beers, but hey, I'm no drunk. It's the hypocrisy I hate."

I felt sorry for the guy and sensed he was a kindred spirit—I myself have very little tolerance for hypocrisy of any kind. Plus, I like a few beers, too. But I'm no drunk. I bought a sympathy six-pack of Diet Coke I didn't really need.

Back in the car, after a few miles, I decided it was time to liven things up a bit. My sister is married to a great guy, Kipp Greene; they have no children. Jeanne, like our Dad, is a gifted and award-winning teacher and a passionate advocate for kids. I informed Jeanne, in a conversational tone to conceal my subterfuge, that David, our brother, who Jeanne often had contretemps with as a child, had taken his eleven-year-old son, Jake, on a shooting outing with David's older boy, Garrett, a Marine. I reported David and Garrett had encouraged Jake to shoot a rifle at his teddy bear to "help him get more comfortable with guns." Now this is the same bright and sensitive nephew that my sister taught to knit while he visited her the previous summer. I thought my story might get a rise out of Jeanne. It did. I'm going to say it was a good fifteen-to-twenty-mile rise.

Later, we simultaneously started singing "Dead Skunk in the Middle of the Road…." Whew! At the same time! And speaking of bad odors, we agreed that siblings did not have to ask to be excused after burping, or worse. Just open the window as required.

We passed vineyards and pecan groves and saw ads for sweet tea. Every cemetery had a sign by the highway and an arrow pointing the direction to the burial grounds. Road signs for life and death, I thought. Right this way to the afterlife. When you're spending time with a sibling, and talk turns inevitably to beloved parents who are gone, you find yourself wishing, "If only there were an afterlife." My sister brought me out of my melancholy with characteristic humor when we passed yet another church, "Hmmm. Lone Wolf Assembly. Hard to assemble when you're a lone wolf."

Near Austin it was sixty-eight degrees, with not a cloud in the sky. We were hitting more four-lane highways as we approached the city. We saw a tan and smiling, but extremely rumpled, fellow panhandling at an interchange. His hand-scrawled sign read, "Why lie? I need beer, women and chicken wings." The mowed grass in the median was a brilliant green for so late in the fall.

Far and away, the most befuddling aspect to traveling Texas superhighways is the on/off ramp system. It is so confusing I'm not certain I can describe it. Imagine you are traveling on a two-lane frontage road, to the left of the oncoming-traffic side of the highway. When you encounter an off-ramp from the highway, the exiting traffic dumps right into, *and crosses,* your line of travel, and you are expected to yield. And in case you haven't noticed, folks who have been traveling, say, seventy-five miles an hour on an interstate don't exactly slow down on the exit ramps. It feels like suddenly being thrust into the middle of the Indy 500, going the wrong way. In general, the best part of driving in Texas is, again, the inherent friendliness. People will pull over and drive on the shoulder on a hill if they feel they are slowing you down behind them. There are signs everywhere along the smaller highways that read, "Drive Friendly." Nice idea. But it doesn't seem to apply on the freeway-ramp system. Those urban Texas cowboys bearing down on me, and blasting their horns when I forgot to yield, did not look or sound friendly.

We arrived in Austin, but kept going south, through the city on I-35, to a suburb called Buda. I had an appointment to get the hitch fixed and a few other minor repairs done to Winnie at the Camper Clinic in Buda. Lucinda, the tough, silver-haired service and repairs boss, talked me into a bath for the Bambi, even though the price was roughly equivalent to a rather expensive spa visit.

Jeanne and I explored Austin. After checking into a motel, our first stop was the "bat bridge." The Congress Avenue Bridge spans the (other) Colorado River and leads to an ultra-modern downtown skyline framing a majestic, domed capital building constructed of "sunset red" granite. Over a million Mexican free-tailed bats spend summer and fall days hanging out under the bridge. We watched the hordes fly out on cue at dusk and form a billowing black cloud. Within minutes there could not have been a mosquito or moth within one hundred miles of the bridge. Some bats can consume one thousand mosquitoes per hour, greatly reducing the need for chemical controls. After the bat show, we caught our own chow at the Iron Works, a funky ribs place, in an old blacksmith shop downtown. It was smokin' good!

The next morning, I carried Betty in my hand so she could guide us as we walked through downtown Austin to the O. Henry Museum, a quaint little cottage the famous author rented in 1893 with his wife, Athol, and daughter, Margaret. We sat outside the cottage for a while, and waited for the museum to open. The day was sunny and warm, but pleasant, not oppressive. At the museum, we learned that the author, whose given name was William Sydney Porter, once spent time in jail on federal charges of embezzlement. I opined to the rather humorless tour guide and the small group of gathered fellow tourists that O. Henry must be one of the most famous and successful felons in the history of American letters. Our guide was not amused. I later learned that Steinbeck narrated a film, released in 1952, titled *Full House,* which dramatized five of O. Henry's stories from his New York period (1902–10).

Over lunch in a stylish Tex/Mex restaurant, I asked Jeanne what she had observed about Americans from her time on the journey. She said that for every "wacko-cracker" dad who wants his own reality show, there are thousands of hard-working, warm, lovely people who simply aren't sensational enough to make the local news.

After lunch, I dropped Jeanne at the Austin airport for her flight home to Salt Lake City. Then I drove to the Camper Clinic

View of downtown Austin from on top of the "bat bridge."

and made arrangements to leave Winnie with them, so I didn't have to deal with her in downtown New Orleans. I got directions from an RV salesman to some back roads that cut the corner from Buda to I-10, which would take us through Houston and on to Beaumont, Texas, on the coast, where Steinbeck spent the night.

Mid-afternoon, we left Buda and headed toward Bastrop. The air was warm; I opened the sunroof just before blasting through a hatch of small moths. Several blew in and landed on the front seat. The pretty little insects were smaller than a quarter and had brown-and-black wings with white dots.

I connected with I-10 west of Houston and then hit Houston at the very worst time of day—rush hour—a misnomer if I've ever heard one. I crept through the heart of that mammoth metropolis for well over an hour. After finally breaking away from Houston, I passed the north end of Galveston Bay in the dark and then saw a sign for Winnie, Texas. I later learned that Winnie, founded in 1895 and named for Fox Winnie, a railroad contractor, is the home of the Texas Rice Festival every October..

On I-10, we made our miles to Beaumont, near exit 851, which, of course, means it is eight hundred and fifty-one miles from the western border of Texas and still not in Louisiana, by 7:30 p.m. An enormous pumpkin of a moon hung over the gulf. After checking in to the Super 8 Motel and taking care of the needs of the little guy, I walked across a shopping mall parking lot to Joe's Crab Shack, with three things on my mind: seafood, beer and baseball. That is, until I met a charming barkeep named Krista. I knew Krista was local and I was surely back in the South when I heard her utter, "Do what?" as a way of asking, "Say that again, please." Krista explained that Beaumont is just a "huge small town of 250,000." She was twenty-three and had been a bartender for five years. Four little Texans sat near the other end of the wooden bar, in their baseball uniforms, and watched the World Series game while bantering with Krista. I overheard one remark about the Joe's Crab Shack slogan "Bite Me" stretched across her chest. The boys were swilling something out of a dark bottle—root beer perhaps. When I suggested that the characters at the other end of the bar might have had too much to drink, Krista said they had been cut off after one beer. "Texas law, if you can't see over the bar, you only get one beer."

The Yankees' pitcher struck out a Philadelphia Phillies batter and the crowd erupted, both on the screen and in the bar. Krista said folks from Beaumont don't necessarily root for the Yankees, but they liked the pitcher because he used to play for the Houston Astros.

Krista had all the well-known qualities of a southern belle. She was blonde, cute and warm as a southern summer night. She also possessed the best-kept secret of many southern belles; she was very smart. *Of Mice and Men* was her favorite book in high school. She really got the relationship, the dream, the tragedy. She wrote several English papers about it. When I told her it was one of Steinbeck's most banned and burned books, she said she remembered parents of classmates who complained to the school about the book's language.

I overheard Krista, by the kitchen door, commiserating with an exasperated co-worker in an "I'm Feeling Crabby" T-shirt, who had been jerked around by a large group of customers at a table, and then given a two-buck tip. The rest of their brief conversation was drowned out by the televised crowd's reaction to a base hit.

"Pretty tough to be treated like that," Krista said to me when she returned to the bar, "when you're only making $2.16 an hour, plus tips."

I paid my bill and tipped, well, perhaps a *little* bit more than usual, and was preparing to leave when Krista said, "Hey, hold on. You haven't answered the Joe's question of the day."

"I'll bite," I said, I hoped with noticeable irony. "What is it?"

"If you were an animal, what animal would you be?"

I had thought about this before, so I answered without hesitation, "A golden retriever."

"Why?"

"Well, because I'm loyal, friendly and love attention. You?"

"I answered earlier when I came to work. I chose a puppy because I'm loyal, playful and a people person." She smiled at me. "Maybe in the next life we can be dogs together. Hey, wait a minute, don't go yet, I've got an idea." She went to the little store at the front of the restaurant.

When Krista returned, she "knocked it out of the park" in terms of Texas hospitality. She told me that Texans "bleed orange" for the Longhorns and presented me with a gift bag. Inside was an orange Joe's Crab Shack T-shirt. I thanked her, we hugged and I left, all aglow. In fact, the next day, I glowed orange in my new shirt all the way to New Orleans.

Chapter Thirteen
Big Easy Ain't So Easy Anymore

While I was still in Texas, late in 1960, the incident most reported and pictured in the newspapers was the matriculation of a couple of tiny Negro children in a New Orleans School. What made the newsmen love the story was a group of stout middle-aged women who, by some curious definition of the word "mother," gathered every day to scream invectives at children.

Travels with Charley

There was something odd about the baseball game on the TV behind the counter. Upon closer examination, I realized it was a cricket match. The clerk who was checking me out of the Beaumont Super 8 Motel explained that the game was being broadcast from his homeland, India, and that the score was very close. His team only needed nineteen runs from seventeen balls to win. He quickly explained how a team gets a run, or several for that matter. It has to do with how many times the two players on the offense can exchange places, over the short distance between wickets, while a single hit is in play, before the ball is retrieved by the defensive team. We Americans find cricket a bit silly, but imagine if one of our baseball players could score multiple runs on a single solid hit alone. It might make the game more interesting. I wished the clerk and his team well, loaded up Max and my gear, and programmed Betty for New Orleans.

Somewhere around Exit 875 on I-10, Texas stopped messin' with me and I entered the whole different world of Louisiana. My first gas stop was just over the state line at a Flying J. I held the door for a large, slow-moving, elderly black woman in a floral dress. I told her I was the Flying J greeter and wished her a good morning. "Well, thank you very much. Have a blessed day," she said. On such a beautiful day in Louisiana, how could I not?

After crossing the Black Bayou, I left the interstate and drove around in the town of Sulphur, Louisiana, in search of some authentic Cajun food for lunch. I passed the Son Shine Christian Book Store and found Richard's (Ree-shard's) Boudin and Seafood. Richard's is in a low, red-metal building, with a monster crawfish perched above a sign

Richard's Boudin and Seafood in Sulphur, Louisiana.

that promises, "Fine Cajun Dining." Several local pickup trucks parked outside indicated I had chosen the right place. As I entered, I noticed a placard that said, "God Bless Us Cajuns." Richard's dining area was divided between two spaces. There were a few tables in the entryway, but it was mostly taken up by the counter for the cash register, and a large display cooler chock full of Cajun treats for cooking at home. I entered the second dining area and sat alone beside a snapping turtle and gator perched on a shelf above my chair. Most of the other tables were occupied. While ordering my crawfish peaux boy, I asked the sweet, slender, forty-something waitress about boudin (boo-dan). She immediately returned with a sizable sample of the pork-liver and heart-meat sausage. After an exploratory bite, I slipped the remainder into my pocket (in a napkin) so as not to offend, and to allow Max to experience this delicacy.

At the table behind me, three small-business types were talking guns. One hundred and one guns to be exact—that's what the primary yakker said made up his collection—12, 16, 28 and miscellaneous other gauges—and that didn't include his pistols. "When I die, she can sell em' all," he said.

I devoured my delicious fried-crawfish sandwich, coleslaw and iced tea ("Sweet or un, hon?" the waitress had asked when I ordered my tea) and then snapped a picture of the stuffed gator, while commenting about being a "dumb tourist" to a lone female diner—sweet, forty-something but not so slender—sitting nearby. She told me where I could go in Lafayette for even better Cajun food and an even larger stuffed gator.

Dining companions at Richard's.

Between Sulphur and Lafayette I noticed something that had become familiar while on this cruise around America, yet another sign for a Lion's Den Adult Superstore. My curiosity was piqued about what it meant to be part of a chain of porn stores. Also, I remembered my friend, Rodney, whom I had met in New York, saying the gambling industry did better in tough times. I wondered if that held true for the pornography business. After all, I thought, this trip is about pushing my boundaries and providing a balanced view of America; why not see if I could get an interview in a Lion's Den? Plus, it wasn't like I had never been in a porn shop before. I smiled, remembering a time when I left Dimmie in the car and went into an adult store to get a joke gift for a friend's bachelor party. When I came out, Dimmie had the windows up and the car doors locked with the engine off, in June, in Georgia. This low-slung Lion's Den was in a wooden building with no windows. A sign above the opaque door said, "The Lion's Den, Your One Stop Shop for Adult Fun. Must be 18 years or older."

It was air-conditioned and cool inside. You can imagine the collection of DVDs and various and sundry toys and potions. The Den was brightly lit, clean, and very well organized by fetish. Several silent men, with their heads down, perused the merchandise. A young, heavy-set woman stood at the counter. When I approached and spoke, she looked stunned, like it was the first time that had ever happened. An older, short, salt-and-pepper-haired woman, perhaps in her early fifties, turned her chair around at the desk behind the counter and smiled. She was dressed for business in a black and white pants suit and was obviously the owner. She seemed pleased to have an "adult" conversation.

The owner informed me that there were thirty-nine stores in the Lion's Den national chain, all with a similar format. I asked her about the impact of the recession on her business, and she said the area had been relatively recession-proof because of Katrina money pouring into southern Louisiana. But recently, as that money slowed, business had been off by about 20 percent. I asked if she thought folks felt better about Obama than the Bush administration, which had been criticized for reacting so slowly to the Katrina crisis. Her response was very interesting. She informed me that there was a company-wide policy that no politics ever be discussed in the stores because that can deteriorate into an anti-porn rant. The mistress of this Lion's Den said she had been lucky out in rural Louisiana, but some of the stores close to urban areas had been picketed twenty-four hours a day, seven days a week, for months at a time. "Now, that," she said, "will hurt your business, big time, more than any economic downturn."

Back on the highway a few minutes later, it occurred to me that all that picketing of the Dens was a little like throwing the lions to the Christians. That was a recurring problem on the trip; I always thought of the best lines too late, with Max as the only audience to try them out on.

Sailing across what was to be my last state on the journey, before turning toward home, brought a great sense of relief and freedom. It was good to know I had no more scheduled appointments or commitments. I could discover the Pelican State at my leisure. I cruised along fourteen miles of interstate-on-stilts across Henderson Swamp, part of the Atchafalaya Basin, east of

Lafayette. Bald cypress trees, buttressed by knees, shot up out of the blue-gray water; hawks perched on high limbs. An occasional swamp boat motored around the tiny islands; herons and egrets worked the shallows, while pelicans bobbed on the surface. It was a beautiful balmy-weather day. In the spirit of Louisiana, I listened to gospel music on the radio. "Only God's rain is fallin' down on me," a choir sang.

After traveling without a major incident for over twelve thousand miles, I felt it was time to pay my respects to St. Christopher, so I had booked a room in the Best Western-St. Christopher Hotel in New Orleans, just two blocks from the French Quarter. I arrived at the hotel at dusk. The St. Christopher resides in an historic brick edifice built on property Paul Tulane gave to Tulane University in 1882. The original pink bricks were exposed, and surrounded the floor-to-ceiling windows in the comfortable and well-appointed rooms.

It bears repeating what preoccupied Steinbeck in late November 1960 when he visited New Orleans. It was a vicious display of bigotry recorded in the national media as the "cheerleaders," adult white women who heckled and harassed small black children attempting to integrate the public schools. I visited the main branch of the New Orleans Public Library and studied both the white and the black press from around November 14, 1960, the first day of federally mandated desegregation. Thirty percent of white students were absent from school, most with parental consent, during the first few days of integration. *The Louisianan Weekly,* an African-American newspaper, described the protest activity as "jeers, catcalls, screaming uncomplimentary epithets, and waving crudely printed, misspelled signs." *The Times-Picayune* described the greeting U.S. Marshalls received while escorting the "negro children" to schools as "hooting and hollering, booing and name-calling, but without the threat of violence." What is most striking about newspaper accounts of the events in that pivotal time is that black children, and their parents, all stated that they were not afraid. I could find no specific mention of the word "cheerleader." In fact, no one I spoke to in New Orleans, black or white, remembered that ironic moniker in association with the tumultuous times of 1960.

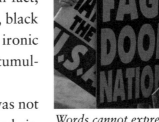

Words cannot express...

It was clear that, in 2009, I was not going to witness the sort of overt and virulent bigotry in New Orleans—now considered one of the most tolerant and diverse of American cities—that Steinbeck did. However, there *were* ads running on local television featuring sports celebrities calling for interracial tolerance in the region. Sean Olivier of Olivier's Creole Restaurant, perhaps in his mid-forties, and with the drop-dead handsome appeal typical of mixed-race people (think Tiger and Barack), informed me that when he stands outside his father's French Quarter restaurant in a shirt and tie, some white visitors cross the street to avoid him. Pierre La France, also a Creole of color, who had driven cabs in New Orleans for over forty years, never attended an integrated school as a child. "New Orleans was more liberated before the Civil War. Before the war, Creoles were known as *Les Gens de Couleur Libres*— Free People of Color. It was the Protestants brought Jim Crow during reconstruction after the civil war," Pierre said. "All that separate but equal crap started then." He remembered riding on the bus to baseball games and, when white boys entered, he was expected to move to the back. "My children and grandchildren wouldn't stand for it today. Things have changed, thank God. Obama is history in the makin.' But it was two hundred years of captivity and we're still not near all the way there."

Today, it is the Baptist church leader who hosts the "Jews Killed Jesus" and "God Hates Fags" websites, who, in my opinion, represents the frontline of vicious bigotry. In

The St. Charles Street Trolley in New Orleans.

fact, while in New Orleans, I learned he was planning a protest at the pending memorial service in the aftermath of the Fort Hood, Texas, massacre. The stated reason for the protest—the U.S. military was "fag-infested." My brother, David, and I have both attended events that were protested by this infamous group—angelic-looking little children holding signs that read, "God Hates Fags"—sad, sad indeed. Two separate friends who have lived near Topeka, Kansas, the headquarters for the "church," have told me that these bigots are scary and dangerous. They apparently get very close to passersby and spit invective into their faces. One father of a slain soldier, whose funeral the group protested, brought a case that went all the way to the U.S. Supreme Court. The case challenged the protesters' right to sully such a sacred and solemn ceremony. The outcome was pending as of this writing.

I was curious about the lingering effect of Hurricane Katrina. Sean Olivier said it was depressing—his mother's house was the only one on her block that had been reoccupied at that time. Many houses were still being bulldozed because it was often cheaper than trying to remodel. My second day in New Orleans, on a walk in search of a library out along the St. Charles Street trolley line, I stopped and spoke with a short, powerfully built, African-American man named Philip, who was painting an iron fence in front of a brick house. Philip looked to be in his early thirties and wore a stud in each ear. His hair was cropped short.

He said when Katrina was bearing down on New Orleans his sister-in-law talked everyone into leaving the family home in the Lower Ninth Ward. After the storm, it was too dangerous to return for three days. When they finally did return, they

Lord, the Cajun food was good at Court of Two Sisters!

found water in the house over their heads. "Were you glad you left?" I asked.

"I was glad I left, but I wanted to come back home, bad," Philip said.

"Has the city fully recovered?"

"I'd say New Orleans is still only roughly 75 percent back to normal." Phillip said. "But, God willing, it'll happen, eventually."

"And they call it the Big Easy," I said.

Turning back to his painting Philip sighed and said, "Big Easy ain't so easy anymore."

I took the trolley back toward my hotel. The windows were down and sun-warmed air rushed into the crowded car. I sat across from two short women dressed as the gnomes made famous by Travelocity ads. They chatted excitedly with two men seated in front of them who were dressed like cops from the TV show *Reno 911*. They were all participants in an urban race, a sort of citywide scavenger hunt. As we whizzed by a street corner, one of the gnomes pointed out the window at a man dressed like an eighties aerobics instructor and said, "There's the guy who won Seattle."

The short, stout, African-American driver of the trolley was barking orders and throwing people around with her abrupt starts. As we jerked away from a brief stop, a woman sitting behind me said, "Someone took the sunshine out of *her* day."

After completing my own urban race, partially on the trolley but mostly on foot, searching for the main library and information about desegregation, I treated myself at Court of Two Sisters. It was, in fact, my sister who insisted I try the jazz brunch there.

A ferry docks on the Mississippi River in New Orleans.

I arrived about 2:00 p.m.; the crowd had thinned out, but a jazz trio was still playing for the remaining diners. I sat outside on a vine-covered patio. Birds twittered about picking over crumbs. I could hear riverboats tooting in the distance. Accompanied by tunes such as "It Had to be You" and "As Time Goes By," I dug in—to what turned out to be the most wonderful meal of my American odyssey: jambalaya, turtle soup, Cajun corn salad, pasta seafood, muffuletta, boiled crawfish and shrimp, Andouille sausage, maque choux—all followed by bread pudding and the deepest, darkest, most remarkable chicory coffee. I remember thinking, while sipping, even the coffee is delicious.

Next on the agenda was a nap at the hotel to sleep off my Cajun meal. While I was conked out, a cool, still evening arrived in New Orleans, as if it had been carried in on the current of the mighty, slow-moving body of muddy water that is the heart and soul of the city. Revived, I strolled out to the river walk along the Mississippi. I watched a ferryboat dock and then, hearing faint music a few blocks away, I hurried to investigate. A colorful procession was making its way to the Canal Street ferry. A vehicle that appeared to be a retrofitted armored car was leading a small marching band, followed by shovel-wielding Caucasian men and women in olive-and-khaki, park-service-type uniforms. While the uniformed "guards" pantomimed shoveling motions to the music, black men in dazzling ostrich plumes, feathers and sequined costumes, known as the Mardi Gras Indians, whirled around them. It was as spirited and eclectic a gathering as New Orleans offers.

During a break in the music, I went over to the truck to get the scoop from the folks with shovels. They said they were boarding the ferry to cross the river and attend a fundraiser for the nonprofit, *Sous Terre* (under ground). The music was courtesy of the Algiers Brass Band. The truck was kicking off what was to be

The Mardi Gras Indians dance for Sous Terre and the health of American kids.

a trip to several cities on the way to Washington, D.C. Volunteers hoped to deliver three million original works of art in the form of "Fundred [sic] Dollar Bills." Sous Terre's mission was to attract attention to the crucial problem of childhood illnesses caused by contaminants, especially lead, in the soil of New Orleans and other American cities.

I wandered into the French Quarter and eventually found myself in a kaleidoscopic crush, the nightly movable binge on Bourbon Street. I was treated to my second jazz procession of the evening; this band led a wedding march. A lovely black bride in a dazzling white dress, accompanied by her beaming white husband, marched under a white umbrella down the center of Bourbon. Other members of the racially mixed wedding party followed, waving white hankies. The crowd shouted words of encouragement and snapped photos. I only mention race in regard to this happy couple because it is a pretty safe bet that, in Steinbeck's time, when a marriage in New Orleans such as this one took place, it was neither publicly paraded nor applauded. A recent Pew study reported that a record high fifteen percent of new marriages in the U.S. in 2008 involved couples of different races or ethnicities. In 1961, the intermarriage rate was two percent.

I ducked out of the crowd on the street and into a crowded and boisterous seafood

A Bourbon Street Wedding Procession.

place on Bourbon. There was a stool open at the bar. A guy in his fifties with glasses and fine, thin, orange hair was perched to my right. While I was enjoying my oysters and beer, he rather noisily sent his order of hush puppies back to the kitchen. He turned to me and said, "They don't do 'em right. They're raw in the middle. You gotta be a redneck from south Georgia, like me, to know how to cook puppies right." We chatted for a while, especially about my time living in Georgia. When I got around to mentioning my trip, he said, "Steinbeck, huh? Sounds familiar, like someone I should've read in high school but didn't."

A middle-aged couple sat down on the other side of me at the bar. They introduced themselves as Mike and Rita from Biloxi, Mississippi. Both worked for the shipbuilding industry and both were, shall we say, somewhat morose. Later—say, roughly some time between three-o'beer and four-o'beer—Rita, a bitter, blonde hairdo of a woman, informed me that "demo-commies" were trying to destroy this country and want to rebuild it as a socialist state. I thought, some vent, some spew, and surreptitiously jotted that in my notebook. As the two got more inebriated and thus more vehement, the tall sandy-haired bartender raised a sympathetic eyebrow at me as if to say, "You stepped in it, didn't you?" Mike, who was balding and paunchy, showed me that he had the Constitution and Declaration of Independence on his iPhone. He said he had been building "war toys" for thirty-five years. He spoke of a ship that had recently been constructed from seven-

and-a-half tons of recycled steel from the World Trade Center towers. "Fox News covered it. Commie Net News (CNN) did not," Mike slurred.

I worry about a country where people are so deaf to opposing points of view and so willing to ignore facts. Back in the day of discussing politics around the potbelly stove in the general store, Americans had no choice but to occasionally listen to opposing views. Today, with so many media options, we can chose only those opinions that reinforce our own, shutting all others out. That applies to my liberal friends, as well as folks like my shipbuilding bar mates. President Obama, himself, has encouraged us as a populace to "expose ourselves to opinions and viewpoints that are not in line with our own" so as to avoid becoming more polarized and because "listening to opposing views is essential for effective citizenship." As to the polarized times we live in, we can take heart from the writings of John Steinbeck, who chronicled two periods in the last eighty years when we were divided as a nation—the thirties and the sixties. America survived both of those difficult decades and emerged stronger.

Okay, I confess I soon tired of hearing Mike and Rita's "opposing views," paid my bill and left the bar. On my walk back to the hotel, I was stopped by a preppy guy who was young, drunk and confused. "Hey man, I'm staying at a hotel with a revolving top. I'm kinda lost," he said. The description did not ring a bell for me, so all I could do was wish him luck.

Another college type staggered by, shouting into his cell phone, "You left me. **You left me!**" Bad night for directions and connections, I thought.

Max was pretty happy to see me after my long evening out. He never got as energized in New Orleans as he did in San Francisco, but he must have memorized every pee-gram in the alley next to the hotel. During our time in New Orleans, we certainly moseyed up and down the alley often enough, stopping at every scent. I decided he was just assuming the pace of the South and the city, walking with all the urgency of an elderly Louisiana gentleman on his way to nowhere in particular. I took him down the elevator and out to the alley to cap off the night. An African-American man wearing a tattered black pea coat and pushing a bike approached me. "I'm not trying to hustle you. I'm a fifty-three-year-old diabetic homeless guy living on the street since Katrina," he said, hustling me, and for emphasis demonstrated that his right shoe heel was flapping around loose. His beard was dark stubble and he was missing several teeth.

"You have a nice bike," I said.

"Someone just gave that to me yesterday," he said defensively. I gave him a few bucks and wished him a good night.

Early the next morning, on the television news, there was talk of a storm, possibly of hurricane force, coming in that night. I was glad to be departing. While leaving New Orleans, it struck me that it is possible to drive into the city on 1-10, stay for several days downtown, near the French Quarter, and depart with the impression that racial tensions are a thing of the past and the city is fully recovered from Katrina. That would be dead wrong. From my experience, brief as it was, I would echo the sentiments of Philip and Pierre, who said that the city is not all the way there yet. I think it's safe to assume that were John Steinbeck to visit New Orleans today, he would be gratified with the progress on race relations and appalled that it was taking so long to recover from Katrina. And if, on this hypothetical visit, he had been bucked around by the wind as much as I was while driving out of New Orleans, he might have wondered if another Katrina was barreling into Louisiana that very day.

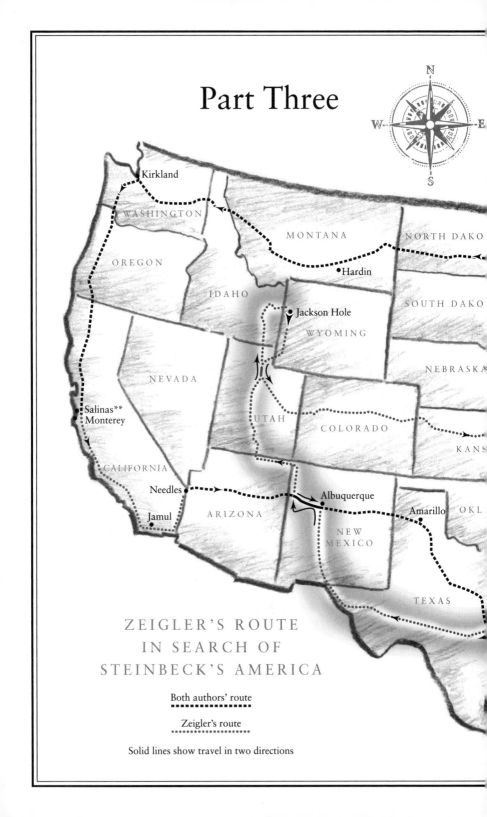

Part Three

ZEIGLER'S ROUTE
IN SEARCH OF
STEINBECK'S AMERICA

Both authors' route
▪▪▪▪▪▪▪▪▪▪▪▪▪▪▪▪

Zeigler's route
▪▪▪▪▪▪▪▪▪▪▪▪▪▪▪▪▪▪

Solid lines show travel in two directions

The Long
Way Home

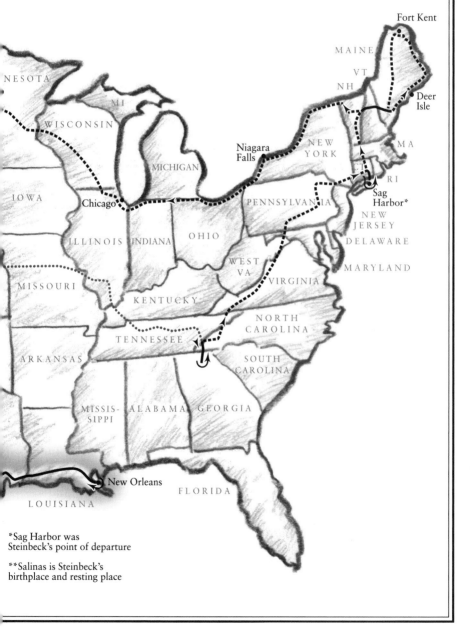

Fort Kent

MAINE

VT
NH

Deer
Isle

NESOTA

MI

WISCONSIN

Niagara
Falls

NEW
YORK

MA

MICHIGAN

CT

RI

IOWA

Chicago

PENNSYLVANIA

Sag
Harbor*

NEW
JERSEY

ILLINOIS

INDIANA

OHIO

DELAWARE

WEST
VA

MARYLAND

MISSOURI

VIRGINIA

KENTUCKY

NORTH
CAROLINA

ARKANSAS

TENNESSEE

SOUTH
CAROLINA

MISSIS-
SIPPI

ALABAMA

GEORGIA

New Orleans

FLORIDA

LOUISIANA

*Sag Harbor was
Steinbeck's point of departure

**Salinas is Steinbeck's
birthplace and resting place

Chapter Fourteen
Texas Redoubtable

America—complicated, paradoxical, bull-headed, shy, cruel, boisterous, unspeakably dear, and very beautiful.

We have failed sometimes, taken wrong paths, paused for renewal, filled our bellies and licked our wounds; but we have never slipped back—never.

America and Americans

On November 8, 2009, I bid farewell to John Steinbeck. Although I would be returning along the course Steinbeck and I both followed from Austin to New Orleans, we parted ways in New Orleans. Steinbeck wrote very little about the South after he left Louisiana. As I've mentioned, he was anxious to get home and was no longer absorbing the experience. There is one interesting counterpoint, however, embedded in that short section of *Travels with Charley* that warrants recounting.

Steinbeck picked up three separate hitchhikers in the South: a very reticent older black man who said little, a white bigot who hurled racial epithets at the author, and a young black man who was impatient to see change in his lifetime. The last two may still be alive today. I found myself wishing I could find the idealist, but Steinbeck didn't identify him in any other way. If that man *is* alive, perhaps he feels his dream of change has at least partially been fulfilled. As to the white bigot, my sister once asked my father why he wasn't a racist like several of his brothers. His one-word answer: "Education." Assuming the hatred churning in Steinbeck's angry hitchhiker didn't destroy him, I'm just enough of a Pollyanna to hope he got educated and eventually recognized the perversity of his ways.

I rushed back across Louisiana, with Hurricane Ida coming in hard behind me, and tried to imagine what it must be like to live with the constant threat of the next "big storm." The accordions and washboards of zydeco thumped on the radio and, speaking in a mix of French and English, the announcer pitched "Slap Your Mama Cajun Spices." He said, "With a purchase of twenty-five dollars or more, you get lagniappe," (pronounced "lan-yap," a small gift or little bit extra). One of the songs was titled "Don't Squeeze My Charmin" and, you guessed it, Charmin was a woman. I remember thinking the Acadian/Cajun relationship between northern Maine and western Louisiana is one of the richest cultural connections in this country.

For only the second time on the trip I was backtracking—this time from New Orleans to Austin. I reviewed Steinbeck's words regarding the differing perspectives on travel: "What I set down here is true until someone else passes that way and rearranges the world in his own style." I realized that's accurate, not only because of the convergence of players and events, but because the scene is viewed through a different lens by a different person with different moods. Give grump, you get grump in return. Although I was repeating a part of the route, it did not look or feel the same. How can going to New Orleans differ so from coming from New Orleans? I wondered.

Mile after mile of fecund swamp sped past. The eeriness of the setting brought on a brief, macabre thought of driving off the road and plunging deep into the tendrils of the bog. In my mind, the water closed around me. Never to be found, my eyes and orifices eventually sprout vines. It was time for a coffee break.

I pulled into a gas station and restaurant and walked past a man wearing a black T-shirt that read "Female Evacuation Route." Humor thinly disguises how close to the consciousness *escaping* must always be in this volatile region. In the men's room I looked in the mirror. There were bags under my eyes. I realized, with amazement, that it would soon be Thanksgiving. I had been on the road two months, and I was tired. I went into the restaurant and considered eating breakfast. Nothing looked appetizing. I was weary of all road food. "Everything tastes like soup, including the soup," Steinbeck wrote in Abingdon, Virginia. I left with a cup of coffee and a muffin in plastic wrap.

I stopped at the Atchafalaya Basin Visitors' Center west of Baton Rouge. There I found my almost forgotten final state postcards. Louisiana was my thirty-fifth discrete state. After Louisiana, every state on the way home was going to be a repeat and therefore would not require a card. In the visitors' center, a mechanical coon rose out of a plastic stump and began chatting with a mechanical snapping turtle about life in the swamp. Suddenly a menacing mechanical gator appeared in the reeds. Every story must have a villain, I thought, while watching this latter-day morality play. Steinbeck wrote in *East of Eden* that a life comes down to one simple story, which asks the question, "Did I do good or evil?" How would the gator answer that question? How would I? I learned from a display that the Atchafalaya Basin, now mostly swampland, was a bay of open water only ten thousand years ago.

In Lafayette, at a truck stop, I saw something that appalled me and something that pleased me. *Appalled*—televisions on the gas islands. (Please!) *Pleased*—a sign, possibly related to the hypnotic allure of the TV monitors, that read: "No Parking On Gas Islands Unless Fueling." After eight weeks on the road, this had become my pet peeve, nay, my crusade: **Move your damn car before you go inside!**

"Working hard today?" a large, thirty-something, African-American man asked me in the restroom. We had one of those totally trivial conversations in terms of progress toward goals, but imperative in terms of the richness of human experience. He mentioned where he was going and that he had intended to get up early enough to get there by noon. "You can see how that worked out," he said, shaking his head. It was already mid-morning and he had a long way to go. "All right, y'all," he said, tossing his wet towel into the garbage and departing.

The Buda Best Western with flags at half-mast for Fort Hood.

"Travel safe and at least get there by dinner," I said.

Soon, Max and I were off again. The day remained cloudy and on the cool side.

Lake Charles, Louisiana, whizzed by as a cluster of refineries, and then I was at the border. I was back in Orange, a city just inside the eastern edge of Texas, where people "bleed orange" for the Longhorns.

On this visit to Texas, the Lone Star flags and American flags were flying at half-mast because of the Fort Hood tragedy. I was reminded that although there had never been a hint of violence in this, my most American of experiences, we do live in a gun culture, in extremely delicate times. West of Houston, I detoured off I-10 and headed northwest to Austin to pick up the Bambi in Buda. It was pouring—no "pouring" is too tame. It was *sheeting* rain! I assumed that Ida had caught up with me, but a native I ran into in a café explained the deluge was a fairly typical occurrence that time of year, when moisture-laden warm air comes off the Gulf and collides with cold air from the north. Great, I'd just paid a lot of money to get Winnie washed, and streams of mud were flowing everywhere, beneath rain that hit with such force it bounced on the pavement.

The Buda Best Western was my choice for the night. I delighted Hilda, the Mexican woman at the desk, with a gift of two limes and two Ruby Red grapefruit from my brother's place in

San Diego. "To remind you of home," I said. Hilda gave me a free upgrade on my room. The rain continued into the evening. Wind snapped the Lone Star and American flags, which, at half-mast, framed the entrance to the motel. I learned with relief on the television news that Hurricane Ida had turned into a non-event for New Orleans.

The next morning the sky was gray and the air moist but the rain had ceased. I hooked up Winnie in the mud at the Camper Clinic in Buda, and then asked for directions to U.S. 290. Bob, one of the mechanics, ("Ask Bob, 'at ole boy knows everthin' there is to know about these local roads.") without a hint of rancor, reeled off several names of roads and road numbers and summarized, "just take a left and a right, two lefts and a right." Fortunately, Betty bailed me out and, after sixteen miles of back roads, I found U.S. 290. My plan was to follow it west to I-10.

The pretty, rolling high country west of Austin is dotted with vineyards, orchards and farms. Back roads have an F.M. affixed to their number. I later learned that means "Farm to Market." I passed oak-covered property with perhaps the most interesting juxtaposition of signs on the trip. A series of severe warnings behind a fence shouted, "No Trespassing! Violators Will Be Prosecuted! Extreme Danger! Active Hunting All The Time." And then I encountered an alluring little sign within ten feet of one of the warning signs that whispered, "Attractive Home Sites for Sale."

My route took me through Johnson City, birthplace of Lyndon B., and past the white stone buildings of historic and strongly German-influenced Fredericksburg, Texas. Soon after, Betty made one of her worst errors of the trip, taking me miles out of the way. I finally found a place to turn my rig around and blundered back toward I-10. On the return, I saw a sign surrounded by pink grass and orange trees that advertised "Show Goats." I imagined the feather boas and sequins.

Some distance down I-10, I made a strong impression at Cooper's BBQ in the town of Junction, Texas, when I asked for the slaw to be put right on the beef brisket. I didn't admit I had

Sign in Fort Stockton, Texas. I think we need that blessing 24/7.

recently learned that technique from a Wyoming transplant from Tennessee, a woman friend in my book club. I, of course, acted as if I'd been doing it all my life. There are three major roads (or a total of six ways in and out) crisscrossing the little town of Junction. I chose to remain on I-10. I locked down my cruise control at seventy miles an hour (only ten miles below the speed limit) and devoured my sandwich while steering. Near Sonora and Ozona I discovered there were no radio stations; I was suddenly out there, in what was rapidly becoming western Texas. Trees were more sporadic. Century plants spiked up toward the cloudless sky and I could see dust trails, at the foot of distant squareish buttes, reminiscent of the old western movies.

I encountered windmills and oil patches, literally right on top of each other, and crossed the Pecos River making its way to the Rio Grande. My goal for the day was Fort Stockton, a mere two hundred and forty miles from the western border of Texas. When I finally arrived, I saw a vet's sign that exhorted, "God Bless America. Monday through Friday, 9–5:30."

The next morning, I drove in a gauzy, fogbound dream world, at times dense and disorienting. At long last, I had only one hundred miles of Texas left to go. I was feeling confident that I'd survived the worst of the desert, so during a stop for breakfast, I dumped my potable RV water at a gas station and improved my miles per gallon remarkably. Still, the end was not in sight.

At a rest area near El Paso, a middle-aged man in jeans told me he and his wife were "bustin' it back to Houston 'cuz she's got a meeting of the bank board."

A large man, who was struggling out of his car and onto crutches in a handicapped parking space, had only one leg. He saw Max and said, "You have your baby with you. He's a beautiful boy."

I led "my baby" into a sandy patch behind the facilities. His back legs collapsed under him. Because of arthritis and other complications, our fear for Max is that his back legs will go first. He looked at me, beseechingly, and lifted one paw, then another. I was relieved to see the ground littered with objects bristling with small spikes. I stabbed my thumb removing thorns as sharp as steel from three of Max's tiny feet.

The thorns notwithstanding, I liked this rest area; it was sunny, attractive and clean. Even though I couldn't connect to the free internet as advertised, I felt grateful for the pleasant break from the trek across Texas. I thanked the female Hispanic attendants for maintaining such a pleasant facility.

I got around El Paso with relative ease and left I-10 for I-25 in Las Cruces, New Mexico. Later in New Mexico, as I drove, I recalled the desperate and trusting look on Max's face as he turned to me for help with the thorns, and a whole well of emotion bubbled over. I felt grateful to Max for his patience and companionship, and indebted to Dimmie for her support and unfailing belief in this odyssey. I thought of my daughter, Jamie, and her passenger—my grandchild—and, of course, of my boys, Alex and Wil, two characters who have chosen the hard road, but nonetheless are making headway. I smiled when I realized a hitchhiker's sign that puzzled me when I saw it in southern New Mexico— "T or C" scrawled on a piece of cardboard—must have stood for Truth or Consequences, New Mexico. (Texas or Colorado? What a flake! Can't the guy decide which direction he's going?)

Truth or Consequences is where I had my emotional

epiphany, realizing that, truthfully, I could not live with the consequences of losing Dimmie—who, in my life's journey, is magnetic north—or for that matter, any member of my family. It will be hard enough, I realized, to lose my little sidekick, Max.

I followed I-25 and the Rio Grande River into Albuquerque. It was a warm and breezy November evening. Yellow cottonwoods lined the river valley bottom.

That night I sat at the table in the trailer with a glass of white wine and called Dimmie. I told her about my day—she told me of hers. I relayed the details of my sentimental insights and said it was my intention to be an ideal spouse and pet owner when I returned home. She said that was her plan, too—for me. I told her I missed her and loved her very much.

After I hung up I poured another glass of wine and drank it while lost in thought. I sensed John Steinbeck looking over my shoulder, chuckling and saying, "To quote the great Bobby Burns 'The best laid schemes of mice and men....'" What I had said to Dimmie, I meant sincerely. I just hoped I hadn't set the bar too high.

Chapter Fifteen
The Land of Hoodoos and Whodunits

When a man comes to die, no matter what his talents and influence, and genius, if he dies unloved his life must be a failure to him and dying a cold horror.

East of Eden

Early on a crisp morning, I left Albuquerque on I-40 and zipped through one hundred sun-dazzled miles of sheer rock buttes and dry, treeless basins, passing the Rio Puerco Bridge on another short stretch of historic Route 66 and the town of To'hajillee, and finally stopping for breakfast at the Kiva Café in Grants, New Mexico. At an adjacent table, a man clad in jeans and cowboy hat said to his friend, "The wife wants to build a cabin but until the economy changes, I'm afraid to bite it off." I ordered huevos rancheros with red chili. After devouring every bite, I went up to pay at the register and had a short discussion with the heavily made-up, redheaded waitress about the relative merits of green and red chili, a dispute that shall never be resolved in New Mexico, nor should it. The waitress reminded me that if I ever wanted both red and green chili to just say, "Make that Christmas."

Between Grants and Gallup I swung in at the Continental Divide (where Steinbeck had camped, heading east) to stand with one foot on either side, just as he had done in Montana. North of Gallup, on U.S. 491, there was a hand-painted sign that read, "Gas $2.97 Sheep $89.00." It was desolate north of Gallup. Periodically I passed a small-box house or mobile home with a power pole, two or three older cars and a propane tank. No trees. Everything was pale brown in color: grass, dirt, even shrubs by the road. I saw some tarpaper shacks and an occasional hogan, the traditional round home of the Navajo people. I couldn't imagine how many acres were required to sustain one head of livestock. It appeared to be one of the toughest places in the U.S. to scratch out a subsistence living. Soon I passed the junction with Route 264 to Window Rock, Arizona. Then the fight began.

Betty and I argued for at least thirty minutes, as she insisted I turn around at every unpaved side road and return to Route 264. "Betty, goddamnit, I told you, we're going to Shiprock!" I even began to cruelly mock her because I had come to hate the way she says the number 2. "Ta-hundred miles, Betty? **Ta-hundred!**" Eventually, I had to concede that she may have known something I didn't—Shiprock was a shipwreck, nothing worked. After visiting two gas stations and trying six or seven pumps, I left to cross the Navajo Reservation with less than a full tank of gas.

The Continental Divide in New Mexico.

One foot on either side of the divide.

I was in writer Tony Hillerman country. I have always loved his novels. Truthfully, I have always loved northern New Mexico and Arizona, and past explorations included such cultural and historical treasures as Canyon de Chelly, just north of Window Rock. But on past explorations I hadn't exceeded fourteen thousand miles and eight weeks on the road. It was in northern New Mexico that I realized I was truly in the home zone. Although I could see it for miles, I had little time to think about the large, discrete formation for which Shiprock, New Mexico, was named. I learned later that the Shiprock itself is a volcanic "neck," or the plug formed when magma cooled in the vent of a volcano. Devils Tower in Wyoming is another notable example. In the town of

Shiprock, I joined Route 64. The New Mexico portion of the road was teeth-rattling rough, but as soon as I passed into Arizona the pavement improved and the terrain got prettier, with pink rock, juniper trees and richer grasses. Route 64 led to U.S. 160, just across the Arizona border.

I sailed by the turn at Teec Nos Pos to the Four Corners because I'd read recently the monument is in the wrong place, and I was worried about how far I had to travel to the next functioning gas station. There wasn't much out there in Navajoland—at least not from the perspective of this road-weary Anglo vagabond. My mind began to play games. I remembered one of Hillerman's favorite characters in his murder mysteries, the Navajo cop, Jim Chee. Gee, I thought, I wonder if Jim Chee liked Cheetos? "Wow. Arguing with Betty—stupid thoughts like Jim Chee liking Cheetos—must be time to get home," I said to Max.

U.S.160 crosses northern Arizona and continues west through the pink and salmon Chuska Mountains of the Painted Desert region, northeast of the Grand Canyon. Towns included Red Mesa, where I thankfully found a functioning gas station, Mexican Water and Kayenta. I snacked while I drove on three-month-old M&Ms and three-week-old pretzels. In Kayenta, the largest town since Shiprock, I pulled behind the new brick Hampton Inn and parked. Two Native American men, one wearing a battered, straw cowboy hat and dingy, cream-colored jacket and jeans, the other in a ball cap, gray jacket and blue jeans, were searching through the litter in the tall, dead grass behind the inn. My guess is they were hunting for discarded and presumably half-empty bottles. The cowboy hat came up to the passenger side window of my car and asked me where I was going. When I told him I was going to Page, he said they were hitching the opposite direction from Flagstaff to Shiprock. He said they hadn't eaten in twenty-four hours and asked if I could spare five or ten dollars. I said I had no cash, which was the truth, but offered food. He politely passed, and they shuffled on through the grass. West of Kayenta, at a junction marked only by the convergence of two roads and the concomitant signage, I turned north on State 98. After the junction, I covered miles of uninhabited country, with

A view of a mountain from northern Arizona.

little traffic in either direction. Of course, when hauling Winnie, because of limited visibility, I can be blissfully ignorant of what is directly behind me, which turned out to be the case that afternoon. A large truck on a straightaway startled me, suddenly pulling out to pass. As the semi blasted by, I made out the words on the side of the trailer, "Always the best price. Always." It got me thinking about what is omnipresent along the highways of this country: Walmart, trains, anti-abortion signs, religious signs, livestock and tons of hay. And casinos, casinos everywhere—what happened to the idea of keeping the good sin quarantined in Nevada? I never had a problem with that, but tacky casinos in every state get tiresome. What's coming to our neighborhoods next, I wondered, legalized prostitution?

Near Page, Arizona, the coal-fired Navajo Generating Station power plant thrust its smoking stacks up into the desert sky like an insulting gesture. I know virtually nothing about power generation or demand, but I can't believe that the needs of the region, even considering Phoenix's desire to ice down all interior space nine months out of the year, could possibly require both a hydroelectric plant at Glen Canyon Dam, and a desert air-polluting coal-fired plant a few miles away.

I arrived around 5:00 p.m. at Lake Powell on the Utah/Arizona border. Pauline, the friendly, roundish Navajo attendant in the

Wahweap Campground store, offered me a site with hook-ups—
that is, power and water, for forty-three dollars—or "dry" camping for twenty dollars. I chose "dry" and found a flat, sandy,
pull-through site, which satisfied my back-up avoidance syn-
drome. The site was clean and close to the lake. It contained a picnic table, a fire pit with a grate and one Mesquite tree. In due
course, I lounged under the tree in a camp chair with my Sponge
Bob pillow tucked into the hollow of my back.

For so late in the fall, it was a temperate evening, with a sunset splashing the red/orange/yellow end of the spectrum above
layer-cake sandstone buttes extending up from the easy waters of
the lake. I felt...ambivalent, which is what I anticipated, and am-
bivalence is the reason I had stayed away from Lake Powell in all
my years of exploring southern Utah. Those waters are indeed
beautiful, but they are not natural. Lake Powell was formed by the
construction of Glen Canyon Dam in the sixties, and it involved
the inundation and destruction of geological, anthropological, historical and cultural features in Glen Canyon. In his essay "Lake
Powell," Wallace Stegner put it best when he wrote, "It strikes
me, even in my exhilaration, in gaining the lovely and the useable,
we have given up the incomparable." After all those years of
avoidance, there I was, camped and conflicted, beside what some
environmentalists refer to as "Lake Foul." There was only one
thing to do—drink wine.

I suppose it is time to admit to my hedonism. The fullness of
the view was enhanced by, indeed paired with, the fullness of my
glass and plate. I built an aromatic and crackling kindling fire in
the pit and heated up a delicious surf-and-turf medley, comple-
mented by most of a bottle of brisk and peppy Chardonnay, for
medicinal purposes. Could I have enjoyed the view over a bowl of
rice and veggies and a glass of water? Perhaps, but nowhere near
as much. I jotted the following in my journal: "Glass of wine,

glassy lake, layer cake, t-bone steak, spicy fish and chips, burning lips. Life on the road—full, large, delicious!"

"Can you grow a garden anywhere in Wyoming?" a man in a black cowboy hat asked as he walked by with a small white dog. Max gave the dog his usual, warm, highly vocalized greeting.

"What's the weather like in Jackson now?" a slight woman with a towel covering long wet hair inquired.

I was most curious about an Asian couple who kept coming and going from the site next to me. They smiled and waved at Max and me and took pictures of the rock mesas poking out of the water, but they had failed, even with dark approaching, to pitch a tent or prepare for the night. I assumed they were neophytes and had to fight the urge to ask if I could help them with their gear.

Around 7:00 p.m. a hush fell over the camp. Primitive, or dry, campers seem to blend naturally into the rhythm of their surroundings. For starters, there are no generators allowed. The desert was silent as were we. Doors were closed gently and people spoke in soft tones. I poked a bit at the coals, polished off my glass of wine, took one last look at the lake glistening in the twilight and turned in for the night.

Early the next morning I awoke and saw the Asian pair asleep on the ground on a thick air mattress surrounded by just the proper amount of gear to travel light. Their camp was impressive in its simplicity and made me feel as if I'd brought along the entire contents of my garage. The day was cool and cloudy, and gray streaks of rain fell across the distant arms of the lake.

I lived in Utah twice during my wandering years and never tired of exploring it in any season. I spent the morning doing one of my favorite things—driving the Beehive State's back roads: US-89 through Big Water, Kanab, Orderville, Panguitch, Circleville and Sevier. Spring is an especially fine time to drive that country, for the emerging green of the valley meadows and stream-side trees creates a striking contrast with the timeless, red rock above, capped by the lingering winter-white of mountain peaks. In au-

A good hair day was had by all.

tumn, the grasses have mellowed to vermillion and the mountains have less snow but, still, the contrast is wonderful. I opened the window to the chilly fall air and let the blast muss my hair.

Southern Utah is a mysterious and mystical land of hoodoos and whodunits. Hoodoos are totem pole-shaped columns of eroded rock carved by water and ice. Hoodoo is also a term for witchcraft. Five national parks protect southern Utah's otherworldly terrain and treasures. The hoodoos of Bryce Canyon National Park are one striking example. Imagine you're a fly on a chessboard loaded with carved pieces, and you will have some sense of the scale and majesty of these red, orange, yellow and white limestone spires, some looming as tall as ten-story buildings. The Paiute Indians believe that the hoodoos were created when Mischievous Coyote froze people into stone.

The Colorado Plateau, centered in the four corners area and drained by the Colorado River, is a convoluted country. Canyons as large and luminous as cathedrals, or as confined and dark as coffins, crack the veneer of the desert and branch like lightning. Desert canyons are scary places to be in a rainstorm; water screams down them with a fury.

As I drove, ghosts joined me in the car.

Evidence of the Anasazi (Navajo for ancient enemy), also know as the Ancestral Puebloans, who anthropologists have determined disappeared sometime during the thirteenth century and reemerged later as modern Pueblo Indians (such as those I visited on Acoma Pueblo), is everywhere. The desert preserves all and reveals all, from Anasazi fingerprints in the mortar of ruins to mortal bones and artifacts. The ancient language of pictographs (paintings) and petroglyphs (carvings) adorns the sandstone.

I first felt a deep connection with the Ancestral Puebloans in January of 1978. I was leading a group of six women from Mt. Holyoke College through Canyonlands National Park. It was cold and one of the students was ill. Because we had no tents, we needed shelter for her recovery. We were backpacking in a narrow dry wash, surrounded by slanting red rock, with a view of the distant snowcapped peaks of the La Sal Mountains. I scouted ahead and found a sandstone alcove that opened onto the streambed. It faced south and gathered and reflected the weak winter sun, yet was deep enough to shelter us from rain and snow.

There was water nearby in "potholes" or depressions in the rock, and plentiful pinion pine and juniper driftwood, for fire building, in the wash. As we spread our sleeping pads and bags on the red sand in the alcove, something shiny caught my eye. I picked up a tiny, white bead drilled for stringing. Everybody pitched in and a little sifting of the fine sand revealed more beads, several small arrowheads, pottery shards and stone chippings. Although we had no intention of keeping these antiquities, this was a momentous discovery. We had happened upon an Anasazi site, probably for the chipping and shaping of arrowheads, and had been attracted to it for the very same reasons the ancients had— shelter, warmth and water—eight or nine hundred years earlier.

Two other phantom passengers came along for the ride as I drove north through southern Utah. One was that of a murdered white boy, the other the specter of a severed hand.

Everett Ruess left the little town of Escalante, Utah, in November of 1934. He was twenty years old—a likable young man from California who loved nature and had been on a "walkabout" for several years. He was traveling alone with two mules. Sheepherders last saw Ruess southeast of Escalante, heading down the Hole-in-the-Rock trail toward the Colorado River. Everett Ruess was a romantic vagabond, but he was also a writer and an artist. One of his woodcuts is the logo for the annual Escalante Arts Festival. Because of his mysterious disappearance over seventy years ago, and after being celebrated by several southwestern authors, Everett Ruess is a mythological figure. His demise was one of the great western mysteries. No verifiable trace of him was ever found—until recently, when the mystery seemed solved.

According to Navajo oral tradition, in 1934, Ute Indians killed a young white man with a blow to the head. His murderers then stole his possessions. A Navajo who witnessed the killing, but had no idea who the young man was, buried the body in a crevice of a nearby sandstone ridge. The Navajo passed the story down to his grandchild, who found the body, and with the help of a tenacious journalist and a forensic anthropologist, proved, to the satisfaction of the missing man's family and the national media, that it was Everett Ruess. The desert preserves all and eventually reveals all. Emphasis on *eventually*—in this case she was not ready to give up her secret. An update on the National Geographic Adventure website in February 2010 admits a stunning reversal in the Ruess case. Further DNA tests and other evidence have revealed the skeleton was not Everett's; indeed, it is the skeleton of a young American Indian male. The remains have been returned to the Navajo Nation. The Everett Ruess mystery continues.

The man without a hand embodies a Utah tale of impulsiveness and self-centeredness, resulting in what is likely to become the most remarkable survival saga of this century. I speak of Aron

Ralston, my daughter Jamie's college boyfriend. Aron was an intense young man in college and his approach to the outdoors always struck me as excessively goal-oriented and competitive. When he and Jamie went into the mountains, I worried he would push her beyond safe limits. Jamie loves the outdoors and is very athletic, but she is just as happy stopping short of a peak and writing a poem about it, as she is to summit it. Aron, in my view, was all about the conquest. Jamie and Aron called it quits during her senior year and, frankly, I was relieved.

A few years later in the spring of 2003, I got an excited call. "Turn on CNN. They're saying that Aron was trapped in a canyon in Utah and had to cut off his hand," my daughter exclaimed.

And indeed, he had. After leaving no sign of where he was going, Aron was scrambling solo down Blue John Canyon near Hanksville, Utah, when an eight-hundred-pound boulder rolled and crushed his right hand. He spent six days trapped in the canyon—with only equipment, food and water for a long day hike—one hundred feet down in a crack not much wider than a casket with a narrow slice of sky above. Although searchers found his car, they never spotted him. Aron knew that any amount of rain on the plateau could result in a flash flood and that greatest of ironies, drowning in the desert. When he was close to exhausting his food and water, as well as all other options, Aron sawed off his right hand with a Leatherman tool, put a tourniquet on his arm and hiked and *rappelled* down the slot canyon to a trail and, eventually, the aid of some German hikers. All this could have been avoided if he had left a note in his car, or a voicemail message with any friend or family member, telling them where he was going. But Aron's courage and ability to correctly analyze and overcome a dire situation cannot be faulted.

Aron has accomplished many amazing feats since his recovery, including writing a book about his ordeal, *Between a Rock and a Hard Place*. After being fitted with a prosthesis (which he proudly demonstrated at Jamie and Paul's wedding in August 2003), he was the first person to solo all of Colorado's fourteen-thousand-foot peaks in mid-winter. That aside, Jamie assures me he has mellowed and his priorities have shifted. Aron's transformation was born while he was imprisoned in the rock of Blue John Canyon. Mustering the courage to cut off his right hand, and thus survive, was driven by a persistent image. He imagined himself, not scaling peaks, but, even though he didn't have a girlfriend at the time, holding a future son high above his head in his left hand. Jamie later informed me that a son was born to Aron and his wife in the spring of 2010.

The further north I drove, the fiercer the wind and more threatening the clouds. Thankfully, my ghosts had departed by the time I reached central Utah because conditions required me to pay better attention to the road. Most of the back roads of Utah follow the center of mountain valleys, parallel to meandering streams, beneath towering peaks. On fair-weather days these scenic byways offer lovely vistas and myriad birdlife and wildlife, although that is the only "wild life" one is likely to find in southern and central Utah. The little towns of Utah are very pleasant in appearance, with their wide streets lined with local businesses, but they have a reputation for being insular and almost impossible to abide if one is not of the Mormon faith. And it is next to impossible to buy a drink.

I drove past Big Rock Candy Mountain, a natural rock formation resembling chocolate sauce drizzled over caramel, south of Sevier, and my mind drifted again. What came first, I wondered, the naming of the mountain, the Wallace Stegner book of the same name, or the folk tune rediscovered by the film *O Brother, Where Art Thou?* (I later learned it was the tune.) I was reminded of a line from the song "Big Rock Candy Mountain," about a bluebird singing at the lemonade springs, which made me think of the bluebird that had landed near me while I was cross-country skiing the previous spring on snow-covered sagebrush flats. The bird was the only color in an expanse of white—blue could have been named for that bird rather than vice versa. Suddenly, twenty tons of steel came roaring toward me in the opposite lane, snapping me out of my reverie. I gripped the wheel to hold the road and thought maybe it should be against the law to *think* and drive.

By Salina, Utah, I was starting to sense a relentless pull for home. Back roads had lost their charm. Road food had become even more unpalatable. Steinbeck hit his saturation point in Abingdon, Virginia. I hit mine in Salina, Utah. Clouds were boiling to the north and the radio was predicting snow. I wanted interstate and I wanted to (a) get past Salt Lake City, (b) avoid I-80 across Wyoming, known as the "Snow Chi Minh Trail," and (c) get Winnie home before snow accumulated. I consulted by cell with the best regional driver I know, my wife, and we agreed I-15 all the way to Idaho Falls, Idaho, was the right route for that day. I passed on an offer for lunch from an old friend in Salt Lake City and just kept on, in the zone, boring north past the city through mixed snow and rain and battering wind.

Chapter Sixteen
Home

The trip had dimension and tone. It was a thing whose boundaries seeped through itself and beyond into some time and space that was more than all the Gulf and more than all our lives. Our fingers turned over the stones and we saw life that was like our life.
The Sea of Cortez

And that's how the traveler came home again.
Travels with Charley

I pushed into southern Idaho late in the afternoon and arrived, after dark, in Idaho Falls. It was cold. There was snow on some of the vehicles in the parking lot of the Comfort Inn, and I immediately began to fret about what I was going to encounter on the next—and last—day as I drove the final one hundred miles to Jackson Hole. One doesn't have to live in Wyoming long to learn, if there is snow in the region, there is snow in Jackson Hole.

On one of my trips into the motel with the dog, a tall, white-bewhiskered man got the door for me. "Looks like you have your hands full with that, uh, dust mop," he said, referring to Max. "I'm with my mother-in-law and she has…one like that. It's been drugged for two days for travel. Just lying around. Kinda nice for a change."

I suggested that perhaps they should make those drugs in time-release capsules for daily usage. The man turned at his door and I went down the hall and into my room, and then, that's it—that's all she wrote. I don't remember a thing about the room, or what or where I ate that night. I don't have a single note about it in my journal. While I can recall every detail, for instance, from that night in Kansas when I shared dinner at a picnic table with a family and two young men and later went catfish fishing, or the morning I had breakfast surrounded by locals at the Lariat Country Kitchen in Hardin, Montana, I remember nothing from the last night on the road. Nothing. I must have been preoccupied. Or perhaps I was on autopilot. Too bad people don't come equipped with little black boxes to check for recorded data. My last night on the road is a total blank.

Friday, November 13, 2009. Max got me up at 5:00 a.m. to go out. The temperature had dropped even more overnight and I was concerned about pipes freezing in Winnie. I lay on my back, in the dark, on the frigid pavement, amidst the ice and snow, and tried to loosen two petcocks that allow water to drain out of the low points in the pipes. One worked, the other was frozen closed. I didn't realize Max was observing me. My fingers ached and the pavement was cold, so while straining to get up, I inadvertently kicked out my foot, launching Max off the curb several feet in the air. He landed hard on his side, popped up and darted around the parked cars, avoiding me. He wore a look of disgust and fear that said, "What, after all these weeks, have I done to deserve this?" I heard a voice from my past, "I told you that dog would never survive the trip." I chased Max around the dimly lit lot, trying to show with body language, since he couldn't really hear me, that it was all a mistake. Finally he let me pick him up and nuzzle him in apology.

Now, I was wary. Typical of Jackson Hole, the last day was bound to be hard. Plus, I'm not superstitious but it was, after all, Friday the 13th.

We got off fairly early on U.S. 26, and I mused en route, as I approached the Teton Mountain Range and the Wyoming border, just how gorgeous and yet how intense and spiritually powerful northwestern Wyoming is. On a break at an Idaho rest stop, overlooking the Snake River winding far below, I saw a bald eagle sitting nearby on a limb. I welcomed the presence of the bald as a good sign, but still felt uneasy; the weather to the east, toward the mountains, looked malevolent. The trip had gone so well, perhaps too well. Would this be the day, so close to home, that the other shoe dropped? Jackson will always test you. Many fail and leave. But, as I said, my wife and I are determined to stay in Jackson permanently and I was determined to get back

The Snake River in Idaho, winding upstream toward home.

home without an incident. I reflected on my ambivalent relationship with the town of Jackson because of what Jackson demands to live comfortably versus what the town offers in a monetary sense to support a comfortable life. But also, I thought about our inexorable attachment to our small spot, four miles north of Jackson, as well as our love of Grand Teton National Park, the southern boundary of which is a few hundred feet from our front door. I remembered a promise to myself to volunteer at least four summers at the Laurance S. Rockefeller Preserve, a LEED Platinum (the greenest of the green) facility and interpretative center connected to Grand Teton National Park. This I must do to justify the carbon I had produced during my fifteen-thousand-mile trip. I wondered if I would keep my promise.

I crossed the broad, smooth back of the Snake River, entered Swan Valley, Idaho, and paralleled the conifer-covered shoreline of Palisades Reservoir. Although there was snow in the trees, the roads were clear and the sailing was smooth. I relaxed a little, thinking back on my pilgrimage as one with movable shrines, some of scenic beauty, some with traces and tracks of the life of "the master"—he who had gone before. I made a mental list of all the beautiful places I'd seen: Utah; Colorado; eastern Kansas; North Carolina; Tennessee; north Georgia; eastern Pennsylvania; eastern Long Island; all of New England; Niagara Falls; Wisconsin; Montana; northern Idaho; Washington; Oregon; Mount Shasta, Big Sur, Santa Barbara, and Pacific Grove in California; Arizona; New Mexico; Texas; and Louisiana. I crossed the Wyoming line.

I stopped for breakfast at our favorite coffee shop, The Coffee Cabin, in Alpine, where I chuckled at a cartoon that read, "Forget health food, I'm at an age where I need all the preservatives I can get." Over a steaming latte that warmed my hands, I recalled my early expectations for this odyssey. I was prepared for some complications and murkiness. I held myself to investigating three issues only: the economy, "Team Obama," and race. Other concerns I anticipated would come up spontaneously did not. I have this sort of bifurcated montage memory of the journey. In the background, blaring from screens everywhere, I heard snippets about swine flu, climate change, terrorists, war casualties— the matters I expected Americans to be discussing. I learned that the media does not accurately reflect the mood of this great country, or the values and daily lives of Americans. Even National Public Radio is guilty of these assumptions. During my travels, I heard an NPR commentator say, "The world is more jaded and full of hype." In fact, in the foreground, in America, people are not jaded and actually talked about baseball scores, winter tires, severe weather, lost jobs, the price of gas and food—safe local subjects all, and quite understandable really. I expected conflict. I met hundreds of people on this journey and observed hundreds more. I never heard a word spoken in anger—never witnessed an angry gesture. Like Steinbeck, I asked the question, "What are Americans like today?" I found the answer: kind, respectful, optimistic, democratic, diverse, becoming more tolerant, and still dreaming the American dream.

Americans live all issues—safe, unsafe, big and small—locally. While the content of each community's issues is unique, two things are true and universal, knitting communities together into a democratic nation: first, we deal with our local issues bravely and humanely and kindly; and second, our local issues have as much potential to be complex and difficult as do the large ones portrayed by the media. We live out our democratic values, not by being preoccupied with climate change or swine flu in the world, but by dealing locally with those and other issues as they arise, close to home, among neighbors, friends and family. My family is the perfect example. Our concern with our son, Wil, is a microcosmic example of the nation's concern about a disengaged, frightened and cynical younger generation, especially boys. I live that problem; I deal with it in the here and now every day. I try—locally and in my own way—to contribute to the solution by serving on the boards of two secondary schools. I am not unique. The church choir, the soccer club, the school board, the library, the land trust, the scouts are all examples of Americans living a democratic life locally. Our explicable insularity aside, however, we Americans do need to remember that we are fighting, and our young people are dying, in two wars.

There was tremendous comfort and reason for hope in the fact that no matter where I traveled across my nation, every group was living the American version of democracy in its local way. That any American can go anywhere in this "monster land," and know that he or she will see that reality in every community, is a testament to the strength of the fabric of this great country. For several months after returning, I led this bizarre sort of dual life. For example, I read a magazine article about activist gun owners visibly packing side arms while patronizing Starbucks. And my initial reaction was, oh my God, what a bizarre state of affairs! Then I paused and thought, wait a minute; I just drove fifteen thousand miles around America and stopped in lots of coffee shops and didn't see a single handgun on a single person. But "thousands of Starbucks patrons observed sipping coffee, unarmed" doesn't make for a good sound bite, does it?

I joined U.S. 89 in Alpine, and followed the undulations of the Snake River through the river canyon to home. Once in Jackson, I passed a runner working out, at twenty-five degrees, on a school track, in his bare feet. After executing one ceremonial pass by the Teton County Library, I pulled into the library parking lot. Dimmie and my son, Wil, who had moved back home, and several of Dimmie's friends and co-workers greeted us with signs, cheers and hugs. I jumped out of the car, carrying Max, and in my excitement left my car running. After a decent interval, my wife gently reminded me I was idling in a no-idling zone. I moved the car, shut it off and went inside the library for the first of several interviews about my trip.

Home, of course, meant many things, rich upon rediscovery. I slept in *my* bed with *my* wife. In the morning, I scrubbed my back with *my* brush in the shower. I slipped into my comfortable "writing" pajamas. Our home is organized, neat, and warm and does not have to be attached to the car. I opened the fridge and it was stocked. I studied the sonogram of my grandson on the refrigerator door. I went out on the front deck with a cup of coffee and stared at the preserve below—and saw elk in a long line returning for the winter. I enjoyed minutes of still silence, broken only by the bugling of bull elk. Steam curled up off my coffee. Steam rose up off meandering Flat Creek in the center of the refuge. It struck me that coffee and cream are the late fall colors of the refuge meadows. Across the refuge, the Sleeping Indian Mountain's headdress was early winter-white. I was home.

But still I dreamed. I dreamed of the road, and places along the road, and I awakened disoriented, wondering what state I was in. I began again to read *East of Eden*, glad I had not finished it before or during the trip. Now that I had visited them, I could envision many of the places mentioned in the book, such as Salinas and the Salinas Valley. Most importantly, I could celebrate the fact that I had accomplished something momentous that can never be taken away. In a country still far more beautiful

Second day home snow.

than exploited and far more welcoming than malevolent, I had achieved what John Steinbeck felt was the most exultant of all the human undertakings. I had exerted my free will in the pursuit of a creative endeavor. "Timshel—Thou Mayest."

On the first day home, I backed Winnie flawlessly up our long, narrow driveway and tucked her within a foot of the front deck. Later that evening, when I unloaded the car, I found seven pens under the driver's seat, and Max's treats cached in every nook and cranny in the rear.

On the second day home it snowed, blanketing Winnie in a thin white mantle, fringed with icy glass beads. I gathered Max up in my arms, looked out the window at the large flakes coating the sagebrush and felt a profound sense of relief. Even nomads have to hole up for the winter.

Questions for Discussion

1. What *are* Americans like today? How have Americans changed since 1960 when Charley and his traveling companion, John Steinbeck, explored America?

2. It is said that in 2010 we are living in a time of great polarization in America. What lessons from the thirties and sixties, two eras Steinbeck knew very well, can be applied today?

3. What personal and external forces were driving Steinbeck while he was driving Rocinante? What motivated Gregory Zeigler to recreate Steinbeck's route?

4. Do you feel Max, the seven-pound Maltese, held his own against his predecessor, Charley, the regal standard poodle?

5. President Obama recommends that Americans expose themselves to opposing points of view in order to be effective citizens. How else might Americans enhance their effectiveness as members of our society?

6. On his trip, Zeigler met with many Americans. Whom do you think was most interesting and colorful?

7. Is change in the American landscape and lifestyle always beneficial? Is change always destructive? How can Americans—even those with limited means—manage change responsibly?

8. John Steinbeck could not abide the changes he saw during his lifetime in his home state of California. List examples of beneficial change in the last fifty years in America. List examples of destructive change in the last fifty years in America. What parts of America that Zeigler explored seem most unchanged since 1960? What parts are most different?

9. John Steinbeck was concerned about economic and racial equality, materialism, militarism, environmental quality and moral integrity. If he could return to America today, what would delight him? What would appall him?

10. What is your impression of how Americans adjusted, individually and collectively, to the recession of 2008 and 2009?

Acknowledgments

How is it that an endeavor that feels, at times, as lonely as writing a book is also such an ensemble effort? The acknowledgement sections of many books tend toward several pages. Were I to elucidate what every person on this page offered in support of this project, it would add another lengthy chapter.

If your name appears on this alphabetical list, you know what you did. I hope you also know how much I appreciate you: Ann and Steve Ashley, Colleen Bailey, Heather Bennett, Tom Bentley, Chris Brueningsen, Betsy Burton, Tammy, Thyrza and Chris Christel, Anne Coldsmith, David Conrad, Mary Correla-Moreno, Mary Cutler, Kelsey Dayton, Laurie and Lindsey Gilbert, Susan Grun, Becky and David Hall, Jim Hayes, Scott Hirshfield, Jay Hoeschler, John Kerr, Jamie Zeigler Laurens, John Marshall and the students of Rabun Gap-Nacoochee School, Libby Mitchell, Arthur Moore, Ruth Ann Penny, Harriette Rasmussen, Gillian Rose, Jane Roth, Margret and John Rowland, Heather Salter, Valerie Schramm, Craig Spitzer, Gail and Thomas Steinbeck, David Styne, David Swift, Teton County Librarians, Ken Thomasma, Colleen Thompson, Dimmis and Stuart Weller, Jake Zeigler, Jr., Jeanne Zeigler, Lori and David Zeigler, Patsy Zeigler Reich, Toni (Berger) and Steve Zeigler, and Wil Zeigler.

And, of course, Dimmie Zeigler and Max Zeigler.

About the Author

Gregory Zeigler, a career educator, has served as an English and drama teacher and headmaster at several schools. He is a trustee for two independent secondary schools and a community theater company.

A life-long passion for communication, both written and spoken, has inspired Zeigler to pursue writing and acting. Zeigler's publications include articles on historical and educational subjects. He is the author of *The Straw That Broke,* an environmental mystery. Both an end-user and creator of educational materials, Zeigler recently worked as an editor and writer for a website for lesson plans and teachers' aids. He was educational editor for the *Jackson Hole Weekly* newspaper (formerly *Planet Jackson Hole*). His articles have appeared in publications such as the *Bend Bulletin* (Bend, Oregon), the *Atlanta Journal Constitution, Mosaic* magazine, and several college and secondary school alumni magazines. Zeigler and Associates offers consulting services to non-profit organizations nationwide.

A popular public speaker throughout his career, Zeigler regularly presented papers at national educational conferences. His love of theater led to work with community groups as an actor and director. Most recently he played the lead in an Off Square Theatre summer production of *Sylvia,* in Jackson Hole, Wyoming. His acting experience extends to film, with appearances in dozens of commercials and educational films. In an Instructional Television production of *Arts Alive,* he acted alongside NFL great Lynn Swann. Zeigler has worked as a first assistant cameraman on a feature film and has written and directed several promotional videos. Zeigler earned a Bachelor of Arts, in English at Washington and Jefferson College, Washington, Pennsylvania, and a Master of Education at the University of Utah, Salt Lake City, Utah.